"Dear Nancy"

The Pattern of American Life
Revealed in Letters

EDITED BY

Nancy Brown

THE DETROIT NEWS

1933

Table of Contents

LETTERS—*Continued*

POEMS

Introduction

THIS book, "Dear Nancy," is the second volume of the story of Experience Column, as set forth in letters contributed to it since its first appearance in The Detroit News, April 19, 1919.

The preceding volume, entitled "Experience," was published in December, 1932, and included outstanding letters which had appeared in the Column during the period from its inception to the end of 1931. The large first edition was exhausted in eight days, necessitating an immediate reprinting. "Dear Nancy," whose title was suggested by a contributor signing himself "Trooper," is for the most part devoted to representative letters published during 1932; but it also contains a number of significant letters dating back to 1920 which, for lack of space, could not be used in the first book.

Experience Column history has included, among other things, a wide variety of activities in the field of social service; the financing of the reforestation of denuded lands in Northern Michigan; the establishment of a fund for the purchase of a picture to be hung in the Detroit Institute of Arts (the result of a "Column Party" held there November 4, 1930, to which some 35,000 gained or attempted to gain entrance); and the sponsoring of six Experience Column concerts of the Detroit Symphony Orchestra.

Nineteen hundred thirty-two saw the continuation of the Column's welfare work; the planting of its fourteenth and final 40-acre plot of pines; substantial growth of the picture fund, and lastly, the publication of the first book.

Outstanding subjects of discussion in the Column during 1932, aside from the individual problem letters, included the kindest acts of husbands and wives toward each other; Columnites' ideas of happiness; comparative merits of early and modern writers, and books in general; childhood memories; why people do not go to church; and the evils (if any) of dancing. But perhaps liveliest of all the arguments was that started over an article by Mary Roberts Rinehart, in which the famous novelist asserted that if she had a daughter she would probably assent to modern moral experiments for her, if the girl wished to make them. Mothers of the Column promptly accepted the challenge, and for many, many days Column space was filled with their answers. Contributors also engaged in a salutary contest to see who could write the best letter in the fewest words.

The "In-Betweens," Column writers of high school and college age whose letters have right-of-way on Wednesdays, fought their own battles lustily, and participated in some begun by their elders. They argued the advisability of "Dutch treats" between boy and girl friends; they joined in the discussion of books; they debated the advantages of higher education; and they argued about the meaning of a wink. Some of their offerings in prose and poetry are included in this, as they were in the earlier Column book.

Even though "Dear Nancy" is primarily devoted to notable letters of a single year, selection has still been difficult. More fine letters have been printed than can be held between the covers of the book. I have done the best I could with my problem, and I hope my Column Family will understand.

NANCY BROWN

Bob-o'-Link

* * *

I

DEAR NANCY BROWN: I am coming with a proposition so unlike many of your admirers.

I am deeply in love with a man, and he is in love with me as well, but neither of us believes in marriage. Nowadays people look with disdain on "common law" marriage, but we both have decided that we are not going to listen to "people" but are going to live our lives as we desire.

Tell me, please, why is it that two people have to be "married" in order to live together and be happy?

This man loves me dearly and I certainly do love him, but never will there be a marriage ceremony. If he should decide that he loves someone else, and the same applies to me, we will simply separate and try to be happy otherwise and, can't you see, there is no divorce to contend with. The very word "divorce" makes me shudder.

Suppose I will be heaping abuses on myself by public opinion but we should worry what other people think. Don't you think I am correct in my theory?

I would appreciate what you might have to say in this matter, and will be watching for your reply in the paper, so will my "husband." Thank you very much.

July 20, 1920   BOB-O'-LINK

P.S.: I am 26 years old and he is 29, so we are not just flappers with romantic ideas.

[1]

IF YOU are in earnest, I feel very sorry for the misery that you are starting for yourself, "Bob-o'-Link."

Why think the whole world is wrong and you are right? There are things that are more "shuddery" than divorce. Your theory is one of them. You really have doubts yourself, or you wouldn't have written.

Don't do it.

* * *

II

DEAREST NANCY BROWN: Terry and I have read your advice in reply to "our" letter, and it has sort of made me stop and think a little bit.

Terry says he thinks we ought to be married and is willing to go through with it, but, Nancy, I simply cannot understand why it is that anyone has to have some one say a few words over you and then you can go through life as husband and wife. I am not narrow-minded, but won't you admit that it is somewhat inconceivable?

I am most willing to do just as Terry wants me to, and we both want to live a good, clean life, so, with more serious consideration of the matter, perhaps I'll submit to a ceremony.

You say I am causing a great deal of misery in my life? Just why, Nancy, dear, why will there be misery? We both love each other very dearly, how could there be misery? But I am going to think this matter over. Oh, I do so want to do the right thing, but honestly, my will power is not submissive to that one thing "marriage."

Couldn't you help me out in some way? Isn't there something I could read up or some life that I could study that would satisfy me? Please help me, won't you, dear? Terry is very anxious now to be married so that we can go away, as this position is awaiting him down in South America, and he won't accept it unless I can go with him, so whatever I do or decide upon must be done within the next week or ten days.

We both will thank you exceedingly for your advice.

July 26, 1920   BOB-O'-LINK

* * *

I'D MAKE that will power subservient to my reason, if I were you.

If you and Terry intend to live together all your lives, what harm can the marriage service do? And you will be living lawfully.

You must know that our laws—especially the old and tried ones —were made by wise people and found to be for the best. Why try to deny them? Can you picture good women drawing their skirts away from you, or good men passing remarks that good women do not want spoken of them, because you choose to defy the law to gratify a whim? The price you will pay is too great.

Your foolish little argument about "What difference does it make to have some one say a few words over you?" has been answered by so many million sorrowful, heartbroken women, who have done as you want to do, that no further answer is necessary. They all started with the same trust and confidence that you have.

Can you imagine the never-ending tangle of explaining which will follow the rest of your life and of your children's lives, if you persist in the wrong thing?

You are an intelligent woman. Use the brains God gave you and don't throw away your life for the sake of being different from other folk. Be married, as the world of good people—and Terry—want you to be, and you have my very best wishes. I hope you will write and tell me that you went to the minister before going to South America.

[EDITOR'S NOTE: *She followed my advice, and is glad she did.*— NANCY BROWN.]

[3]

Slim of Black Canyon

* * *

I

DEAR NANCY: Pardon this rather intimate salutation, but as I have no relatives to my knowledge, you will *have* to adopt me.

Like the two ex-cowpunchers, "Sagebrush" and "Bill Cactus," I, too, am hitting the trail for God's country and it seems fitting and proper to write and thank you for the many pleasant hours your Column has afforded me since my coming to Detroit. Your Experience Column has been part of my daily life and so it is "sort of a part of me."

May I burden you with another account of a "punctured romance"?

In the summer of 1915 I met the only one, when she was touring the West with her parents. At the time, I was a forest ranger. We corresponded regularly and in November, 1916, I came east to work in "papa's" office in Providence, R. I. Preparations for our wedding were well under way when the War came on. I enlisted and went to France shortly afterwards. Soon after getting into the lines, I was badly wounded and held prisoner until after the Armistice was signed.

After arriving home, broken in health and spirit, one sleeve empty, and my physiognomy mussed almost beyond recognition, I went back to Providence to see Helen's father. He said that the Government had reported me killed in action. It seemed better for me to remain killed, than to be a burden to anyone, so he finally promised never to say a word about my return. Through him I got a job in Detroit and have been here ever since.

About three weeks ago he wrote me and said that Helen was to be married February 12, so I went there again just to see for the last time the sweetest girl in the world. I sat in the choir loft and bawled like a kid during the ceremony. I don't know who the groom is, but he is a wonderful looking lad.

In the spring I will pull my freight for good old Montana and the old job, and spend the rest of my life enjoying single blessedness. No "Sunshine" and "Smiles" will be at the depot to weep salt tears all over my hard-boiled collar.

Now Nancy, when summer days come again, and you sit at your desk melting with the heat, straightening out love affairs, or writing consoling words to some poor fellow whose girl kicked the daylights out of some perfectly good manicure set he gave her, just pause and see a little coulée in the heart of the Rockies—peaceful and quiet except for the distant murmuring of a little creek, or the night breeze singing through the pines up on the mountainside, and the whole sky turning crimson and purple and finally golden in the fading twilight.

Then see a dilapidated ex-soldier huddled up close to a camp fire dreaming of days that were, and finally having a good laugh on the whole world.

I suppose I should sign "Enoch Arden" to this letter, but will close, with

Your loving "pseudo-nephew,"

January 29, 1921   SLIM OF BLACK CANYON

* * *

I TAKE off my hat to you, lad, as I am sure all readers will. You did one of the finest things I ever heard, in not allowing "that sweetest girl" to know you were back. That, and your war-service, entitle you to a high place in heaven and on earth.

[5]

I shall think of the little coulée among the Rockies when the summer months are here, and will write you if you wish, just as I do my other nephews. It might help to pass the lonely hours. And I know that the Column Folks will be glad to hear from you.

But you know, lad, there is no reason for you always to live the life of a bachelor. There are lots of lovely girls who would not think of the empty sleeve when they knew the fine spirit underneath the coat. Please don't forget us.

* * *

II

Dear nancy brown: Many times since leaving your fair city I have thought of you and your large family, but have deferred writing for the reason that there has been nothing very interesting to tell you.

All spring and summer I was with the Forest Service, surveying most of the time, on the move all of the time, so that it was practically impossible to send or receive letters.

I read the answer to the letter before I left Detroit.

So you think that there are lots of girls who would marry me? Well, Nancy Brown, I reckon a girl would be taking a big enough chance if I were all together in one place; then again, my face is a pretty rough looking affair, since the war, and would be a tiresome mess to look at across the table three times a day.

My pardner and I came down here for winter supplies and we leave today for the tall timber. The forestry work is done for this year so we are going to hunt and trap during the winter. It is about three days' journey by trail. After the snow gets in, there is no way to get out until spring, so will sit in the old log cabin during the long evenings, toasting our respective toes, murdering the time with rummy and chess and much tobacco.

I had intended sending you a present, or rather a remembrance, but in the hurry to get down here forgot and left it up at the shack.

You see I used to dream of acquiring a wife and eventually a considerable family, and when they're grown, thinks I, I'll drag forth this trinket and say, says I, "Children, this is the *Croix de Guerre* that France gave me for winning the war." Now that isn't to be. There is no one here to show it to. Shorty, my pardner, saw more of the war than I did, so he doesn't enjoy it any more and I'm tired of lying to myself about it. Those are reasons enough for you to accept it. It doesn't mean much to me. It was presented in Paris after the war for no particular feat of bravery—just on general principles it seems.

If the snow doesn't drift in too heavily, it will be possible to make the trip down here on foot for Christmas mail and this *croix* will be sent to you, then. For reasons of my own, I want you never to tell my name and above all my address. One "certain person" must never know that her "Long Boy" came back from France.

Shorty and another fellow have just pulled up in front of the store where I have written this letter and that means that everything is ready. From the pickle barrel where I sit, I can see two of the seven packhorses that are loaded down with clothing, grub, guns, traps and snow shoes.

Don't waste your valuable space by publishing this. If you think that anyone would care to hear about me, just say that Slim says "Hello."

Respectfully yours,
SLIM (*formerly* OF BLACK CANYON)

Somewhere in Montana,
Somewhere about September 12, 1921

[7]

There is no use to answer this letter as the lad would probably not see it. But if he sends me his address and the package, I can only thank him for the honor, and tell him the "trinket" will be kept for him, at any time he should want it.

*

Wind Before Dawn

This morning the wind blew, blew wild and free,
And I flung wide the window, for it seemed I should see
Bare branches tossing in a wet, grey sky
And the wild geese flying endlessly by.

Seemed I must hear the dark earth waking;
Seemed I could smell the black earth breaking;
Seemed I'd see the river rolling restlessly down
Through bleak old hills to a little river town.

Through marsh land and bog land and tangled wild plum
The river rushes downward, and herons come
To wade among the rushes; killdeers scream
And sweep the shining surface of the deep, brown stream,

But across from my window is the house next door—
Brick walls and twisted chimney, a gate—and nothing more.
Now, when the wind blows I shall shut my eyes
And keep my dream of river and of wild grey skies.

February 19, 1933   HOLIDAY

West Virginian

* * *

DEAR NANCY BROWN: May I answer "West Virginia Snake's" letter through your Column? Have wanted to ever since I read it, for they are kin of mine, since West Virginia is my mother-state too. I left there a good many years ago and have seen a good bit of the world since then, but just as one feels toward his Alma Mater or his country, I think we feel toward our birth-state. The others are all right but our own is just a little bit the best.

"West Virginia Snake," I'm afraid that you have given the Column Folks the impression that we could be quitters—could whine. I, too, have seen the sunsets among the hills; I have heard the wind whispering through the great trees; I've lain on my back and watched the clouds drift across a summer sky and called them ships on which I was going to sail out on into the world beyond our hills; I have stood in the lonely places at night and felt awed by the seeming closeness of the star-studded heavens; I've climbed our hills by day and gloried in their beauty; I've driven over them at night, and stopped on the top of some high one to look at the almost unearthly panorama of moon-flooded valleys that lay below me.

I always like to think that from our hills I drew to myself courage, endurance, squareness. Life hasn't been all easy for me—not by a darned sight—but I have played that each day was a new world with fresh opportunities. And one thing I can tell you all—if I should ever start to back down I'll never put West Virginia to my signature.

March 11, 1922   WEST VIRGINIAN

I, TOO, know and love the green slopes of your West Virginia hills, and their sunsets. One of the happiest times of my life was spent there, though that is not my native state. Your idea of making each day a fresh world is a good one.

*

To Little Sleepy Folks

Peregrine White in a cradle slept,
  You can see it in Plymouth Town.
Jacob slept under the open sky
  And his pillow, they say, was a stone.
And one Little Baby slept on the hay
  In a manger bed, far, far away.

But I have a little white bed for myself;
  My windows are opened wide;
Over me blankets are softly piled
  Till I'm snug and warm inside.
My sheets are fresh, my pillow is small—
  And sometimes I have no pillow at all!
                    (*Quite cheerfully*)

Jacob dreamed of a ladder that reached
  From the earth right up to God.
Over the manger a Great Star shone,
  And the angels sang aloud.
And through my window the stars shine bright,
  And God watches over me all the night.

March 2, 1930   TRUDGIN' ALONG

Jobber

* * *

DEAR NANCY BROWN: "Detroit the Dynamic" has heard her praises sung many, many miles distant and has undoubtedly brought many people here from many lands, as well as from other parts of this country, seeking, if not their fortune, at least the betterment of their condition, possibly socially but probably financially. Some of the latter may expect to find in Detroit a gigantic Aladdin's lamp, or expect to become here a Midas. However, when its call came to me near Manchester, England, a little over two years ago, I expected to find an opportunity to make an honest living by giving in return an honest day's work.

You may wonder what prompts this letter, but I feel that some one should defend Detroit, the city of my adoption, from the attacks of "Smiles," "Easterner," and possibly more to follow. I am not in accord with their plaints. I believe that if they will sit down and analyze themselves, they will find that as the result of an honest analysis the fault and cause of their misfortune is within themselves.

My experience has been that human nature is much the same, wherever one may travel. Commercially, there is the law of supply and demand. If one has something to sell, whether it may be his labor, the result of his labor, or a commercial commodity, if he seeks industriously and intelligently, he will find a buyer.

I came here a stranger, without a friend or even an enemy; had heard, of course, of your great motor plants. I therefore went to what I considered the largest one, stood in line with many others, stated my qualifications which are very few, and after a few attempts, got a job. I then worked diligently trying to convert that job into a position.

[11]

About this time I met a lady who was the cashier at a restaurant where I ate occasionally, and after two months courtship, was married. She insisted on retaining her position temporarily, until our finances were in better shape. I might state that upon my arrival here, I had between two and three hundred dollars. I had saved a little and my bride augmented this amount by $440, her savings, so that when the layoff came, as it did during the depression for myself, and as it did for thousands of others, we had about $900 in the bank as well as a small equity in a lot my wife had induced me to buy on contract.

Reading in THE NEWS about the construction of a new building, I went to the location thinking that I might obtain a job. I found that there were no jobs. There were, however, some old buildings to be wrecked to make way for the new one. I bought one for $150, hired a man, tore it down, moved it to my lot. I sold about $200 worth of this material in the neighborhood, and saved enough to rough in a small house on my lot. I very soon after sold this house at a very good figure, $500 down. I still have the contract which brings in $40 a month.

I bought many other buildings to be razed and sold the material. After several months of this business with very good success, the thought came to me of selling new building materials to contractors. There are, you know, many different commodities used in building construction. I secured the Detroit agency for one of them, not exclusive, and went to work. I now have an office in the Penobscot Building, three salesmen working, have a modern complete home and am rated from $15,000 to $25,000 in Bradstreet's and Dun's, good credit, and still growing.

Of course, much credit is due the sweetest and best little American girl in the land. But without the opportunities a city like Detroit affords, I never could have had the small success I've had. The razing of buildings in England is a rare thing indeed. The construction material is in the hands of merchants who have handled it for years. In England what I have done here would have been utterly impossible. In Detroit it has been easy. I feel that I could start now with nothing, and accomplish as much again.

All of this is not written in a spirit of braggadocio but for two purposes, to defend Detroit, and possibly to help "Smiles" and "Easterner" and their families.

Detroit is to me, an Englishman in the process of becoming a citizen, the finest city in the world. If a foreigner can come here with a limited education, a total stranger, and accumulate $25,000 honestly in a little more than two years, a man of the type of whom "Smiles" writes can do a great deal more, if he wills so, and if, as "Smiles" writes, he can't get a job—well, why go elsewhere?

Remember, "Smiles," it is sometimes necessary to start at the bottom. Best luck.

You have a wonderful Column, Nancy, and we enjoy it immensely.

November 20, 1922 JOBBER

* * *

I BELIEVE that your letter recounts the most encouraging and practical experience that has ever come into the Column. It can't help but carry its influence to many a man who has lost courage. It is so cleanly straightforward and sensible and practical. I wish I could have more of them. It is the kind of letter men need who have lost, temporarily, grip on themselves through the bad times that must come to every man.

Even though all men cannot have the business ability that is yours —and the helpful mate—they cannot help but be impressed by your resourcefulness and success.

[13]

When I read your letter, I wanted to go right out myself and buy an old house and wreck it.

It was good of you to write it to the Column. I know that

"Some forlorn and shipwrecked brother,
Seeing, shall take heart again."

Won't you please write again? You can do more good than you realize. Thank you.

*

A Song Eternal

(*Lines written to "Tippity Wicket"*)

What is this song? 'Tis a nameless melody
Sung softly to beloved ones everywhere;
An ageless song; a deathless, poignant air,
And blest by Time with immortality.
Ah me, sometimes it is a threnody,
Sobb'd bitterly unto a heedless world
By one who clasps a small, still'd form that's hurl'd
Her soul forever to eternity.

This lullaby the swaddling Shakespeare heard.
'Twas the dumb paroxysm of joy that sway'd
Beethoven, Handel, and Mozart to sleep!
A song is this that knows no critic's word;
For even ere sere History'd been made,
Its notes each night from throbbing throats did leap.

October 23, 1932   BENI-DICK

Alley Cat

* * *

Dear n. b.: Well, here's little old "Alley Cat." Seeing that all the old contribs have written lately, I may as well write too. The trouble with me is that once I start, all the little ideas that dwell in the spacious regions above my eyebrows, supposed to contain gray matter, begin to tumble out fast as they can, eager to spill themselves out on fair white paper just like Jack Daw's cherries jumping out of the bottle and into Chocolate Lake.

Spring days are here and with them the old longing. I believe I voice a trouble not mentioned in the Column, and that is trying to reconcile the different parts of a complex personality. Honestly, I am pulled this way and that by so many forces that it is like a problem in physics—the sum of these keep me stationary.

The complex person is often the gifted but perhaps the least liable to achieve success. His mind strays in too many paths and there is but one to success. You know that dope about a straight line being the shortest distance between two points.

I am tired of these little houses sitting cheek by jowl—tired of narrow streets endlessly segregated and so incredibly dirty.

Fortunately I can place the blame for my discontent on my ancestors. Mine came from a small green island, set in a stormy sea. Poor, little isle—it has rocked with the struggle of faction and faction, the tread of oppressor and usurper. Still it is a magic isle, and its people by some enchantment have been made just a little different from the other people of the gray old earth, a bit fey perhaps. I love them, though—they are so darned impractical. Your Irishman is ever the knight errant—maybe more Quixote than Galahad, but he is never ridiculous, for alongside of his cause your Irishman places his life and counts it not in the balance. There can be no greater gesture than this.

My grandfather was a man of property and culture—the last of a noble name. Romantically enough, he married a peasant girl, beautiful but illiterate—my grandmother. In my mother are blended the practical traits of her peasant ancestry and an interest in world politics and kindred subjects that would do credit to a great lady. My father's people were just average, industrious folk, "good mixers" all.

Superimposed upon my Celtic heritage I have many of the traits of this, my own land. I have the American love of success in material things, the American love of small diversions. I adore all the childish amusements extant.

I find life very interesting. I used to think that after the first flush of youth, life closed in on one, so I crowded my youth-time to get all the savor of it, but I do not find this to be true. I would say, rather, life opens out like a great, gorgeous flower.

I know I can write a little but I doubt if it will ever get me anywhere. I tell myself sometimes, "What if life binds my hands today—beyond the horizon of today lies the vision of tomorrow." Still, I think I'm only kidding myself.

Tomorrow is for the dreamer; today for the people that count.

By the way, Nancy, why bar the intelligent woman from motherhood? And why perpetuate only the morons? Again, why so hard on the wimmin? Why don't you give them a fifty-fifty deal and not a ninety-ten? Honestly, the best-loved women I have ever known haven't been those who would turn the other cheek. Not perceptibly.

Is marriage such a safe institution nowadays that it automatically insures a woman against toil? Is it nobler to take in boarders or to work in Ye Five and Tenne? "This Freedom"—poppycock—a palpable over-straining of cause to produce a desired effect. All right, maybe, for our English sisters or for those who take their opinions ready-made from the nearest print (their name is more than legion), but not for your up-to-date American with a mind of her own. Gosh, Nancy, I've worked for men years enough to gather that they had no monopoly of brains, although it was always my good pleasure to make them think so. It's not hard.

Well, I'm in a cynical mood—I'll quit picking on you! Really, I do admire the way you handle your tumultuous Column children. When things go wrong we would all, like old Omar, "Grasp this sorry scheme of things entire and mould it nearer to the heart's desire."

I must say that those who declare these letters the work of some one on the NEWS staff credit said staff with remarkable versatility. It can't be did. After a while you begin to "feel" the writers behind the letters, just as you would feel one of the great fiction writers. I subscribe my assurance that my letters are written by a small person who has never been near the NEWS office.

My discontent arises not from the fact that I am so dissatisfied with my place in the sun. On the contrary, I have many of the things for which the Column people crave—a congenial mate, lovely children, cozy home, even the background of family. It is perhaps because of these things that I feel the urge to achieve. According to my convictions, if I only do the usual household tasks and bring up my young ones to maturity, I am only accomplishing on a little higher plane what our animal friends accomplish with less fuss and more despatch. My brain has not really functioned to its capacity. A few years and my children are grown, and at a time when men—statesmen, diplomats, doctors, lawyers, writers, etc.—are doing their best work I become a supernumerary—must needs tread a narrow path between high blank walls, ending at the grave. Oh, death in life— not me!

Of course, the individual conviction must govern. "Childless" feels that it is worth a life to be a splendid mate to a splendid man. I think so, too. My insistence is only for myself.

I have many messages for the Columnites but will have to postpone them. You see, it is even as I said—I can't get near a typewriter without writing a ream or two.

Anyway, I have been much interested in the Column lately and am so glad to hear from all the old writers.

April 24, 1923   ALLEY CAT

* * *

EVER since I read your letter, Mrs. "Alley Cat," I have pondered and pondered to discover what I have ever said that would lead you to think that I "barred intelligent women from motherhood." Quite the contrary. It has always been a hobby of mine that they should have children. I can't believe that you read the Column very closely if you have drawn such a conclusion. And about "turning the other cheek"—nope, I never advocated that, either.

I do advocate a woman compromising in her home for the sake of peace and happiness, because generally the average man will not compromise. And I do believe that the average woman can find ample scope for her mentality in managing her home and bringing up her children. There are exceptions, of course, as there are to everything else in the world.

I do believe that it is a worth-while life to be a splendid mate to a splendid man. I voiced that very sentiment in yesterday's paper. I do believe that the very zenith of womanhood is reached when she bears and brings up children—not, however, in such great numbers that it over-taxes her strength, and the family finances are not sufficient to care for them properly. I believe that is neither fair nor just to the mother or to the children.

Guess you have no monopoly on the feeling of restlessness these days. Not one of us, who has a drop of red blood in his veins, but craves to get out into the open, build a fire with crossed sticks and watch the smoke curl through the sunny air; hear the birds sing and watch the beetles crawl out of the warm earth—and oh, everything else that comes with the warm spring.

No, life does not "close in on one" after the first flush of youth. The very best of life comes with mature years. We are at our very best just at the time when the end of the road is in sight. Seems too bad, but I suppose it is right.

Why don't you write in earnest? You surely wield a deft pen and have an apt vocabulary and phraseology. You have very fitly expressed the right idea of the Column letters. It seems to me it must be a very dense person who cannot, as you say, "feel the writers behind them." They are certainly not written by the NEWS staff.

*

Confession

You look at me askance, I fear,
From out those eyes of blue—
Because I cannot sing and dance
For joy, my dear, like you.

But I've a secret dark and deep
That you have never guessed:
My heart still sings, and dances, too;
There now, I have confessed!

July 10, 1930   ANNE OF DIXIE

Ex-Flapper

***

D EAR NANCY BROWN: Please let me thank you for the pleasure your daily Column has given me. I enjoy the published letters of your correspondents and find in them a poignant sincerity that goes straight to my heart.

I am a stranger in your city—a bride of recent date, with a dear little apartment and a wonderful boy-husband. Sometimes after a perusal of other people's problems, I feel as though I have a monopoly of the world's happiness. My only sore spot is loneliness for my mother. We were very close friends, she and I, and the thought that half a continent separates us now is not a very cheerful one. I miss our twilight conversations and in lieu of them, I have turned to your Experience Column in THE NEWS, with something more than pleasure—a real need.

I want to comment on a letter that appeared signed "Reformed" —the girl who attended wild parties through fear of losing her "only one." My sympathy goes out to that girl. I know of hundreds such. Pretending recklessness, drinking, smoking, countenancing road-side petting parties just to be in with the rush. Afraid of being called "slow"—it is an old story these days. In a set like that, every girl is guessing as to how far the other girl goes—and no one is sure.

My knowledge of these things is first hand because my marriage meant to me deliverance from that crowd. I just happened to be lucky where "Reformed" was unfortunate, and now my hubby and I are ideally happy in each other's happiness. We've both sowed our wild oats—and we got tired of it, so we quit. My mother trusted me, and in the real sense of the word I proved true to her trust—though no one would have suspected it.

I was in Rome and did as the Romans did. Three a.m. was no unusual hour, and cigarettes never made me sick. Even after my engagement was announced, Hubby and I went around a lot together and separately. I never slacked up till the day of the wedding, but it is well over and done with now. Personally, I am none the worse for my experiences and I honestly believe that at least 80 per cent of the modern young people react as I have done. There are many who fall by the wayside, either from ignorance or from curiosity. Very few, I assure you, are knocked down by force! The survival of the fittest has been the slogan of the world since man was man—and applies here.

Of course, I grant this—we are over-sexed these days. From the shrouded and veiled mystery that Grandma knew, we have reacted too strongly and are now at the other extreme of vulgar display and a harsh frankness that appalls most of us even while we pretend to take it all as a matter of course. Sometimes it seems as though we have lost all sense of delicacy and are wallowing in a slough of realism whose quicksands threaten to drag us under.

There is no rule of conduct, but God gave every one a tiny inner voice called intuition, instinct, or conscience, as you will, and that was my only guide. Mother counselled, advised and admonished, of course, but in the long run I was thrown back upon my own resources in my dealings with the men who made up our crowd. Not one of us was really bad, at least I don't think so, and I know that the sacred ambition of one of our wildest "neckers" was to have a home and a baby. And that's that!

I didn't mean to write at such great length, but now I'm glad I did. I had the urge to explain—and oh, I hope, Nancy Brown, that you understand I am not discussing something I know nothing about, but something that until three months ago was my own life. I insist that I had a marvellous time, but that I'm too glad for words to be definitely out of it. And every blessed one of us felt the same way, though I would never have admitted it then any more than they.

Thank you for the precious time I've taken up, and believe me a sincere well-wisher. May I come again?

September 6, 1923   EX-FLAPPER

* * *

You have truly struck the keynote of a girl's ability to choose between the moral and the immoral.

Mothers may admonish and teach, as all mothers do, but in the end, it is always the girl's own instinct or conscience which must decide at the crisis.

As you say, there are thousands of girls like "Reformed," who play the wild parties solely because they think the men they love admire that. Yet all the time these men are being disgusted with the girls' laxness of morals. It is equally true that many and many a young man likes to take girls to these parties but would never choose for his wife the girl who attends them, never giving a thought to the fact that perhaps the clean girl might demand the same cleanness from him.

I am glad you wrote this letter. Thank you.

*

A Tanka

O Spring, you are a rare old wine.
With shining amber stealth
You waft me to intriguing heights,
Then leave me dazed
In languorous bliss.

May 15, 1932   NAIAD

[22]

Dotted Swiss

* * *

Dear nancy brown: It seems to me that my troubles are as the stars in the heavens—numberless, and to solve all the difficulties would be a task as great as to try to put out those twinkling lights.

I am but 18, and my dear husband 20, and in just another month we expect a little stranger to come to us. I'm afraid that it will be an unhappy little mite, because I have cried so much and worried incessantly. I truly try not to, but how can I help it?

Honey-Boy is just as sweet and kind and patient as he can be, and helps me in every way he can, and I don't want to be unhappy all the time, for it makes him blue and discouraged too. But Nancy, he gets just $25 a week and we just have money enough in the bank to pay for the coming doctor's bill, not the hospital bill. We pay $10 a week rent for two rooms and $5 for food. The rest we have spent in buying clothes for the little one and ourselves, and in making the two rooms cozy and comfortable.

We have only been in Detroit three months so things are still pretty strange to us. Christmas is near at hand and we have managed to get little remembrances for each member of our two families, and oh, Nancy, there isn't a cent for me to get my darling husband a present with, and it will be awful to go through Christmas Day without giving him something. He said a kiss would be all he wanted, but you know he'd be happier with just a little something from me.

And I try not to be a coward about the coming event, but is it as awful as everyone says it is, Nancy? I am healthy and well, at least, and that is something to be thankful for.

Can you in any way help me, dear Nancy? I'll look for an answer to this incoherent mass of words and if I do not see it, it will be another disappointment to add to the long list of others.

December 11, 1923   DOTTED SWISS

* * *

THOSE little troubles look pretty big, don't they dear? Maybe we can reduce them in size. I can tell you just what to do, so that there will be money enough for the sickness and perhaps even a little bit to buy that good husband a Christmas gift.

Go right down to the Women's Hospital, corner of Forest and Beaubien, and make arrangements for them to take care of you during your confinement. Don't hesitate to go. It is a place we have for just such disturbed little wives and mothers-to-be as you.

Now that reduces one big worry, doesn't it? Let us take the next one—the fear. Why, my dear little girl, there is nothing to fear. You say yourself that you are well and healthy. To have a baby is just one of the natural things of a woman's life—just as natural as living or breathing. Put away all of those foolish fears, and think only of the happiness you will have when that soft little mite is in your arms.

I know what I would do, if I did not have any money to speak of, and wanted to give my husband a Christmas gift. I would go down to the five-and-ten cent store and look around. You will simply be surprised to see the things down there that will appeal to any man, woman, or child. There are lovely little ash trays, pipes and other smoking accessories, books, pictures and handkerchiefs, which you would never suspect were only a dime or a quarter,—and other things that you will see that will interest him. Just try it. You will go home with your arms full of little packages and your eyes shining, and know that it doesn't lighten your pocketbook very much.

Once I knew a little girl who wanted to give me a Christmas gift. She didn't have any money either. She confided so, herself, to me. I

[24]

say little girl—she was 16. I told her that I would show her something that I would enjoy very much and which I knew she could afford to buy me. I took her to the five-and-ten, and pointed out two little glass vases for a nickel, just the size and shape you use for small bouquets, or for two or three posies. She did not want to buy them because they cost so little, but finally agreed. That was fifteen years ago. I am still using one of the little vases and the other I accidentally left somewhere, when I went away. I presume that it may still be in use.

You can see what enjoyment I have had out of the five cent gift. It isn't the price that makes the pleasure, is it? Just the fact that it is useful and helpful, and carries the loving thought with it.

Instead of thinking of the troubles, think of the blessings you have. That sounds quite trite, doesn't it? But after all, it is a good old-fashioned remedy. So many, many young wives like you write to me and tell me how unkind their husbands are to them, never remember them in a pleasant way, never love them or sit at home with them. You don't have any of those worries, do you?

Now I want you to cheer up and for the rest of the time before that little mite comes to earth, give it that which will make for it a happy disposition. That is the kind of baby you want, isn't it?

I would like you to send me your name and address just for myself, if you are willing.

Rag Carpet

* * *

DEAREST NANCY: The loom is creaking dolefully and threatens to break down. The warp tangles and ravels. The Hand that guides the weaving surely does not waver in its purpose, yet the pattern is uncertain and great unlovely knots appear. A touch of brilliant color here and there serves only to accentuate a shadowy strip of grays and browns and somber greens. Such is the latest strip, Nancy and "Moon Calf"; scarcely interesting, but such strips must be—always are—in every life where we see it whole at last.

Not that I am much of a philosopher. Just another "Baffled Little Girl" grown up, but I have always been, as Stevenson says, "Conscious like all Scots, of the fragility and unreality of that scene in which we play our uncomprehended parts; like all Scots, realizing daily and hourly the sense of another will than our own, and a perpetual direction in the affairs of life." So I am trusting that this strip which seems all awry will be all right, and at heart I am quite happy, too, as "Moon Calf" is, in spite of disappointments and yearnings—those growing pains of the soul, I think they must be.

"Moon Calf" wrote not half enough, so selfishly intent was she on wriggling her soul in the sunshine. But we love her that way and only regret the letters she said she destroyed because of Pollyannishness. You know that word was invented by critics who cheaply vie with each other in cynicism (for lack of more constructive qualities, perhaps). One who is not afraid of them—Joseph Conrad, to be exact—says that the cynic sees with one eye only.

I am wondering about "Moon Calf's" stories that would end as tragedies. Perhaps she is happy because she has discovered the secret of the happy ending. I think I should write some stories myself were it not for a constant preoccupation with the "cheaper cuts," and everyone of my characters I would steal bodily from Experience Column. Visions of "the great American novel!" I would be the Dickens of America. Had I not been so unfortunate as to miss your radio talk, dear Nancy, I might have received the inspiration that would have started me on my literary career in spite of frenzied housekeeping.

For Nancy—the fascinating paint and cretonne are laid aside, and the garden—well, there isn't going to be any, unless it is a sort of Topsy garden that just grows. The Little House is quite, quite neglected and forlorn and apologetic for the unadorned newness that hangs about it like a misfit garment. Just a difficult place in the weaving. A lesson to be learned, perhaps. Sordid money cares—and sickness.

If the story were to end here, it would end on a tragic note, "Moon Calf." One of those deadly realism stories, full of germs and bills and dishes to be washed and dust on everything—but just around the corner may be "the" happy episode. Who knows?

My love to "Daughters Three," and to you, dear Nancy, and to all my Column friends.

June 2, 1924 RAG CARPET

* * *

THE web of every life, dear "Rag Carpet," has big knots. They seem unlovely but in the untangling of them we run across the most beautiful colors, and weave from them the finest pattern. You know it is so, don't you?

There is no life that does not have sickness and sordid cares of some kind. It would not be life without them. But you know and I know, and all the grown-ups know, that life is not all sordid cares and sickness. There is just as much of happiness and cheer and loveliness as there is of the sordid.

[27]

I am sorry that the little house is neglected and forlorn, and the pretty cretonne and paint are laid aside, and there is to be no garden. Perhaps, though, they are only put away temporarily. I am quite sure of it. Some day something lovely will happen that will make you forget the "cheaper cuts" and the many cares. Every morning when you wake up and start the day, think that perhaps something nice is going to happen. It surely will some day, you know, and the thought does help a little bit when we are blue and things go wrong.

Shouldn't wonder if you would be away past that stretch in the loom where the warp tangles and the knots appear. I hope so, anyway—for you. I am so glad you came back. Please don't stay away so long again.

*

Recompense

If I can say a little word
    To one whose heart is sad,
That carries, like a homing bird,
    Some thought to make it glad;

If I can lend a helping hand
    To lighten some one's load
And make him know I understand
    How weary and long the road;

If I can know because I've lived,
    And done some simple task,
That this old world's a happier place—
    Then, that is all I ask.

July 5, 1930   ANNE OF DIXIE

Drifting Down Detroit Lake

* * *

To NANCY BROWN Who Ans. letters for people in trouble: Dear Nancy, I know I never can be a member of your big family for I am a poor disgraced girl and Nancy I know you don't want anybody in disgrace to belong and become a Column member so I will just write you a letter to answer but not to try to belong.

Oh good lady ans me please I am so sad I cam to Detroit from a small town eight months ago left 4 little sisters and two brothers at home. My good dear parents are poor just a small little home on an old dirt road there is no work there Nancy for girls so I came to Detroit and worked as a maid in a doctors home here been getting 8 dollars and board send mother 4 every week but what my trouble is I can't work much longer Nancy in two more months I will become a mother unmarried and the Dear Boy I liked so well has fled to Canada thats what he says in the letter I received the other day.

Oh why don't mothers tell their daughters those things before they let them drift off by themselves I was such a good girl and so innocent before I came to Detroit my Mistress is so stern to me and she says I must leave in a few days and go back home which I never will do I am thinking very much of taking my own life coward that I am but my pride has got the best of me the Detroit Lake I am considering.

Maybe in a few days you will hear of a 19 year old girl old-fashioned with long hair it will be me Nancy I am a firm believer in God yet I don't feel afraid to meet my maker leave this cruel cold world Nancy ans me do you think a girl that makes a wrong step could ever be respected again not in our town I would die a thousand times before letting Dad and Mother know.

April 17, 1925   DRIFTING DOWN DETROIT LAKE

No NEED for the Detroit Lake for you, my little girl. There is a better way and a better place. Come right into Column House where the folks are friendly and kind and want to help you, and we will talk it over and I will tell you what to do.

Down at 583 Elizabeth Street, East, is the Florence Crittenton Hospital, a lovely place built in memory of the girl for whom it is named, for girls who have made the mistake that you have made. You go down there and ask for Mrs. Palmer and tell her that I sent you. Tell her your story just as you told it to me. Perhaps you might take the letter with you and show it to her. After she has heard your story, she will tell you that there is a place right there for you to be cared for immediately, and until after your baby comes. No one will know anything about it, and it will not cost you a cent. The only compensation you are expected to give is to stay there for a time after your baby comes and help care for other girls in the same predicament. You will be glad to do that, won't you?

And now don't feel frightened any more. Try and see how cheerful you can be, because you know you want that baby of yours to be a good baby, a sweet baby, and a healthy baby, don't you? And oh, you will love it so when it is in your arms! I know you will want to keep it, and Mrs. Palmer will talk with you about that, too, and help you decide. Will you go right away, not waste a single day thinking about it? It is just the place for you, dear. Will you please write to me and tell me what you do? I want to help you.

Of course you can be respected again, and that is what you must look forward to. Hold fast to your faith in God and the surety that you can "come back" and compensate by living the sweet good life that you want to live.

[EDITOR'S NOTE: *A factory-worker who lived in Cleveland, and whose wife had died, leaving him with several small children, wrote to me offering to marry the girl in my office, if she would mother his children. He promised he would have her send me a monthly report of his care of her. The offer was not accepted.*—NANCY BROWN.]

*

Prayer

Sometimes I dare not pray
   For fear that I
Might ask of life more in a day
Than is good for mortals
   Such as I!

Some days I dare not pray
   For fear that I
Might selfish seem, and what I say
Would make the Lord think I am greedy,
   And my plea deny.

Sometimes I dare not pray
   For fear that I
Might ask too many blessings—
More than would warrant a reply
   To such as I!

August 4, 1932   GEE DEE

Chaos

* * *

DEAR NANCY: Once more you have been chosen as an outlet for heartache. However, I don't really believe that anyone, even you, can be of assistance except to offer sympathy, for within myself lies the only possible solution and as yet that is not forthcoming.

I am engaged—or supposed to be—to a man eight years older than I. I am entirely out of his social sphere. That part of it doesn't bother me in the least, because I have no social aspirations. It is the result of his social position that affects me. Night after night, dinner parties, theater parties and other parties. He lives at an exclusive club and his friends are male almost exclusively, except for the wives of some of his closer friends. This sort of thing has been going on for two years. He assures me that there are dozens of invitations that of necessity he cannot accept.

Of late, about one evening a week has been reserved for me. Even that could hardly be called "reserved." As a matter of fact, a few hours are squeezed in between numerous other engagements and usually he is so tired that we don't even go out, but stay at my apartment and read. We haven't gone to a theater for a month. In the summer, when society is not active, we did manage to go to the theater once a week. Possibly we might even have dinner together twice a week. Your conclusion from that would naturally be that I should not complain. But it puts an entirely different aspect on things when I say that I never know until an hour or two before whether I am going out or not.

But now it's winter and everything is changed. He pleads that so many of the affairs are formal, and that members of his family are going, and that he cannot well refuse to go. Please, don't misunderstand: I realize that he must go to these functions. But when evening after evening I must stay home while he goes to all these places to which I do not have entrée, it seems that I just couldn't be more unhappy. Last winter it was the same, but somehow I managed to get through, but each month has grown more and more unhappy and discontented. I have tried innumerable times to explain to him. I am sure he understands, but he offers no solution.

Now an even more interesting phase has presented itself. He has been chosen as groomsman at a very prominent wedding to take place the first of the year. You can picture the result, I am sure. At least twenty dinners are planned, at which his presence is required. To that I have acquiesced with the best grace I could muster, knowing it to be unavoidable.

Just this morning I talked with him over the telephone at quite some length. He was very sweet to me and promised me the loan of his car over Thanksgiving. I didn't ask for it, and I do appreciate the offer because I know that he is inconveniencing himself to loan it to me. He does try to do nice things for me to compensate for his inability to see me oftener. But it doesn't help at all somehow. I can picture ahead of me weeks and months of this association, and in doing so I become all but desperate.

Everything seems wrong. There seems no way out. I cannot be accepted in his social sphere. Even if he was willing, I don't feel ready for such an ordeal. I am constantly studying and improving myself, but not having had the advantages of college life and resultant association, it is rather an up-hill job. Anyhow I need to travel and acquire the culture that comes from association with all the better things before I can think of attempting to be accepted.

But even aside from all that, if I could get a firm foothold or a firm basis from which to work, I wouldn't mind all this lack of admittance to the social register. But I'm slowly but surely breaking under this battle to keep my position in his affections. This constant worry and loneliness when I can't see him is taking my courage.

Can you understand, Nancy? There is one way out of it, and that is not to see him any more. But the result would be that he would gradually fill up the void which my absence would bring, with other pleasures and other friends, until in an incredibly short time he could forget me. While for me there is nothing left. I am not a flapper and it has taken a long time to bring myself to the realization that I do love him, and nothing can make me forget him. Once before I cared for someone, years ago when I was a mere infant—from my present point of view—and I never quite forgot, but forced myself to become interested in other things until I no longer remembered the heartache. But this is so different. I can vision things now, and know what life would be without him. And isn't it better to go with him, as matters are now, than to break off entirely with absolutely no hope? If I weren't so sure that he cares for me I just wouldn't have the courage to go on. I could manage to go to some other city and start over again and try, in spite of everything, to forget. But the knowledge that he *does* care keeps me chained here with no way to turn.

I fear I am not thinking coherently right now, although I know that if I were writing to you 24 hours later I would say exactly the same things perhaps in a little different way. You see I have grieved about it so much that even my heart is full of tears. I have tried everything—coaxing, storming, just waiting, making myself inaccessible for one or two days, anything that might possibly offer a solution, but the only result each time was a temporary respite, and even that was marred by the thought that the old routine would soon be in effect, and I have never been disappointed in this respect.

Something definite must be arrived at soon, for last week I broke down and was in bed for a whole day, extremely ill and the physician said it was acute nervousness. Now I'm recuperating and back at work but am fighting to prevent a recurrence. I shall have plenty of time to study your answer—and possible solution—for I expect to be at home every evening as usual. Other invitations have been refused, because I should not like to accept unless I could be an agreeable companion, and that would be quite impossible under the circumstances.

I would so appreciate an answer soon.

November 30, 1925   CHAOS

* * *

I UNDERSTAND the situation, my dear, and I sympathize with your loneliness and know how helpless you feel to combat what seem like overwhelming obstacles. On the other hand, I do believe you have brooded over the matter until it has become an obsession with you —believe that it seems greater to you than it really is.

And I think you make a mistake in the mental attitude you take toward your ability to hold your place in the social world of your fiancé. Any girl who could write the intelligent letter you have written me would find no difficulty in taking her place in any social rank. College training is not necessary to being well-bred. If you go through the ranks of the social register, I am sure you will find the greater percentage of the women are not university trained.

It seems to me the man is selfish or—thoughtless. It is hard for a man to realize the woman's viewpoint in so many things. That, sometimes, is excuse for him. Could you not ask him plainly if he will not set aside two or three evenings a week for you? Surely he would not consider that unreasonable.

Moreover, there is something wrong in his being invited to so many places without you. If he has told his friends that he is engaged, social courtesy would demand that you be included in the invitation, except to the "stag" affairs. You speak of your fiancé's family. Have you met them? It would be only ordinary courtesy for them to include you in their social activities, even to having dinners and parties for your special benefit in order to introduce you to his friends.

I believe I would have a very frank talk with the young man on the subject. Tell him that you would like to meet his family—if you have not already done so. Ask him if he has told his friends of his engagement. Don't mention, of course, that his family might present you at some special social functions. He understands that.

You say that you realize that he must go to these functions. Why must he? It seems to me that consideration for you should stand before a mere party.

You belittle your training, and that is a bad mental condition. You know what good table manners are. You know how to meet people. You know the ordinary rules of etiquette—and courtesy is only kindness, you know. With this equipment, it is easy enough to pick up the knowledge of the little social details—a knowledge of which fork or spoon to use—a recognition of caviar or other dishes, that are served in ordinary life. It takes but little time to learn these things, and remember, my dear, you do not stand out alone, the observed of all observers in any place. You are simply one of the mass. You can follow the lead of others without attracting attention. After a brief experience, you will not need a leader. Believe me, you should take your place with your fiancé in his social world.

As for the twenty dinners to be given to the bridal party of which he is a member, it is not necessary that he should attend them all. If he says that it is, it is because he is selfish. I believe that my spirit of independence would demand that I take my place with him. You are to be his wife. He should help you now, even as then.

Why is your marriage delayed? I would not wait because of any

foolish notions about my own fitness. To my mind the best thing
that you can do is to have the wedding set at a very near date. I certainly would not give him up if I loved him. Some way will open for
you to take your place at his side—but I would give that sense of in-
feriority short shrift if I were you.

*

A Little While

A little while, and then the dawn
Will grace the farthest hill . . .
A little while, and I shall see
The sun is shining still.

Right now, a shower . . .
No light in view . . .
The skies are grey
That once were blue.
No song to sing . . .
No tune to play . . .
Just rain and shadow
Day by day.

But what though clouds hang very low,
And tempest out of night be born,
A little while . . . then comes the dawn
That follows after every storm.

June 12, 1932   FORGOTTEN

Lady of the Evening

* * *

MISS NANCY: Such a strong desire have I to get into your Column, that I would sacrifice much. But I can only expect to be turned away; shoved into the depths where I belong. If you do not see fit to publish my letter, will you please just send a few words of cheer? When you read the next paragraph, please do not brand me with hatred. I am sorry for all my past.

I am a woman of the underworld. Am but 27 years old but ah, feel twice that. When I reached the eleventh grade of high school I could stand no more of the gossip that I was an illegitimate child. I got in with a wild crowd who did not care about my rearing or origin. They welcomed me—treated me right—in their own way. I fell lower and lower and did not realize I was bad until my first visit to a dive.

It is too late to turn back. My life is nothing, and will never be. The "dicks" don't know me at heart. My swearing and vile talk are a force of habit. It reveals the darkest side of my character.

When I read in your Column about young girls petting, wanting clothes, and ready to leave home because their folks want them to obey, I just sit down and cry . . . heart and soul. I have clothes, both beautiful and expensive, but I would gladly exchange them for what these flappers run away from.

My heart is black and hard, as cold as stone. I hate men! I loathe men! Ah, it is wrong of me to speak that way to you but it is true. Perhaps it is because I regret the fact that I cannot have a real one of my own. I regret to see fine young men throw away their lives the way they do and regret it afterwards. They suffer just as we do . . . sometimes more.

If I had fought against the fact that I was an illegitimate, it would have been much better, but I was blind, so very blind and inexperienced.

I am a good looking woman, Nancy, but my soul and thoughts are scarlet. My skin is painted all the time, and except for my features, my face is ruined. I am too far gone to reform. And no one wants me to or will care. It isn't much for a mortal to build his hopes on, but I have lived this life nine hard years, surely I can stand the remaining amount.

Words of encouragement will help, but what I really write this for is to help others. To warn your young writers of life's cruel pitfalls. And to those who are married, let them be thankful and contented. This is my first real talk with a worldly wise woman. Your position in life is important and honorable. I look up to you.

I shall understand if you do not pay much attention to an outcast. I believe that I am the first woman of my kind to try and enter your Column . . . I shall wait and see if I'm turned away. I shall not be hurt; life is too hardened before my eyes for that. Do not let my joining frighten away your highly honored members. . . . I will not ask to join; just allow me to visit.

With hope,

September 12, 1926   LADY OF THE EVENING

* * *

YOU are welcome to the Experience Column. You will be simply a woman among women. The Column is not devoted to any one special kind of woman. It is open to us all.

There is no woman on earth who could not be better, and a good woman if she tries. What if you have had nine years in that dark, mysterious place known as the underworld? There is nothing to prevent your crossing its boundaries back to the upper world of sunlight and fresh air. And after all, what and where are those boundaries? Thinking good thoughts and establishing them as your law of living carries you across the unseen lines, even without your knowledge.

It is entirely a matter of your own volition. You can force yourself to think good thoughts hard enough and often enough to carry you into the world of good women. If you truly want to change, why not go to another city where you are not known and start over? You are young, quite young. Your habits are not irrevocably formed.

Your reason for undertaking such a life was not a good one, was it? You see that now, and you warn other young women against it. Why not put your good warning into execution for yourself?

You are not "too far gone" to reform. There is someone who wants you to, and will care. I do. And there will be many, many more who will read your letter who will want you to. Doesn't that help some? It *would* have hurt if I had not used your letter, wouldn't it? And I would not hurt you for the world.

*

"Toyo"

A "Noble Lady"
Whispered, " 'Toyo' no longer
Exists. He is gone."
A piquant charm of Column
House—a prismed light flicked out.

"Toyo" lives again.
In each new cherry blossom
And peach bloom of spring
I glimpse his quick, subtle smile,
And hear his quaint phrases stir.

March 4, 1932   FRIEND OF THE FAIRIES

Most a Hundred

* * *

DEAR NANCY BROWN: I am sorely in need of advice and as I have no one to turn to, may I come to you, Nancy, please!

A year ago this June I was graduated from high school and a few days later Mother and Dad were killed in an automobile accident. As I had no relatives excepting a married sister living in Detroit, I came here to make my home with her.

Last January Sister gave birth to twin girls and passed into the "Great Beyond" a few days later, leaving the twins, and four boys 16 months, 2½ years, 5 and 6 years. I promised her, just before God called her away, that I would care for her children and try to be a mother to them. Since that time I have continued to live with my brother-in-law, keeping house and caring for the children the best I could. Am only 18 and have never had anything to do with children before.

A little over a week ago a group of neighbors came to see me for the first time since Sister's death and informed me that I was immoral, and a few other things which hurt me to even think of, never mind repeating. I didn't realize I was doing wrong to continue to live with Brother-in-Law after Sister passed away. Anyhow I had no one to go to, and what would six babies (and they are all almost babies) do with no one except Daddy to care for them? Brother cannot afford to hire a housekeeper, as it takes every cent of his salary to feed so many and to pay the hospital and funeral bills for Sis. I told him what the neighbors had to say and he suggested that we marry as a way out of the difficulty, but although I love him dearly as a brother, I could never consider him as a husband.

Am practically engaged to a young man who also finished school last June, but as he is only earning $18 per week, marriage is out of the question for some years yet. And anyway, I could not expect him to care for so many youngsters, although he loves them as much as I do.

Oh, Nancy, what shall I do? I want to care for the youngsters as I love them so and they love me—call me "Muvver" and hardly seem to miss Sis—and the twins need someone to mother them.

Shall I continue to live as I have been, innocently enough, but get my character besmirched? (Believe that is the word my neighbors used.) It was hard enough to keep my courage up before and keep going, but now I just feel as though I couldn't go on living. Guess I'm too young to have so much responsibility.

Please Nancy, be my Column Mother and tell me what to do. I do want to do what is right. Will sign what I feel.

May 26, 1927   Most a Hundred

* * *

You are a dear plucky girl to undertake such responsibilities and to carry them on so bravely. You are indeed, as you say, too young for such a burden.

Now about the great problem. In a way, little girl, the neighbors are right. Perhaps a kindly motive prompted them to caution you, a young girl, against a possible danger that had not occurred to you. Scandal and unpleasant criticism are pretty sure to follow such conditions as those under which you and your brother-in-law are living, however innocent they may be in reality. Your neighbors know that attitude of the world and wanted to caution you against it.

You should not, above all else, marry your brother-in-law, since you do not love him, and because there is the boy whom you do love. The right is yours to live your own life. Also, there should be some older woman in the house with you.

You say your brother-in-law cannot afford to hire a housekeeper. Neither can you afford to have your reputation marred. Better spend a few dollars to have a woman in the house than to have that happen. Besides, the work is too much for you to do alone. The care of six small children and keeping house for eight people would be too much for more experienced housekeepers than you. The responsibility is your brother-in-law's, to produce money enough in some way to have a woman help and protect you. It need not necessarily be expensive help. If you could find a middle-aged woman who would come for $7 or $8 a week—there is a possibility you might find one for even less—your brother-in-law should accomplish it in some way.

If, however, I am asking the impossible in that direction, would it be possible to rent a room to an older woman who would serve as chaperon in the house? There should be someone, my dear, and it can be accomplished if you and your brother-in-law make up your minds about it.

Here is something I would do, if I were you. I would call on those different neighbors who came to you, and appeal to them for help in your difficult situation—help in this way, that the condition is something that cannot be avoided at present, that there is no wrong in it, and ask them if they will not please try to smooth over any attempt at gossip. A plea to them individually for special help will win their championship, which is far, far better than their enmity. Above everything else, my dear, do not antagonize them. Tell them that you appreciate the kindly motive with which they came to you, and will do the best you can to have an older woman come, when you can find a suitable one.

Be very discreet, dear, in your movements. Give as little cause for gossip as you possibly can—and go your way with a free conscience.

Happiness

* * *

To have a wee house far from madding crowds,
 Yet near enough to mingle there with men
And share their moods, and work and play a while—
 But always to come home to peace again.

To hear the ringing voice of childhood's joy,
 To have a clinging hand to clasp my own,
To share a hearth-fire's warmth and cheer with him
 Whose love and courage builds for us a home.

A fringe of bright-hued blossoms 'round my door,
 A background of old trees that face the gales,
A flare and dash of color through the rooms,
 And worn books marked and pregnant with old tales.

To have a three-fold task to do each day—
 A bit of work with brawn, and some with brain,
And yet another portion with the soul
 In kindling fires to glow through dark and rain.

This is my goal of peace and happiness,
 An Eldorado sought through all the years,
And found for one brief moment on the heights—
 And fear to lose through mists of happy tears.

December 25, 1931   FRIEND OF THE FAIRIES

Laughing Cavalier

* * *

Nancy brown: Here I am with broken arches—tried working in a department store after the theatrical job didn't pan out so well. No! I'm not clever enough to be a performer, but I did rather like the booking racket . . . that is, legitimate booking, and the said office was that. However, show business just isn't so *forte* at present. Department store is okay for some people but this person couldn't learn to like it for $16 a week . . . and the arches didn't think so much of the job either . . . so both the child and the arches dug out . . . leaving the $16 for someone else . . . But just ask me if I like my new job? . . . *and how!!*

I've got the tiniest little switchboard away down under one of Detroit's large downtown hotels where all sorts of engines hum a million melodies in the big power plant . . . where electricians, carpenters, plumbers, painters and locksmiths rush hither and yon, and the bosses call down and want this and that immediately. (The funny part to me is that they get it immediately.)

Well, I answer to the name of "Trouble"—nice, eh what?

A sweet voice calling in my good ear: "The guest in 1928 is locked in, do send a locksmith, at once." . . . Two minutes later: "This is the nineteenth floor calling. Is the locksmith on his way up here? . . . The guest is very impatient." . . . I want to tell him to keep his shirt on . . . but I don't.

A gruff voice growls, "This d——n window won't shut, get a man up here to fix it." I hope his wife puts cracker crumbs in his bed. . . .

Another guest calling and putting in his own complaint (evidently he is pie-eyed and the operator is sick of his hounding her): "Did you say you were 'Trouble'? . . . I've got all the trouble I want up here. . . . I just reached across the table to get a drink and I got a shock from the lamp. . . . Yesh, I'm having a shocking good time. . . . but Gee I'm lonesome . . . and I'll be in this darn hotel until 4:30 p.m. tomorrow . . . and tomorrow is tomorrow . . . and tomorrow is the Fourth of July . . . . Where is your department? Wouldn't you help me to celebrate? . . . You're sorry? Well then send up an electrician if you have one down there loose . . . one who can talk English. . . . If you do, I'll send you down a nice big drink . . . Sure you can. I won't tell your boss. . . . Won't you talk to me? . . . Bet you haven't a thing to do," etc.

I didn't have, but I didn't see where his conversation was particularly uplifting. Sent the big, blond electrician up to the talkative guest's room. When he finally returned the service order, he took out of his light-box a glass filled with Scotch and ginger ale . . . and set it on my desk. We both laughed at the generous guest, and I held my nose and asked him to take it away. "Sech" is the life of "Trouble."

I'm just in the mood to write a "sob story"—but who cares about the problems of one of the mob. But honest, Nancy, Fate does give one a dirty dig now and then—and its poor sportsmanship to squawk, so we just fool the public and laugh it off. But Conrad writes, "Every age is fed on illusion, lest man should renounce his life early and the human race come to an end."

I'm a bit fed up, but then the most inexpressive of human beings must have said to himself at one time or another, "Anything but this!"

Regards to all. Just a

July 12, 1928   Laughing Cavalier

[46]

I DO not believe that anyone with the strong sense of humor you have need ever fear being "fed up" on anything in particular, or life in general.

You have a good subject for a feature serial in your trouble department.

Please send us some more of your experiences.

*

Grammy's Lonesome!

Just a sturdy little rocker, he left standing on the lawn,
Neighbor's children often sit there,
But Charlie is gone.

It was painted bright and yellow, like the sunshine, 'cause you see,
That would please a little fellow,
Almost three.

Cared for, watched him, how I loved him, just as if he were my own,
But he's gone to live with "Mummy."
I'm alone.

Death is hard, but sometimes, living, we can lose our loved ones too.
Often "losing" means just giving—
I've found true.

So I hope that he is happy. Wish he'd come before I'm gone,
To his Grammy and his rocker,
On the lawn.

January 30, 1932   GRAMMY

Toyo

* * *

PLEASE NOBLE LADY: Toyo he write vere nice poem in Chinese style an although Japanese do not love Chinese individuals, Toyo he wish to become American like an friendly, so he like very much to dedicate this one to Chinese boy Wing, body servant to eminent Column writer Mister "Friend of the Poets," an he hope Wing will deliciously like an enjoy humble effort. Here it is:

Yesterday while strolling through an old orchard, a peach petal, carried by a midday zephyr caressed my cheek, then fell at my feet. It was a good omen an I shall place it among my treasured bits.

A bat, aroused from slumber by some unusual happening, winged its way past me from its sacred roosting place. I was indeed fortunate in witnessing this daylight occurrence.

An did not my generously inclined employer present me with a luscious pomegranate for a good deed I considered too insignificant for compensation?

Last night I dreamed of a successful combat with a fire-spitting dragon!

Does not a peach petal signify long life; a bat much happiness; a pomegranate many children, an a dragon great power?

Could a youth of the Orient such as I, born of humble parents, wish for greater fortune?

August 25, 1928   TOYO

* * *

I AM sure Wing will deliciously enjoy your lovely poem, "Toyo." There is a possibility, however, that he may not be in the city.

We all enjoy it, though, very, very much. Surely no youth of the Orient could wish for better omens.

Irish

* * *

Everybody's friend: Well, 'tis an awful mess I'm after being in. You see it's like this. After going along beautifully happy for lots of years, I get the idea that I ought to be having a baby. Why will people look for trouble?

Being the good honest Irish lass that I am—of unquestioned character, that is, no one ever questioned me about it—I takes me duties very seriously, so sez I to myself sez I, sure I'll be after gathering lots of books on the subject and be showing the ladies of our crowd the proper way to be doing this.

The first hefty volume tells a lot about life's greatest experience, which by this time strikes me as being a bit over-advertized. Howsomeever, thinks I, I will just go on with me books.

The next one says read poetry to give the child an imagination and a love of the beautiful. No Irishman was ever born without imagination—that's why we lie so beautifully—but maybe this would be true about the beauty, so I takes care of that with Kipling's "Ladies" and "If." Then it says to look at lovely pictures that he may be handsome. Down I goes to have a look at some of what Rico calls Rembrandt cartoons. Not so good. The old timers had whiskers and don't look as if they had "*It.*"

Belike this is the job! How do folks ever have a dozen?

Then she said read of great characters, and I did. Now I am all mixed up. Teddy Roosevelt was the peppy sort of person, but I fear he might be hard to live with. People who are always raring to go, tire me. Then I read some more of Washington, and to me surprise I was after learning that 'twas a bit of a ladies' man he was.

'Tis me thinking "Glory Be, all this time wasted,"—and what

with thinking of what his father will say should he look like Roosevelt and write poetry! Still, feeling that I owe the creature the best, I do be after reading a bit by Irvin Cobb on poker, for his Dad will have too many "wild cards," and thinking that this might not be so bad, if a person could create a good poker hand, it might be all worth while.

Then remembering the race a girl gave me years ago for the privilege of using me present calling cards, thinks I, better read a bit about flirting. Memory going back a bit on my own side, I reads two of those.

One day recently I'm after telling the doctor that 'tis all arranged, and what with me music and me pictures and me books, I'll give the world a treat. 'Tis a turmoil I'm in the now. Sure he tells me that the picture that takes, may be the one I saw at the fight one night recently. But anyhow, he sez he will take a hundred off the bill 'cause he's going to tell it at the Wayne County Medical Meeting.

Sure I was wailing like a Banshee when all at once, sez I, I'll call this a misdeal, and I'll be after concentrating on me husband who's after having a tenor voice that would charm the birds out of the trees and has enough "*It*" that he could sell roaches.

Me order is in for a boy with black curly hair. I'll probably get a red-headed girl—or worse yet, a blond. What a life! I stop—overwhelmed.

September 29, 1928   IRISH

* * *

WISE idea, Mrs. "Irish," to concentrate on the good husband who has a tenor voice that would charm the birds off the bushes.

And you will find that the "trouble" will all be forgotten when the baby arrives, whether it be a curly-headed boy or a red-headed girl. Whatever it is, or whatever it does, it will be exactly O.K.

[50]

Fleur

* * *

I

DEAR NANCY BROWN: Have been waiting for a chance for ever so long to fling my hat in the ring and be accepted in the Column fold, but it doesn't seem as if I'll ever have a problem serious enough to admit me, and can I merit it, regardless?

Long ago I believed I had journalistic tendencies and began by taking shorthand. Here I was advised "to take a chance and write something up." That ended that.

How different life is from what we plan, and how often so much better. If we could realize this when disappointments seem most bitter, what a help it would be!

How I cried when my father refused to let me go on the stage in a dancing act. I was so sure of success. I saw myself as millions have before me, tripping the light fantastic, or rather the ultra exotic, for the pleasure of rows and rows of spectators, and striking a spark of enthusiasm in the stoniest of critics. The fact that I had no voice to speak of did not prevent my starring (in imagination) in continued musical successes. How pleasant are the fantasies of youth!

Well, father knew best. I realized that, some years later, when I visited a vaudeville house and saw the dancing act just about where it was when I started. Thus ended my theatrical aspirations, at least in the dancing line. There is still the sneaky desire, after attending a Barrymore or Cornell première. Perhaps my children or grand-children are destined—who knows.

November 27, 1928   FLEUR

I GUESS all grown-ups know how right you are about life being so different from what we plan it when we are young. Of *course* you thought you could be a journalist, a grand-opera singer, a dancer—and usually there are added nurse and actor, and especially movie actor, in the present age. And probably nine-tenths of these enthusiastic feminine planners of future careers, turn out to be perfectly good wives and mothers and home-makers—which is as it should be.

Please do come again.

*

To "June"

If April skies had smiled and wept upon you,
    Or rough March winds had blustered at your birth,
Perhaps it would be harder, now, to love you,
    Without so fair a sweeting for your worth.

If May's gold disks of lavish dandelion
    Foretold to me the wealth of joy you mete,
Or if July had blazed your trail with fire,
    Or silken poppy banners, drowsed in heat—

God's alchemy that wrought midsummer roses
    Had not attained His far, majestic goal,
Till flawless etching of a cloudless June-time
    Revealed the radiant beauty of your soul.

September 16, 1932   FRIEND OF THE FAIRIES

Wind Along the Waste

* * *

DEAR LADY NANCY AND COLUMN FRIENDS: Darn! I've been sitting here fifteen minutes with that line written, trying to decide where to begin this tale.

The logical place to begin, I guess, is the day in late April when, from my hammock slung in the forward deck of a chugging little river steamer, 2,200 miles up the Amazon Valley from the Atlantic ocean, I got the first glimpse of R— de M—, the last outpost of civilization on the Brazilian frontier, where the Javary and the Itecoahy Rivers meet, 30 miles above the Amazon itself. Across the Javary lies Peru—away to the south and west countless miles of totally unexplored wilderness, jungle and swamp.

R— de M—, a tiny collection of corrugated iron, palm thatched huts on stilts, above the river bank—or rather, above the spot where the river bank should be if there was one. (As is common along the Amazon and its tributaries, this region is inundated almost throughout the year.) A more God-forsaken, disease-infested hole than R— de M— has yet to be found, and yet, how vitally important it is to the few rubber planters who dare the terrors of the Javary, commonly known in South America as "the white man's grave."

Our faces, however, were turned to the Itecoahy, which has never been traced to its head waters, and which borders a totally unexplored region. By launch, and later by native dugouts, we proceeded upstream.

On either side, the forest presented an unbroken wall of living green, made brilliant by myriads of butterflies above the huge tropical flowers growing on the parasitical vines which almost hide the trees. Our course lay through the center of the stream, to avoid the insects and alligators which infest the banks beneath the trees, leaning far out over the water.

We were very near the equator, and the whole country is a steaming cauldron during the heat of the day, so we did most of our traveling at night, running the risk of being capsized by drifting branches or unsuspected sandbars, as being infinitely preferable to being cooked alive attempting daytime traveling. Imagine, if you can, creeping through that enveloping darkness into an utterly unknown land through the silent night.

Did I say silent? A silence filled with a million sounds. The croaking of millions of frogs; the menacing, terrifying roar of the howling monkeys. It is almost unbelievable that such an utterly weird and blood-curdling cry can come from one small, gray, and comparatively harmless creature, crouched in some tree top near the shore. On still moonlight nights a new voice joins the chorus—the cry of "the Mother of the Moon," as the native calls an owl which leaves its nest only on moonlight nights, and whose cry is so like a human soul in agony that I never hear it without a tremor up and down the old spinal column.

At last, far up the Itecoahy, we left the canoes, cached a few supplies in light steel boxes brought for that purpose, in a "tambo" (a native shelter composed of little more than a roof on poles) on the only dry spot we could find, and faced the solid wall of vegetation, apparently impenetrable, which is the jungle swamp. Paths are unknown and the mass of tree trunks, giant ferns, climbing vines and llanas so thick that the only possible way to get through was to send "the boys" ahead to make a path, using their machetes, huge native knives that in their hands accomplish wonders!

We made from 15 to 20 miles a day and, in case some of you veteran hikers laugh at this point, let me tell you that this is remarkable speed through virgin jungle. Remember that the floor of the

jungle is just a vast morass, treacherous as only swampland can be—
a mass of twisting roots and rotting vegetation, with the ever-present
menace of the millions of poisonous insects that rise in swarms, and
the deadly jararaca—the most common and the most dangerous of the
Amazonian snakes. We six whites were protected somewhat by our
heavy knee-high leather moccasins, but our "boys" were barefoot.

It is one of the marvels of the tropics that the Indians can go
through these places half-naked and apparently unharmed. Even so,
the mortality from snake bite is simply enormous!

For ten days we splashed on through the gloom (for the sun never
penetrates into these depths), with the 'gators, snakes and monkeys
as our only companions—pestered almost unendurably with the
insects, and faced with the problem of possible mutiny among our
natives. For we were now in the depths of the cannibal country, the
home of the Mangeromas—Indians against whom we had been
repeatedly warned. We had as yet seen no sign of them, although, as
we later learned, they were fully aware of our presence and keeping
close track of our progress. I can easily believe it to be true.

It may give you some idea of the density of the vegetation when I
tell you that a man could stand two yards away and be utterly lost
to your sight. Each day saw our "boys" become more terror-
stricken, and the Major more determined to go on.

Finally, there came a day when we stumbled through the barrier
and found ourselves on the banks of an unknown river, apparently
on none of our maps. Almost directly opposite our point of exit rose
an island in midstream—the first real dry land we had seen in weeks.
I never was so glad to see anything in my life! We made camp and
rested for a day while the Indians hastily threw together a raft, and
poled across to the island which was to be our headquarters, although such was not our intention at the time.

We found ourselves in a deserted Indian village—the huts in a state of disrepair which indicated that they had been unoccupied for a long time. I momentarily expected our Indians to desert, since it was evident that this was one of those villages deserted by the inhabitants because of some imagined "evil spirits" and declared taboo. However, on the contrary, our "boys" seemed contented for the first time in days. It developed that they figured that in this one spot, if in no other, they would be safe from the cannibals, who, having once deserted the village, could not be prevailed upon to enter it again.

As for the evil spirits, our head "boy" explained that since the said spirits were inimical to their enemies, the Mangeromas, these same spirits were undoubtedly friendly to all other Indians. At any rate, they accepted their supposed presence stoically, as the lesser of two evils—a lucky break for us whites. I shudder to think of what might have been the fate of our expedition had the Indians deserted at this point.

For the past week we had all been suffering from fever in its various stages. Doctor Mac was kept busy with his quinine, day and night. Mickey—the second secretary, the youngest of the men and my boon companion—was delirious. I was beginning to feel distinctly low, although at the time I think the doctor and I were in the best condition physically of the lot. We lost one of our "boys" with "beri-beri." It was evident that there was no time to be lost if we were to accomplish what we had set out to do.

The long trip had made serious inroads on our supplies, although we had meat in plenty, tapir, monkey, fish and an occasional jaguar. (We had one very exciting jaguar hunt—wish I had time to go into detail about it.)

Then one night my personal boy, Joao, came to me with many grunts of "sucuruju." My heartbeats quickened. The "sucuruju"—anaconda, or, as you will recognize it, the boa constrictor—is without a doubt at once the terror and the fascination of the Amazon wilderness.

Ill as I was, I couldn't resist the lure of that magic name, and, together with the Major and Doctor Mac, fared forth. Our way led downstream to a sandbar perhaps a quarter of a mile from camp. As we neared the bar a faint, black mass was discernible. We landed on the opposite edge of the bar and cautiously approached.

I can feel the horror of it yet—here, in this quiet lamp-lit room high above the busy streets of Detroit. I close my eyes and stand once more on that sandbar in an unknown river in the far southland and face that monster again. A quivering, glistening, scaly mound, it lay coiled to a height of over five feet, the great head with its yellow, glowing eyes swaying out from the bottom of the coils. I can feel that numbness creeping over me yet, as the great snake began to uncoil.

Fortunately for us all, the Major, a veteran of the swamps, who was quite proof against the hypnotic powers of the brute, emptied his automatic into the great head. That broke the spell and brought my Winchester 30–30 to my shoulder none too soon, for the ugly thing was only infuriated by the round of shot from the Major's automatic. The soft-nosed bullets from the Winchester did the job, however. High in the air it flung in its death agony, a twisting column glistening in the starlight, and then fell, still writhing, into the river. We had to wait until morning to examine our kill.

You, who shudder at a garter snake, what do you say to one 42 feet long, 18 inches in diameter? Can you picture that? Oh, I have heard of boas reaching a length of 58 feet but white men rarely see them. They do their feeding at night and sleep all day. Some day you folks may view the skin of this specimen.

Look where I am, Nancy, and I've just begun. I could go on and tell you of days of fighting the fever, of apparently recovering only to go down again. Of long battles through the jungle—of our first meeting with the cannibals and how we made friends with them—of being lost six days with Mickey, and stumbling at last into a strange Indian village (it was this little adventure that wrecked your girl friend)—of the primitive "telegraph" that saved us at a critical moment from becoming a more or less tasty meal—of our return to our island—but what's the use?

I could write a book and not tell you the half of it. Perhaps, if you wish, my friends, I'll come back and tell you the rest when Nancy has a "dull" time (if ever) in Column House.

As ever,

January 20, 1929   WIND ALONG THE WASTE

* * *

YOUR story reads like the chapters from the adventures of "Monte Cristo," dear woman. I was sorry when it ended.

Please do come back and tell us more of your experiences in that wild, strange country. We shall look forward to them.

*

A Puzzle

So much in life
   There is to learn—
Of fancy, fact and folly,
   Of hiding tears
When pain is felt,
   And trying to be jolly.
I thought I knew so many things,
   And knowledge brought me joy,
Until I proudly started
   Being Mother to my boy!

October 11, 1931   HELENA

Stout Fella

* * *

CHEERIO NANCY!: I have been away a long time, but now I think I am here to stay.

Can you ever hope to imagine the feelings I had on that day which was supposed to be my last of life? It was like what a soldier might have once felt—almost certain death ahead, a desire to defy it, and a yearning to escape it.

Life is sweet when you look at it through the eyes of youth. And I wanted to prove the doctors were wrong by a rather foolish method. I wanted to flaunt in their faces the realization that they could not dictate to anyone whether he should live or not; and I wanted to make them regret the anguish—the agony of suspense, during those six months, that they caused me. Oh, they tried to break the bad news to me gently, but I forced their admissions.

Death in six months! Who can tell when it will come? I was determined that if I were going to die, I'd meet it halfway. I'd be in the air. And then your words: "Be a sportsman." What could I do? I stayed out of my plane, haven't been in one since, and spent that day tramping through the woods and over hills until I was exhausted. So I faced the truth at last—Kismet. As far as spirit is concerned, I am quite my own man again.

I went on a trip after the reaction came. I wanted to try and forget. I wanted to wake in the morning and find interest in new surroundings instead of thinking "Only a few days left!" If you only knew the help the thought of you was during those days! Now that I am back, what can I say? Thanks? Well, rather!

Have you heard further from *"Coeur de Lion?"* He is *un brave.* Perhaps by this time a little luck has come his way. Carry on, fella.

That's all I can say to "Goofy," too. Keep your chin up. It helps.

And now I must face Life. I wonder if that will be as hard as facing Death. You helped once, Nancy, so don't forget.

December 17, 1929   STOUT FELLA

* * *

SUCH a lot of good news we are receiving from our Column sick folks this week, "Stout Fella!" "Another Kim" came back Saturday and told us she would walk again and is going to marry David soon. And now you, lad, come back and tell us that you are still here and able to take your place in the world. I was sure you would.

It was a lot of suffering you endured all for nothing, wasn't it? But I would not criticize the doctors too severely, son. You say yourself you forced an admission from your physician which meant that he must tell you what seemed to him the truth, or else a falsehood. He was a truthful man and his conscience would not allow him to tell you what he did not believe to be true. We all make mistakes. Besides, it was just a bit exaggerated on your part to mark the day on your calendar on which you expected to leave the world. No human being could tell us as definitely as that.

You are indeed a "Stout Fella." You played the game like a good sportsman—and won. But lad, be a good sportsman still further. Take care of your strength until you have nursed it back to normal. Don't go tramping through the woods and over hills until you are exhausted. Don't run for street cars. Take your time and live leisurely for a while.

If you were in business, and an expert told you that a certain method would ruin it absolutely, and another method would build it up to firm financial standing, you would not hesitate about which method you would choose, would you?

Your health is more important than any commercial affair in the world. In fact it is the most important possession of mortals, especially young people. Don't abuse it. Care for it as you would any other valued possession.

You will come to our Column reunion, won't you? And even though most of us know your story, there will be some who do not know why you happened to come the first time. You will tell the story, briefly, won't you?

Maybe you will meet "*Coeur de Lion*." We are hoping so. He has never written since his first letter.

Life is not hard to face if you face it bravely and happily.

I shall watch for you Christmas Day. It will help me very much if you will write early.

*

To "Rag Carpet"

Oh, weary weaver, bending o'er thy loom,
   Fret not that here with threads of drab and gray
Thy shuttles click, 'tis now but life's high noon
   And presently, with threads of colors gay,
The interchanging plaiting warp shall weave
   Gay shapes, to match those ones that went before
All done according to plan—and leave
   A pleasing, finished product on your floor.
For drab and gray and red and green and blue
   Must take their turn, to make the universe.
From distant points we get a better view
   As graceful forms appear and mists disperse.
Stand back! Look up! All thoughts of failure ban—
   The Great Designer will not mar the plan.

July 2, 1932   CZAR

Jerry's Sallie-Dear

* * *

Dᴇᴀʀᴇꜱᴛ ᴏꜰ ɴᴀɴᴄʏꜱ, ᴀɴᴅ ᴄᴏʟᴜᴍɴ ꜰᴏʟᴋꜱ: Here we are, all five of us, Jerry, Sallie-Dear, Jan, Joan and—small Derek, born Aug. 14 at 5:30 p. m., just outside Oslo, Norway. Derek, bless his small, soft roundness, is known now to everyone, including the stoical Chloe, as "Rikky."

Nancy, the twins are walking now. They have seven teeth, each, and lovely silky reddish gold curls. They said "Mummy" to Jerry and me the other morning!

This letter will be taken up with the arrival of wee "Rikky," and the astoundingly dramatic manner in which he came into this world.

First of all, we leased for the season a lovely old home about 15 or 20 miles outside of Oslo—and Jerry made trips around the country while Friend and I were content to dream away under the trees.

One hot August day Jerry was out walking, and when it became quite late Silly Sallie became worried about her Jerry boy and set out alone along the road in a little gig drawn by the rather skittish horse that we had dubbed "Horace." We—"Horace" and I—had gone about three miles along the road, when all of a sudden something (some small animal, I think) darted across the road, frightening "Horace," and he began to run away with me. Try, if you can, to imagine my feelings and thoughts, while hurtling along that narrow, deserted road. I had visions of meeting some other conveyance, possibly an automobile, around a hairpin curve which we were approaching at a sickening speed. I tugged on the reins like a mad woman and screamed my heart out.

All of a sudden we turned the curve, and there were Jerry and Phil! I thought "Horace" would dash on them before they had a chance to save themselves—and then everything went quite, quite black. The boys had each jumped at "Horace" and hung on until he had come to a standstill—then turned to the assistance of poor Sallie, now curled in a limp heap on the bottom of the carriage. Jerry sent Phil post haste toward the house for Friend and the nurse, and while they were gone Rikky-boy came into the world.

After a long while, it seemed to me, I was back in my own wide, soft, white bed, with the dear old Norwegian doctor beaming at me and telling me (according to Jerry's halting translation) that I was one of God's bravest—and he never hoped to see a finer baby. Finally everything was as before, and in the third week of September we were all back in our own dear homes.

I can look out of my window now, down into the garden. The sun is slanting through the trees on placid Chloe, contentedly peeling potatoes on the stone bench near the fountain. The twins are lurching gleefully along the flagged path with Whig and Tory, the Scotties, walking sedately beside them. In their little pink and blue rompers they look like animated hollyhocks.

Nancy, my own dear Nancy, did you miss me as much as I missed you? Those long summer days I would sit out in the Oslo garden and read THE NEWS and wonder about you all. Nancy dear, tell me that they haven't forgotten me in these five months.

October 7, 1930   JERRY'S SALLIE-DEAR

* * *

Now, "Sallie-Dear," you know we have not forgotten you. How could we? You and those twins and Jerry have established yourselves very firmly in the hearts of the Column Folks. And now we are making room for little Rikky. His arrival into the world certainly was dramatic. Too narrow an escape for comfort, for our "Sallie-Dear." I breathed a sigh of relief when I finished the story and found that you were both all right.

[63]

Sed

* * *

Dear nancy lady: I've learned a very bitter lesson, and it's so hard to take. Only you mothers and high-school girls will understand.

I am a popular girl, and I have paid—dear, dear, dearly—for the dances and shows and parties I have attended so often during the past semester. Now, examinations are over—people have passed, and I, Nancy, the girl with the ambitions, have failed. I can't graduate! It will mean another semester. Oh, it makes me sick. Look at "Rippy." She has passed—graduated with the rest of her class. Now she is free to go to college or complete her career, like I want to do so badly—and Nancy, can't you see—I've failed.

What do parties sum up to when you can't look your mother and your father in the face—and when you avoid the eyes of your teachers and make excuses to the students? Can't you see? Now, when it is too awful late, I repent, and acquire a vigorous desire to study. But I'll do it—pass—and I'll show 'em, Nancy!

Would you give up your summer vacation and stay in summer school during those warm months? I have made up my mind to do it, but Mother and Father think I need a little vacation.

May I add—I'm 17 and in love. Could that be the trouble? I don't go steady, as I don't believe in it, but in my heart I want to.

Do you like me, Nancy? Do you think that I am a silly, little nitwit that doesn't know anything? Do you suppose that I am the only one failing like this? I tried to swear off dates, but it was too hard.

I hope I grow up. At what stage does a girl become a woman? S'pose I'll ever have as much sense as "Anne o' Dixie"?

I have a darling brother in college. He has so many brains and so much personality! He is going to become a doctor. This is his third year.

I want to be an artist.

Do you think that it is good for a girl who has been brought up at home all her life, to go away—far away to college? I think it would be good for me to go away and live on my own for a while. It should be an experience for every girl to go through. That is what I want to do. Are post-graduate courses good? There certainly is a lot for a girl to think of when she leaves school, isn't there? But I didn't, I failed.

February 11, 1931   Sed

* * *

NEVER mind, "Sed." Gather up your courage and start over again like a plucky little girl. You have made a mistake and learned your lesson. It has been expensive but expensive things are usually worth while, aren't they? Out of this lesson you will learn many, many things which will be of value to you all your life. Whenever you find yourself with an inclination to slack your work in the future, for the sake of your parties and other fun, you will remember this experience and it will save you another mistake.

Going back with the next class for your work again will be hard, very hard, but there, too, you will not lose entirely, for you will acquire added courage for facing a disagreeable situation.

Here is something else, too. Your work will not be quite as hard for you the second time. Therefore, you will have time to do it more thoroughly and learn a heap more. Perhaps you might even be able to take up an extra subject. I suggest typewriting. It is always a useful thing to know, and is not difficult to learn. It would fit in nicely with taking your regular course a second time.

I should not wonder if being in love had much to do with your failure, dear. If a girl is in love, her mind fixes itself pretty steadily to one place. It is an effort for her to concentrate on school work. But you are only 17, "Sed," and love affairs should not be taken seriously. Perhaps you think it *is* serious. All girls do at 17. All girls always have, and always will.

But after you have passed 17 and then some, you will look back and smile at what you thought was so serious and wonder how it ever could have happened. Perhaps you will not believe this either, but you may forget even the name of the boy who means so much to you now.

"At what stage does a girl become a woman?" It varies with the girl. Sometimes, she becomes a little woman at 15, or even younger when trouble and sorrow come into her life. Sometimes she is 25 or even older, when she is protected and cared for and only the happy things of life are hers. No need to hurry to be a woman, dear. There is time enough, when it comes of its own accord.

I *do* think that it is good for a girl to go away to college all by herself—one of the best things in the world. She comes in contact with so many other girls from so many different homes and learns so many different things. Absence from home makes home itself, and Mother and Father, even dearer than if she had been with them constantly.

I see no reason why you might not have "as much sense as 'Anne of Dixie.'" But one must use one's mind, you know, little girl, in order to be thoughtful and to develop good judgment.

What indeed do parties amount to, if you can't look Mother in the eye, and face your teachers because of them? Indeed I *do* see exactly what it means. And now that *you* see, you will attend different kinds of parties, or none at all, won't you?

I like that sentence of yours—"But I'll do it—pass—and I'll show 'em, Nancy."

I think that the plan of taking a summer course is all right for you unless it interferes with home plans that Mother has made. If it will mean her staying home for you to take up this course, I would give it up and consider that part of the price of failing.

I like your pluck and determination to do your work over again and do it right—like it, oh, so much, little girl.

*

All I Ask

All I ask is a little home,
The walls all lined with cheer,
The trusting love of a happy pal,
And a couple of babies dear.

Not a lot of riches,
Just enough to carry on.
What's the use of money,
When you're dead and gone?

And I'd like a few free hours
Out of every blessed day,
To do the things I want to do,
To read and laugh and play.

And I'd like to have the feeling
That no matter where I'll be,
I'll always see a friendly hand
Come stretching out to me.

May 23, 1931   COBBLESTONE

Cherry

* * *

I

Dear nancy brown: I have been an amused, delighted, touched and bewildered reader of your Column for about two years, but have never ventured to write before. However, the time has come, as the Walrus said, and in talking of many things, someone who calls herself "Hawthorne" asks about furnishing an apartment on very little. Please, may I just have a line or two of your precious space to tell her it can be done, indeed it can, and beautifully? And may I have another few lines to tell her how it was done, in one instance?

How your suggestion of dotted Swiss curtains and rag rugs brought it all back to me! The fact that someone else has the apartment now, and the two who lived there are two tempestuous years older, and oh, so much wiser, has nothing to do with the case.

We met two weeks ago (he who was Head of the House in that little apartment, and I), accidentally, and were very casual, asking meticulously after each other's health and welfare. Nancy, with all your experience, perhaps you can tell me why two people who adore each other can break their hearts thinking they're doing a gallant thing? How often is gallantry only pride—stupid, silly pride?

To get back to the apartment. To begin, you sit down with a paper and pencil and set down the things that you absolutely cannot get along without. Then set down the things you really need, if you have enough money left. Then the list of things you are going to get from the family as wedding gifts (or things you already have, if you have some of your own).

Next make a round of several stores and price the articles that are essential, writing down the names of the stores and the price of each article and its points of superiority. When you finally come to do the actual buying, you will find that you waste no time in fruitless decision, only to find afterwards that you really would have preferred the other one.

Let me warn you that every minute of careful planning you do beforehand will pay you dividends when you spend your money. Don't spend a nickel before you have all your purchases outlined and priced or you'll have a lovely living room, perhaps, and have nothing left for the bedroom, or *vice versa*. I wish I could help you, and I wish you as ecstatic a time with your apartment as we had with ours. I've always wanted to try another—in putty color, perhaps, with burnt orange or robin's egg blue—you know that odd shade of blue green. I'd have black candle sticks and black frames on my pictures for accent. But all the fun (almost) of planning an apartment is having someone to plan it for, *n'est pas?*

May 17, 1931   CHERRY

* * *

IT IS, "Cherry," it is. Having someone to plan for is the supreme pleasure of all the planning of the home.

I have an idea that your letter will play an important rôle in the lives of more than one young couple who are contemplating marriage at present when the financial background is not as good as it is some days.

"Why two people who adore each other can break their hearts" thinking they are brave when it is only silly pride? Maybe it is perversity. Maybe it is just being human.

Believe if I was one of those two people, and realized it was only "silly pride" that was keeping me from my happiness, I would toss it a derisive "Pooh for you," and sit down and write my heart out

[69]

to the other of the two; or else I would inveigle him into my home and tell him about it, until he was convinced beyond the shadow of a doubt.

Try it, dear "Cherry"—it is worth it.

And please write to us again.

* * *

II

DEAR NANCY BROWN: You invited me to come back, you know, and were so awfully sweet about it, I'm going to tell you my tale of woe. Perhaps you can supply me with a telling argument which will convince the Head of the House he's being stubborn and silly and altogether ridiculous, and make him listen to reason—which I assure you is all on my side.

I followed your advice and gave Pride a derisive "Pooh for you," and talked it over at great length, but Head wouldn't give in an inch, and there you are.

Here's the story: H. H. (Head of the House) is just beginning his career and makes $200 a month, $50 of which he sends to his mother, who lives in a small town, leaving us $150 per month. Not much, you admit. He has a fine future, but it will be very slow for a while, hence our very modest beginnings in the matter of an apartment. We can live on $150 a month of course, if we have to, but—

Before I was married, I lived in a small town and wrote sweet, simple little tales of love and what have you for farm papers, needlework journals and Sunday School papers, etc., averaging between $1,500 and $2,000 a year and lots of time left over. I've got the trick of it now, know my markets, and I really think that it's lots of fun, but—

H. H., with true male egotism, feels that a man should support his wife and support her entirely, come what may. I provided all the linens for our newly established household and a few jimcracks in the way of vases and pictures, etc., but beyond that, the Lord and Master paid for everything we bought. It was fun, really, seeing what we could do with as little as possible, but after we were married, he continued to be silly about my money. If I paid a household bill, he paid me back.

He says the stuff I write is silly rot (which doubtless it is) and surely one of my mental attainments (this is my cue to sniff) does not seriously mean to say that I enjoy writing it. I cannot convince him that I do.

He cannot say that I neglected him or my wifely duties about the house because of my work. He has never seen me at the typewriter since we were married. He did not come home to lunch, so I had my days to myself.

As I said before, we can live on $150 a month, but we can have so much fun with extra money! Two thousand dollars a year can buy so many little luxuries!

I suppose I could deceive him about it; men are so stupid about what things cost, but somehow I feel that we would be building on shifting sands, and when I got found out (which I would eventually), that would be something which I could not explain away. It isn't any fun just to put money in the bank. He wouldn't even hear of my buying clothes for myself with it.

Please Nancy, what would you do if you were in my place? We've quarreled about it bitterly, and have gone our separate ways, and we both admit we are unhappy and that we did have such fun together. I feel that we are being so foolish, and yet it is hard to go all the way, too.

If he were being merely stubborn and horrid about it, it wouldn't be so hard, but I know it's because he wants to do it all for me himself, and when I want to spend my money, he feels that I am not satisfied with what he can give me. I *am*, in a way, but what I earn is the difference between not having quite enough and having some left over.

He says that there isn't any difference between me and the woman who goes out to work in an office or a factory; the principle is the same and no woman is going to support him. He wants a little clinging vine, bless his heart, who "doesn't know a thing about business, my dear, not a thing." Now I'm getting all worked up again.

I know that you do not approve of wives working, but don't you think that in our case the dear male crittur is straining a point? Please tell me I'm right, Nancy Brown, and bolster up my weakening courage.

I forgot to say that the $50 he sends to his mother cannot be reduced, and I wouldn't have it for the world. She has her home in a small town and the $50 we send her, and does a little nursing now and then, so she manages. She's a darling and we would like to send her more. There is no one else to contribute to her support. I send her gifts when I can, but if I sent her money, the Dominant Male would flay me alive.

Who said marriage was a 50–50 proposition?

June 7, 1931   CHERRY

* * *

I THINK you are right—but I would give in. Wouldn't you be happier with him, giving up selling the stories, than living as you are now?

Long years ago, I remember a dear old lady telling a girl who was about to be married that the giving in must be done by the wife in most cases, and that she would be happier to let her husband have his way, even though she felt that she were right. The girl never forgot it. It helped her to smooth many a road that would otherwise have been rough.

[72]

Moreover, I have a strict old-fashioned notion that that promise "for better or for worse, until death do us part," is a pretty sacred line.

You are married, dear "Cherry," to a good man who loves you and whom you love. You are separated and both unhappy because you both want your own way and neither will give in. It does not sound very sensible to me. Personally, I should prefer to skimp along on $150 a month, until he is able to earn more, rather than to break up my home as you two are doing.

Go back to him. Build up your home again. Write your stories in your spare time, and file them away. Some time he may be at least willing to compromise; or a time may come when he may be glad to make use of this talent you have. Then you will have your material all ready.

Breaking up a home is a very serious matter, you know, my dear. Only the most serious reasons in the world should effect it. You are wasting a lot of years in which you might be happy with him.

Suppose something should happen to either of you. What an everlasting heartache the other would have!

You say his mother lives in a small town and is able to do nursing now and then. Knowing something of the expense of living in a small town, I think you are wrong when you say that she could not manage with less than $50 a month. Forty dollars would keep her quite happy and comfortable.

But if the Head of the House will not listen to that either, I would let him have his way again.

I hope that you will write soon and tell us that the home with two happy people in it is opened again.

The Gas

* * *

NANCY BROWN: Despair drives me to your door. But let me start from the beginning.

Nine years ago I fell in love with a cultured, good looking young man, one year my senior. I was 20, good looking, too, but ignorant. In fact, I never went to school up to that age. We were married after six months of courtship and we were both extremely happy.

Three months after our marriage, a brother of mine came to live with us. My husband and my brother quarreled and I took the side of my brother. My husband and I had many fights, and we both tumbled from heaven to the inferno. But in spite of the continuous strife, our love for each other survived.

True, I did not give as much as I received, being of a rather reserved nature, and having the mistaken idea that the man has to cater to the woman all the time. He was a wonderful lover, affectionate such as one reads about only in novels. He loved me as one loves a goddess, but I often pushed him away, and did not respond to his ardent kisses.

The child came, and we seemed to get along better. We had a common interest, and the child became a tie between us. He was rather sickly and needed more care than three children of normal health.

I forgot to tell you that right from the beginning of our married life, I went to night school, and about two years ago shifted over to the day school. Finally, last year I graduated from high school and in the fall entered college. I worked feverishly to the point of neglecting my husband and my home. I was no companion to him and no wife. When he came home from work, I put his supper on the table, and proceeded to prepare my lesson for the next day. I had never a minute to spare, no Sundays, no holidays—just lessons all the time. My home wasn't dirty, but wasn't clean either, and often when visitors came I was more than embarrassed, but continued following the same path.

Nancy, I don't know how this will strike you, but I swear to you that I thought I was right. I lived like an ostrich, or rather just existed, for if I couldn't make my husband happy, neither was I happy myself. It takes two people to make a happy home.

About five months ago the child fell ill. We thought it was tuberculosis. He coughed, and the doctors could do nothing for him. Finally one advised that I go to a warm climate for the winter. My husband urged me to go for the child's sake. Before I went, I said that I would not be back until September, to which he gave his consent.

But Nancy, after two months' absence, he started to write me pleading letters, begging me to return immediately. He said he was so lonesome that he could not be so long without his family, but I turned a deaf ear and kept on staying there. After a while, I was lonesome too, for I had nothing but a brother there, and could not go to places on account of the child. But I would not give in. True, I was influenced greatly by my family. They said my husband was selfish to call me home from a place that did so much good for my child's health. (He recovered completely.)

My husband and I exchanged some harsh words through the mail, and from that time on our relations grew from bad to worse. I showed my brother his letters and my brother helped me to write as effective letters as he could. The result was that my husband had the impression that I did not love him at all. He was in despair. He was in need of someone, and you know in those cases the "someone" always appears to "console" and "understand." She is a relative of his, a woman who always admired him and looked up to him. An affair started between them and she fell madly in love with him. What he feels toward her, I can not tell definitely, I can only go by what he says. He claims that he has a deep affection for her. Isn't that identical with love?

He says that he wronged her, and owes her much. He says that she needs him as she has no one in this world except him. (She is a divorcée with two children.) He says that he must see her, and if I refuse to let him, he'll do it anyway. So you see, I'd rather consent to this than bring about more trouble. But I said that he can't see her alone, so each time I have to drag along.

I wouldn't mind, Nancy, for oddly enough, I have no hatred for her. She suffers, too. But it is humiliating. It seems that my job for the future is to sit and watch with anguish their faces. I had one of these visits recently and I almost collapsed under the strain. Probably the rest won't be so hard, but oh, this was so terrible!

She says that I lost my security and that I am afraid of her, and that I should be thankful to her for giving me back my husband. She says that she could have taken him for good, but she was too nice to me, and that I have more luck than brains. I don't know. I can't see clearly. The pain and agony of these weeks have blurred my mind. Perhaps she is right. What do you think? My husband thinks that she has a sterling character. Is a woman who steals another woman's husband to be praised?

I want to tell you that as soon as I suspected what was going on, I took the train and came home. I lost my faith in him, but I came home, because I love him desperately. The shock changed me completely. I gave up my outside interests, my family, and even certain friends he did not like, and made up my mind to settle down and make a real home for him. I became affectionate and loving, but alas, I see that we changed places. And it happens that when I want him to kiss me, he says that I am full of pretenses, and then something dies in me.

What do you think, Nancy? Can I succeed in winning my husband back? I know that I could not live without him, and if I fail my fate is

August 31, 1931   THE GAS

* * *

I AM afraid I cannot speak with authority on the question whether you can win back your husband, but he is worth trying for, anyway.

He seems to me rather lukewarm about the other woman, inasmuch as he consents to your being present at their meetings. That is rather a unique situation, you know, the wife being a third party in a triangular meeting of that kind.

I believe, if I were you, that I would relinquish the right of being with them whenever they meet. Make no comments. Just tell your husband that you have decided to let him see her whenever he wishes. Be a bit mysterious about your decision. Don't let him know what is in your mind. His curiosity will be aroused and that will distract his attention from the other woman. I would not scold or criticize, or make any comment whatsoever on the affair.

Make your home and yourself and the child especially attractive. Have something to talk about when he comes home—some piece of current news in which he is especially interested. Cook the things he likes. If there are friends he likes to have visit you, ask them to come to dinner, or to spend an evening. But let him feel free to go whenever and wherever he pleases. Sometimes an overdose of "the other woman" will seal her doom.

He still loves you, I think. The mistake was yours to refuse to return when he asked you. And then you increased your error by

[77]

writing him disagreeable letters. If the subject is ever broached, I would tell him that you made the mistake, and you are sorry.

I would not describe the other woman in the case as a "sterling character."

You accomplished a wonderful achievement in acquiring the education you did after your marriage. It seems to me a woman with such ambition and persistence will be able to succeed in solving her problems.

The problem that you present in this letter is like "Unfaithful's," which has been under discussion for so many weeks in the Column —only reversed, the man being the offender in this case instead of the woman.

It would be interesting to have the men's solutions to your problem, inasmuch as they offered them to "Unfaithful." I am wondering if they will condemn your husband as they did her—for the most part.

*

To Nancy and My Family

May Santa bring you glasses,
    That you may never see
The many faults and foibles
    That Nature gave to me.

And may he tint them rose-bright,
    And polish them with care,
So you may glimpse the love-light
    That's always shining there.

December 8, 1928   ISABEL

Ozymandias

***

M̲Y̲ ᴅᴇᴀʀ ɴᴀɴᴄʏ ʙʀᴏᴡɴ: Here I am. And with a problem.

My friend and I grew up together, went to college together. Together we were in turn atheists, anarchists, syndicalists, stoics, students, and sinners. Together we tore down existing conventions, reconstructed the world (which, by the way, is the same as it was then), denied theology, wrote modernistic verse, picked Pope apart, turned ourselves inside out over Kant, considered Plato, and became intoxicated Saturday nights.

After college, he went home and went to work. (And a philosopher, too!) I stayed on, took my Master's, and went to Europe a year before my Doctorate. There I taught a year in a school established by an American for sons of wealthy Americans' sons who want the "English atmosphere." After that I wandered.

Feeling my long desire to write (oh, you might have expected it!), I bought a little hut on the outskirts of a quaint old French village and—wrote. Fate. I had a book finished; three chapters I expected to add, that was all. And I awoke one morning; it was but a morning, one like this morning, and—I had nothing. Every plastic thought, any emotion that I might have harnessed and put down (Ah! what that once meant!), everything, do you understand? Everything was gone. And I was left alone, coldly, utterly alone. Barren. Truly, I was the remains of "Ozymandias": "'round the decay of this colossal wreck, boundless and bare, the lone and level sands stretch far away. . . ." What avail was all this? Why, O God of creation, must I of all be the maimed one? Strong art, and strong art alone, was now a thing to envy from afar.

Then I tutored a wealthy American lady, taking a vacation from her husband. I was forced to resign when my employer wanted to be tutored at all hours. I then returned to America, where I made a fizzle of editing a small-town newspaper. By this time, as you can well imagine, my finances were rapidly diminishing. And then Fate, like a pitying taskmistress, again appeared on my horizon. My mother died, leaving no heir but myself. It was fortunate that the old minx had met a sudden death or else she would have left it all to the swine of a chauffeur she'd been supporting for 20 years.

Once more I returned to college. This time I took my Doctorate and was offered a seat as the professor of English Literature. In order to have time for my reading, I accepted. And this time I stayed. That was five years ago. Today I have a supposedly high position in a little college west of the Rockies. Although the college has an excellent library, yet there lingers that eternal gap.

I, who once vied with the gods, standing before 25 simpletons and explaining as euphemistically as I can the relationship between George Eliot and Herbert Spencer. And spending evenings away from my books, contemplating life with erudite philosophy professors who have never been outside their own state and consult their text books for definitions.

This year I had free. And I came here. And then it was. A woman-hater through all these years, I had found consolation with Schopenhauer and Nietzsche. "Listen," I would emphatically declare, "a man either has a career or he marries. I'm above that. Marriage—a jumble of words spoken over you by a minister who has never before seen you or much less cares. The only thing that really matters is reason. Damn you, Zeno, thou prophet of falsehood!"

And my friend of whom I had had but little news was here. Visiting a young lady whom he hoped one day to ask to become his wife. The years had been kind to him; he had seen the limit of rationalization and had stopped. And now the vast gap that loomed between us was evident. The college intellectuals were no more. Our paths had diverged; although he probably was as far as I. I met him one day in your library (it's very lovely) and he invited me to "her" house. I went. We entered. And when that radiant vision entered the room, I knew that here at last, after having traveled the world over, was my Ariadne. We looked into each other's eyes and both of us knew. But he did not. And he loved her, I knew. And she loved him, I knew. And greatest of all, I loved both of them.

Nancy Brown, I stayed. I'm here yet. All my knowledge and pseudo-wisdom are of no use to me now. Like Hamlet, I have lived among the shadows of life's overtones, rocked by the music of the cosmos. And now that Fate has again overtaken me, I am powerless, powerless in the rose-like grasp of Love. Little did I conceive this end. I thought that reason could always reign. How inspired was Emerson: "We know better than we do." And, Nancy Brown, she loves me. She says that he, the other, has no more place in her heart. And that I am the one. I could have taken her and fled, gone any-where. I could have. But remember, I still love him.

Now I think I shall go. And try to leave them as they were. Of course, returning to the college is out of the question now. I couldn't bear it. What I'll do, I don't know. I am as much at a loss as the sim-plest and giddiest of your contributors. A failure and his love! A failure and an empty shell. With all my knowledge, what have I? Is there no limit to this irony?

November 3, 1931   OZYMANDIAS

* * *

I DO not see that you are either a "failure" or an "empty shell," sim-ply because you have fallen in love, dear man, even if the girl does happen to be the sweetheart of your life-long friend. Such things will happen. You have just as much as you had before you fell in love

[81]

with her and the love thrown in, and believe me, love is one of the best individual developers in the world.

The solution of your problem seems simple to me. Let the girl decide it. If she loves you, she certainly should not marry the other man. Her only move, I should think, would be to tell him that she has found she has made a mistake. It is not an unusual occurrence. He will be hurt, terribly hurt for a long, long time, but Time does cure even such grievous wounds.

I think you need not be alarmed about the temporary loss of your power to write. It happens occasionally, I believe, to every writer. In time, the power will come back with renewed strength. Surely with the fine educational equipment that you have, there should be no question about what you can and cannot do. The power, and the means of doing it are yours. It lacks only the will to materialize the strength.

If the girl tells your friend that she has made a mistake (as I am sure she will), then I believe I would go frankly to my friend and tell him that I loved the girl, too, and ask him what is to be done about it. I think you need not fear the final verdict. Please come back and tell us the next chapter.

*

To Other Pilgrims

My dears! That I might help you on your way—
Might fill your groping hands with what they seek,
Or furnish some support, however weak,
When you are faint! But I can only pray,
For only Christ can comfort your distress
And give you what man lives for—Happiness.

April 6, 1929   A PILGRIM TO PARNASSUS

Blue Feather

* * *

DEAR NANCY: Your request to talk about happiness put me up in the air. One cannot talk wisely from that location, and as I am still up, there is still no answer. I have discovered that I am a very happy woman, but for the life of me I cannot tell why, so there we are! Anyway, I am wishing you, Nancy, and all of the beloved Family (especially "Holiday"!) the best of the New Year's graces.

I "crossed the New Year," as the Chinese has it, all alone. There were several places I could have been, but this aloneness was my own choice.

That above statement is only relative, of course. One is never "all alone." One cannot be, unless one is insane in a special sort of way. There was no other body in my quiet room, but I cannot even list the numbers who paid a visit before the night was done. You came in, Nancy, and sat quietly in the chintz chair, your hands folded and your bright eyes watching. "Holiday" leaned against the battered old chest of drawers, and the spark from her cigaret flashed in the mirror of the old dolphin sconce. You two, my dears, were in company with an eminent host, including Dr. Beard, Elinor Wylie, two or three newspaper people, a little Dutch farmer, a poet-business woman (from Saginaw), two trappers, my mother, a soldier, Dr. Hu Shih, a Coast Guardsman-poet, Isabel Paterson (of New York), and a nine-year-old girl. What d' you know about that!

The wind was swaying the old house. We had a "green Christmas" this year; no snow at all, excepting a little in the swamps and deep hollows. I knew that the waves of Superior were dashing against the black rocks at Marquette and the red rocks near Munising. I knew that the moon peered down ghostlike on the hidden coves at

Seul Choix—you say it something like "Sish-Wah"—and the bay at Fayette.

At midnight the church bells rang. I finished my coffee, closed the magazine, smiled at Mother's picture over the desk. "Holiday" and I agree about happiness being a lot of little things. They change from time to time, but some things among them are stationary. For this person there must always be the hand-clasp of friends, unlimited horizons and a tall tree beckoning.

Northwoods,
January 8, 1932   BLUE FEATHER

* * *

I AM glad I was one of the chosen few with you in your quiet room on New Year's Eve, "Blue Feather." I loved my hostess and the guests, and felt myself in honored company.

I liked the wind outside, and the dashing waves; and I liked the church bells that rang at midnight, and the chintz chair by the fireplace, and "Holiday" with her cigaret and her cup of coffee. I liked to be with you all, and the friendly hand clasp was good. Thank you.

*

Christmastime

When the shadows come a-creepin' round about, on Christmas Eve,
On the hearthstone flames are leapin' and the romances they weave
Always seem to start me wishin' for the friends I used to know,
And the heart bends low to listen for a voice from long ago.
The past becomes a present and the future seems to blend
With the joyous effervescence that a friendship likes to lend,
And Christmas wouldn't be the same if it should come to be
That friends I name with glad acclaim were ever lost to me.

December 30, 1928   JIM

I Can't

***

Dear nancy: Personally I'm not in any particular distress, but after our interesting letters on happiness, kindest deeds, women smoking, etc., I have been wondering what the next subject for general conversation would be.

I hope you don't think I'm unreasonable, but would like to know just what your opinion on women and mothers drinking is, that is, consuming liquor and allowing their children, from almost infants up, to drink whatever the adults are being served, thinking it—well, rather clever—and providing the guests with amusement as the children become somewhat intoxicated. Personally, I do not think it amusing.

You see, Nancy, I'm trying to draw a picture of our middle class young American homes.

Three years ago, 18 young couples, a few married, some engaged, others with no definite future, assembled for a New Year's Eve party, entertainment being mostly dancing, some cards, and a delicious lunch at midnight. Later the guests departed gay but sober.

Two years ago the same group assembled at another home. A few more were married and engaged and some were proud parents. But during the past year, recipes had been distributed for wine, the result being everybody sampled everybody else's recipe, until the women began to giggle, and men were inclined to be affectionate. However, no damage was done.

One year ago we assembled at still another home. Guests were escorted to the basement where a four-piece orchestra furnished music for dancing and laundry tubs were filled to capacity with ice and bottles. A table served the purpose of a bar. Beer and wine were consumed in large quantities and before the midnight hour had arrived, lamp shades were being worn for bonnets and beads, and the hilarity was more than natural.

This past New Year's Eve we assembled at a home (a scene of many in-between parties), but instead of wine and beer, gin seemed most popular. Shortly after the guests arrived, couples became quarrelsome and stubborn, even hysterical, and much weeping was done. When the midnight hour arrived, most of the guests, as well as host and hostess, had passed out completely.

Nancy dear, can you tell us what the next watch night party will be like? Frankly,

January 11, 1932   I CAN'T

* * *

YOU have traced very well the evolution of the New Year's Eve party from its normal round of pleasures up to the present orgy. Perhaps by next year the pendulum will begin to swing back. That is what happens when it has reached the limit of its natural swing.

Your picture of young American homes where the children are allowed to partake of alcoholic drinks until they become intoxicated and furnish amusement for the guests, does not seem quite as true to form to me as the rest of your letter. Perhaps it is because I have never happened to be in a home where such conditions existed. I cannot imagine any normal person deriving amusement from an intoxicated grownup, for that matter. I should think that parents who permitted such conditions to exist were not themselves quite normal. And I cannot believe that the condition is prevalent.

My opinion of women and mothers drinking? It is difficult to express myself in black and white without seeming too bigoted or too broad. An outstanding objection to women or anyone else drinking at present seems to me to be the fact that there is a law forbidding the sale of liquor.

[86]

Though personally I am not an exaggerated prohibitionist, I do approve of being law-abiding. And certainly, whether it is legal or illegal, it is a repulsive sight to see a woman under the influence, ever so slightly, of intoxicants. It stands for more than just a repulsive sight. An intoxicated woman destroys every ideal of womanhood that man has ever created. That seems to be sufficient answer to me to the question.

Perhaps the Column writers can give you other reasons.

*

"Fleur"

A comet this,
Leaving a cloud of radiance
Over our careworn world;
Throwing a kiss
To Gaiety, yet withal
Serving our mistress, Poetry.
Envy looks longingly
Upon this glittering versatility,
Covets the breeziness
Of its volubility,
And aches for its charm,
Peeps at new worlds
Of luxurious abandon.
Ah! to explore them
With such a companion!
Alas! back to earth
All too quickly we pass;
But still there is star-dust
Thick in the grass.

April 22, 1929   JUNE

Varangia

* * *

NANCY DEAR: Your answer to "Sad Old Woman," 65, who thought her children did not want her to live with them, interested me very much. You are quite right, my dear. History has proved that no house is large enough for two families; but this life of ours has an uncanny way of forcing us into these impossible situations; then seeming to stand back grinning at us as much as to say: "Now get out of it if you can."

Possibly some of the things I have learned from several years' experience in having my mother-in-law in my home may help some of these people who are forced for economic reasons to "double up" in these difficult times. The same rules apply in any case where two women—I believe the women are most affected—are forced to live together.

People who are constantly thrown together are bound to get on each other's nerves. When the situation seems unbearable, separate for a while—even if you have to lock yourself in a closet or the fruit cellar! A few hours apart does much to relieve strained nerves, and resourceful people can always find some way to spend a few hours alone every day.

Don't try to boss and don't allow yourself to be bossed. There is much unnecessary suffering caused by trying to make perfectly good people over. So may "Live and let live" be the motto of each.

When my husband's mother came to live with us there was no other way. She supported herself until she was 75, though. I decided to make the best of it, and I must confess that I feel the same little thrill of pride at having successfully solved this "impossible" problem that I feel at having accomplished any other difficult task. I soon found that one grain of common sense plus two grains of kindness changed her from a liability to a real asset.

She loves to wash dishes—honest. I don't—and of course I allow her that privilege. She likes to mend—another of my pet aversions—and who am I to deprive her of that pleasure? She has lived through many trying times and what she doesn't know about making over, and saving, just isn't worth knowing. I never sewed on even a button until I was married, but I've found I'm real handy and by following her able directions have made coats, hats, suits, etc., out of discarded garments; and the little Varangians are much better clothed because she is with us.

And her stories! We all love them. I read "Grandmother Brown's Hundred Years" and so did she. She was delighted with it and kept exclaiming, "She's just like me," or "That very thing happened to me." But Grandmother Brown's life was tame compared to my mother-in-law's. Her life contained color, romance and heroism, much of which she takes simply as a matter of course, utterly unconscious of the bravery involved. She follows me about, telling these marvelous tales and I work to an accompaniment of them.

She tries, with rather indifferent success I fear, to keep my feet on the ground when my soul longs to soar to the skies. I came home not long ago from a most inspiring lecture, just aching to put some of my surplus inspirations to work. "Oh," I cried, "I wish I could do some great big wonderful thing." She smiled quietly and said: "Never mind, my dear, there will be lots of little things you can do." And there *were*—and *are*.

Six days a week I am "the model homemaker;" but for years I have religiously set apart one day a week to satisfy my Varangia (Viking) personality. I close the door resolutely on my cares and worries and set out blithely in quest of "gay adventure." When we were rich, comparatively speaking—we never were millionaires,

[89]

just much richer than we are now—I used to go to luncheons, matinees, bridge parties, etc. But now I only spend 14 cents. It is sur-
prising the fun to be purchased for two street car tickets and a couple
of transfers.

This week I went to the Art Institute to see the "Michigan Artists'
Exhibit." I enjoyed the "Armistice Day" parade from a second story
window. I liked the marching men, the bands in their colorful uni-
forms, the Knights of Pythias in their Princess Eugenie hats; but
best of all enjoyed the breaking up of the crowd. I usually end my
day at the main library where I select books for the entire family.
I read 50 books last year—that I can remember. Many of these we
read aloud in the evenings to such members of the family as were
interested. When I get real blue, I read "Impatient Griselda." Ever
read it, Nancy? The main character loves her husband and he wor-
ships his first wife; the other characters follow suit; such topsy turvy
love affairs. Well I love Mr. Varangia and he loves me, thank goodness; and I'm glad.

January 14, 1932   VARANGIA

* * *

I AM hurrying your message right on into the Column, "Varangia."
Any letter that can carry constructive suggestions for two families to
live happily under the same roof is worth passing on to the world.

Your suggestion that two women in separate families, living together, should try to give each other frequent hours alone, is the
keynote, I believe, to what will keep harmony between them if anything will. Even though they may like each other, they do get on
each other's nerves. When one goes away and leaves the other
behind, the solitude gives the jangling nerves a chance to recover
themselves. The two women may be fine characters. Each may recognize the virtues of the other, and yet they should not try to live

together. If they do, however, they will be wise to do as you did, to keep the common sense and kindness recipe always in working order.

There are many people who are substituting the fun that may be purchased with two street car tickets for lunches and matinees and bridge of former days. And perhaps they are enjoying it just as much. It depends upon the person.

I have not read "Impatient Griselda." I was interested in the fact that you read 50 books last year that you could remember. That is about a book a week. I think it made me rather wistful. However, I must admit that unless books are very interesting I do not remember them as I used to in earlier days.

*

The Art Center

Shrouded in the mist
Covering the wide avenue,
Two giant forms loom
In their ghastly paleness;
Man's tribute to Art.
It is the mart
Of the living
In search of Life!
The ghosts of the past
Stalk forth, within those walls,
Serving the present strife.
It is their hopeful hour—
Knowledge is power.

March 13, 1932   A. K.

Just Pretending

* * *

DEAR NANCY: I may be foolish in writing you this, and I have a pretty long story to tell, so hope that you will not be bored to death while trying to read and understand. The whole thing has gotten beyond my control, even though I have been trying to go on just pretending for the last ten years.

I started going with a girl back in 1916. We went together up until 1921, when we were married. Several times I tried to break up our friendship, and just two weeks before our wedding day I made a final break. Then I received a letter that made me think I was a cur or something. My people thought that she was the only real girl I ever went with.

So I finally made up my mind to go through with it—which I did. And no one knows what I have gone through since, trying to make her happy. It is driving me mad. I am 32 years old, always worked every day, bought her a home and car, and have always made good money, but here is the trouble: No matter what business I go in or what I start to do, my mind is so worried that nothing goes the way it should.

Several times I have tried leaving her at home down in the South, to see if there wasn't some way that I might work things out. I don't run around, as you might think, and there isn't any other woman in the case, but the idea of knowing that one of these days I will break under the strain, and then everything will out, is the hard part.

She has been a wonderful wife; would lay down her life for me—and don't think that I would do anything wrong—which I haven't; but there has got to be a change, for I am beginning to feel the strain of it all. That is why I thought I would write and ask your opinion.

Do you think it would be a good idea to go to her and tell her the whole story or let her stay there at her home and me here? I seem to make it very well when I am away, and never miss her in the least.

I know that it is not fair to her and it sure is making an old man out of me. Would like to explain it all thoroughly, but it would take up too much time.

I thought that if we had a youngster it would make a difference. We have one, but it only makes it all the worse to endure. The boy is six years old now and a swell kid, but God knows what I have gone through!

Will thank you in advance and trust that you will be able to understand and give me just a little advice anyway.

Will look for an answer in your paper soon, by Sunday if possible.

January 24, 1932   JUST PRETENDING

* * *

You have a very real problem, very real indeed, but yet an intangible one for solution. As you say, present conditions are not fair to your wife, and are supremely difficult for you. I wonder if you would be any happier if you should leave your wife and child. I doubt it.

You obviously are a conscientious man, with a strong sense of loyalty. I have an idea that you would feel that you had been a quitter and were disloyal if you chose to abruptly break all relationships with your wife. The fault of the whole matter lies too far back to make consideration of it of any service now. It was your weakness in allowing the engagement and marriage to go on. But since it did, I believe you will be just as happy to continue as you are, using your mind to try to reason yourself into a better outlook on the situation, than you would be to break it off. I realize it would take a very strong character to carry on, but think it is the best solution, if it can be done.

I believe also that frequent absences of your wife would help. If she would go home to her parents and visit, perhaps twice a year, it would make conditions easier.

I would not tell her how you feel, unless you intend to get a divorce from her, and I cannot see that you have grounds for that. Also, as I have said before, I do not believe you would be happy.

The summing up of my solution would be to stand by and make the best of what you yourself brought about.

*

Girlhood Prayer

(*Dedicated to the Feminine In-Betweens*)

'Tis not for fame or fortune that I kneel, dear God, to pray;
'Tis not for aught of worldly things I ask of Thee today.
I do not plead that all my future should be free
Of grief or want, discomfort, trials, or yet of poverty.
But please, dear God, bend near Thine ear,
And list to what I say:

I want that I should grow to be a woman, strong and true
To those who call me Friend, and to myself, and You.
I want that mine may be a courage ne'er to fail,
But to hold me straight and steady, God, to weather every gale.
I want that I may gain in faith and understanding, too;
That I may have a beauty come from spirit shining through
This outer mask. And when at last You bid me go,
I hope that I may rest content, and say, "He wills it so;
My work is through; I've done my best; it pleases me to go."

May 24, 1933   JUDY

Ever Striving

* * *

WHAT, O Happiness, are you? I cannot see, hear, or feel you. Therefore shall I say, "You are not real"? But I have experienced you; and also the lack of you, Unhappiness. Thus I conclude that you are, like Faith, Hope, and Love, a spiritual gift; and although invisible, inaudible, and intangible, nevertheless real and infinitely desirable; the goal which all mankind is constantly seeking.

Where, O Happiness, may you be found? I found you in the humble little cottage home where my "Best Beloved" and I started life together, and where our little daughter was born. I did not find you in the most costly mansion in which I have ever lived, because love was absent. So I know that you are not dependent on a large sum of money, but very dependent on love. I have found you in an inspiring book, a beautiful picture, harmonious music, and the beauties of nature; in glowing health when mere living was a joy; in a church where I felt the presence of God; in an interesting task well done; in a service unselfishly rendered; in a group of congenial friends; and in many, many places.

Yes, O Happiness, you are real, and because my life has held so much more of you than of your opposite, Unhappiness, I am most thankful.

And it will bring me additional Happiness if, during the coming year, I may draw up my bench in front of Column House fireplace, and keep on

EVER STRIVING

[EDITOR'S NOTE: *This is one of a number of letters giving Columnites' ideas of happiness. They were printed without salutations or answers.*]

Lethe

* * *

DEAR NANCY BROWN: I am hoping you can help me, as the problem I have threatens to break up an otherwise happy home.

Husband and I were married 16 years ago and are blessed with a fine son just 14. Every year was happier than the one before—and there is nothing my husband does not do for me, nothing in his power, I mean. We so wanted a little daughter that when Son was five years of age we adopted a two-year-old baby girl. She was so lovely and we were so happy! But she and I just seem to live at cross purposes. Any order I give her is ignored or scowled at or muttered about. If I tell her to hang up her clothing, she washes her face; if I tell her to wash her face, she brushes her teeth; if I tell her to brush her teeth, she will study her lessons. It seems to be rebellion to my authority. If I tell her to return at a certain hour (always giving 15 minutes leeway), she will be sometimes as late as an hour. She lags through dressing, eating, or any other task and then always has an alibi, sometimes good, but more often no good. Posture and eating habits are getting simply impossible. I have tried to ignore these things, but if I do not speak of them she will tap her plate or shake her milk glass until my control has left me and then I scold—and then my husband chides me for getting so cross. And the young lady smiles and it is all over—she has obtained her desire—to see me put in the same plight I put her.

I have asked my husband not to criticize me before her, telling him I will be glad to take any criticism in private. Of course, Son is taking up cudgels also and he gives orders and advice no child of any spirit would accept. So, in a measure, we are a house divided against itself.

Unfortunately, my husband would never consent to telling the child she was not our own, and Son has no knowledge she is not his own sister.

To be fair in the matter, I am afraid the child has so got on my nerves that I can never be really a good mother to her. I love my husband so, and in our life together this child is the only thing of any importance upon which we have differed.

Please do not tell me I am jealous of my husband's love for this child, for I am not. He loves her most because he is so sorry for her —he was an orphan himself.

This daily quarreling (for it has become such) is making a nervous wreck of me. I find myself saying, while mending her clothing or making her bed, "How I hate her!" Nancy Brown, that is a sin. Can you help me? I try so hard—and fail so deplorably.

February 4, 1932   LETHE

* * *

WHAT would you do under similar conditions if the child were your own? You will probably say that conditions would not be the same, that you would love your own child. There, probably, is the key to the whole trouble. You do not love this child as you do your own, and she feels it. Children are sensitive creatures. Instinctively they know when people do not love them.

Whether you can bring yourself to love this child is a question that no one but yourself can answer, and I do feel that love is the only solution to the problem. She will not try to aggravate you if she loves you, and she will love you if you love her.

Can you look back over the years that you have had her, and see wherein you have failed? See where the trouble began? See wherein the first symptoms of your lack of love for her occurred? That would help much. It is not too late to remedy the difficulty. A child of eight or nine will respond quickly—especially to love. If you hate her as you think you do, you cannot possibly take her in your arms and cuddle her and love her. She knows it. And although her child-mind has not crystallized the thought, she is bitter and resentful.

I believe if you will begin to do things for this motherless little girl—things that you know will especially please her—not just once, but all the time—that you will begin to love her. Human nature is like that.

It will take time to win her over. She will be suspicious, and you cannot break through her resentment and bitterness all at once, but if you have patience and continue, I am sure you will succeed.

You say that she deliberately annoys you, and then smiles with satisfaction when she accomplishes her purpose and puts you into the same plight that you have put her. If you have annoyed her, you should have understanding of her feeling when she annoys you, and accept the lesson you learn from it.

If you begin your course of kind acts to win her love, and she still displays this naughty tendency to annoy you, I would never let her see that she accomplished her purpose. If she continues to disobey, quietly send her to her room to stay until she can be a good girl.

Never raise your voice in talking to her. Never allow yourself to speak in sudden anger. You will say something for which you are sorry.

You have adopted this child. She is just as much yours for the rest of her life as your own son is. Therefore the only way to bring happiness into your discordant home is to win her love, and you cannot do that by thinking, "I hate her." Your letter does not sound as if it came from that type of woman.

Keep right on trying. Take yourself in hand each morning and make up your mind that you are going to do something for that child that will make her love you. It will not be long before you will see a difference.

Janne

***

I

Nancy, nancy: I've come to you for help. Will you give it to me? I have no one else to advise me impartially. Or will you feel that because of what I am, you cannot print my letter—that you and those others, "Kim," "Toyo" and the rest, must despise me? I hesitated to come—you will see why. I only hope that you can help me. Shall I start at the beginning?

Six years ago, when I was only 15, I came to Detroit with my brother. We were orphans—had been for years, and the grandmother who had brought us up was just dead. I was a junior in high school and brother worked. Among the friends we made was a young man 23, who was very lonely. He had been married when he was 19 and, three years later, after illness and mental attacks, he was forced to put his wife in an asylum. She was older than he. He did everything for her that he could; specialists were consulted, but there was no chance for her recovery that they could see. He did not love her, though he was almost ill with pity and worry. He has often told me that she was not the woman he married and he could not force a feeling that was not there. You *do* see, don't you?

For two years he hadn't gone out with other girls. There could be no divorce as his wife was insane, and there was no apparent release, since she was young and physically strong.

Then, all of a sudden, before we could realize it, my brother died. That left me alone—all alone—with a small income and his life insurance. At this time the person who stood by me was Bart. We were both lonely and rather scared with so many years ahead of us, and apparently nothing in them. At first, I stayed with him and helped him as I had Brother. I finished high school. And, Nancy, we found we cared for each other. It all happened so suddenly that we couldn't foresee it, and yet I remember that we both felt it was right. There was no question of his taking advantage of my being so young. What we did, we both willed. Six years, all told, we've loved each other. To both of us they have made up for those earlier years which were so bitterly empty. Bart has taught me so much; the joy of reading; I have tried to write—poetry—and he has given me some of the background a girl loses when she has no parents.

Can you see what is coming? It is the future we both fear. We have grown up and we realize that we stand so alone. We are both condemned; he for taking a lonely, unloved girl and giving her a meaning for her life; I, because I love him and wanted to make up for all the things he otherwise could not have had. We are not bad—circumstances made us what we are, and because we have tried to build up for ourselves a little happiness where there would only have been void and pain, we are censured.

Nancy, we want out of life what other people want, security and a little happiness. We want love, and that is each other, and we want safeguards for our love. At first, we were so conscious of being happier than ever before that there was nothing more to be desired. Then we grew up and found that there were other people in the world—so many of them—and they are interwoven with our lives. We cannot live absolutely alone. And the laws of society say that we are bad, immoral, indecent, even unnatural. Nancy, we are so natural that we are tearing our hearts out for children and a real home. We are more deeply in love than ever. We have served our apprenticeship and adjusted our lives and we want their fulfillment. But I guess we can't have it.

I am so frightened. Things can't go on like this and I can't see anything better ahead. I suppose some people would say that we should be content to love each other, but our household is shorn of its natural completion. Every day it is harder to face people, to hear them say that Bart belongs to another woman, to be refused service. And the final straw came a month ago when Bart's employer asked him to give me up.

We had a long talk that night and tried to find some compromise. I am alone except for him and untrained for anything except being a housewife. I have tried writing poetry and sometimes it seems pretty good, but I have no one to show it to. And lately I have been practicing typewriting, but it is slow and I am unskilled. Bart told me what his employer had said. He wasn't complaining, but obviously something had to be done. There wouldn't be another position in these times. He said he worried only for me—he knew it was hard and being out of work would make it harder. I would have more trouble than he in looking for a job and I could not support myself. It seems as though we would be parted.

Bart blames himself, but how could he foresee this? Anyway, he was young and inexperienced. His idea is that for my good we should separate and he would give me an allowance. Then—I can hardly write this—some day I would get married to someone else and find all the things we can't have together. I am young, but I know that I shall never love anyone as I do Bart. No one else will ever be a part of me as he is. And if another man should care for me, how could I marry him? Not with a lie on my lips, and if he knew the truth there would be no question of marriage.

And what is there if I leave Bart and we both are alone always—for 40 years, or however long we live (we are both very healthy)? We have no friends and any we could make would despise us if they knew our past lives, and the people who would tolerate us would not share our ideals and interests. I can't bear to think of living all those years without him. If one of us had stopped caring, it would be different. I love Bart so much that I would do anything that would make him happier and more secure.

I have tried to tell you everything, but there are so many little tiny ties and so many shadows that are threatening them. Perhaps it seems obvious to you—I have prayed for a way out. We live in a little house, where we have percolator coffee and the newspaper at breakfast. We aren't different; we live honestly. Are you scorning us? We go to church. We like some movies and love plays. We read the same books and listen to the same songs over the radio. Our lives are like hundreds of others in detail, only we seem to have more to bind us together than most people. Shall we deliberately give up all that we are blessed with? Ah, can't you help me in some way—you, Nancy, and anyone else who knows I am not wicked?

February 5, 1932   JANNE

* * *

No, I AM not "scorning" you, "Janne"—not at all. I am thinking of nothing but your happiness. You cannot find it living under present conditions, can you? Therefore, the only way is to make a change of some kind.

First of all, I suggest that you and Bart go at once to a reliable attorney and tell him your story. He may find a legal way out for you.

I doubt if as many people condemn you as you seem to think. It would be a narrow-minded person indeed who would consider you "bad" or "immoral" or "indecent." I believe there are but comparatively few who would not be broad-minded enough to understand the situation into which you and Bart have drifted, and the conditions that led you there, though I do agree that you might find difficulty in making friends, living as you are now. People might feel friendly toward you, but there is no use in trying to evade or deny the fact that many homes and intimate friendships would not be open to you as they would be if you and Bart were legally married. It is the price that must be paid for ignoring the law.

It seems hard that a young man or a young woman should be legally denied the natural right of having a mate when the husband or wife is hopelessly insane, though a thoughtful person can see the reason for the law. If it were otherwise, there might be too many people in the asylums who did not belong there.

Of course you want out of life what other people want—security and happiness and safeguard for your love. There is only one way to have it, dear, as far as one can divine at present—and that way is closed, unless the far-seeing eyes of the lawyer may sight something for you.

If he does not, the only way is Bart's suggestion—a separation. It seems terrible to you at present, but you are not happy under existing conditions, and that is the answer.

Don't try to think of "living all the years" without Bart. Just think of it as a day at a time, or a week. That will not seem so long and something might happen that would bring you together rightfully and happily.

Don't try to think too far ahead into the future—just hopefully, day by day. You will find it is not so hard. Maybe "This, too, shall pass," and the coveted happiness together will come. I hope so.

I had to change your signature a bit. We already have a "Joan."

* * *

II

DEAR MISS NANCY BROWN: You didn't say I might come again, but you need not let me in unless you choose. I would like to tell you what we are going to do.

I don't believe that even you could know how demoralizing it is to have no one cheering for you—there are too many people who care intensely about you. The thing that I have felt most lately is that I am terribly young; young to have so much behind me and so little ahead.

Nancy, don't you think that the mutual courtesy of intimates is a fine competition? Bart and I still love and respect each other, I think, because we have tried sincerely not to break faith with each other. We redeem our pledges. But it is going to be harder. We went to another lawyer, and he said that there was nothing he could do—there's no loophole.

So we have planned to separate. Bart's employer is transferring him to an office on the Pacific Coast. I will stay here and live on Bart's allowance until I can support myself. We will sell most of our things, and I will move into a room somewhere so that my expenses will be as low as possible. Bart wants me to accept money permanently—he feels that he wants to make things as easy as possible. I think he would be more contented so, but I can't take it as "heart balm."

We are trying to make this an absolutely clean break for at least two years. Until then we will not see each other, nor communicate except through lawyers (barring emergency). In two years we are to make a decision about the future.

It sounds so complete and easy on paper—so unemotional in black on white. But, Nancy, will you tell me what I am going to do after he is gone? I am trying to be courageous, and to say to myself that this is going to be a new life, that I am young and strong, and there is no reason why it should not work out satisfactorily. Bart will have his work to think of—he has always been interested in it. What will I have? I can't put myself into typewriting as I have into making his life comfortable—or trying to. I have looked for work, but you know how many vacancies there are at present. And there won't be anyone to talk to or work for.

I wanted to ask you one more question. When I have started again, how can I do it honestly? I don't want to hide Bart, but won't that separate me from others? When I find work, should I tell my employer what has happened, if questions are asked concerning my background? I would rather do so and be able to feel that I was honest and sincere. It is going to be so hard to find myself worth living for, without deceiving anyone. I hadn't thought much about it from that angle until I read your response to "Oracle's" letter, about the Ten Commandments. Is that how you think of me— branded with the "scarlet letter"?

Nancy, the other night when I was reading your Column I saw how much I could have had of sound contentment if there weren't this problem. I would still read your Column, and perhaps shed tears for some poor foolish Janne, who had been a lost sheep, and I'd have written you a definition of happiness, and maybe even have asked "Toyo" for a book-mark—though without Bart there might not have been any books. It would be wonderful to feel that you had a right to make friends, and had something to give for favors.

Goodbye, Nancy, and thank you. I will think of you so often, and of "Drifting Sands," and "Oracle." I shall remember that you were kind.

Forward,

February 29, 1932

* * *

JANNE

I CAN imagine how demoralizing it would be to have no one cheering for you, "Janne," dear, but I doubt if there are very many in this world who are absolutely without someone to cheer them on. Certainly if you count the intangible friends that you make in the Column as worth while, you have plenty of cheerleaders.

[105]

I believe not a single letter that came commenting on your problem—and there were too many to publish—did not carry some word of encouragement and understanding.

You are young, dear—very young. Had you been older, you would probably have understood better the situation in which you were placing yourself when you agreed to go with Bart. I am glad that you have decided to make a clean break—for at least two years. It is the only way to solve your problem, the only way to bring new happiness. And it is only of your happiness we are thinking—all of us, who write about you, "Janne."

"What are you going to do?" Just what you tell me in your letter you are planning to do—find work as soon as you can, and throw yourself into it heart and soul. Until you are able to find a position, it is all right to accept the support which Bart offers you. There is no thought of heart balm in it. It is yours by right. I know how difficult it is going to be in spite of the "unemotional" appearance in "black on white." But somehow we always find the strength to live through these life tragedies. And you will, dear. It does not seem to you that the years can ever bring healing, but they can and they will. Time and work are wonderful healers.

I see no reason whatsoever, why you should ever tell your story to anyone unless you wish, some time, to take someone into your confidence—someone who will never betray you.

As for telling your employer—certainly not. He would not want to hear it, and it would make no difference in the work you would do for him. It is not deceit—just simply good taste and a matter of individual rights.

Certainly I do not think of you as branded with the "scarlet letter."

You will keep in touch with us, won't you? And remember there is only strong, tender, friendly feeling for you in the Column.

Tippity Wicket

* * *

I

DEAR NANCY BROWN: Here I come, dashing in where angels fear to tread. There's been so much talk lately about drinking that I thought I'd heave in my half-penny bit.

I guess I'm one of the degenerate younger generation, Nancy. I'm 21, white, and as free as anyone, possessed of a darling husband and as sweet a little almost-two-year-old as ever was. I belong to a crowd of which I am the youngest. The oldest is 29. We are all married and have children. We girls are all, in varying degrees to be sure, in love with our own husbands. Our homes are clean and attractive. We take pride in our menus and make them attractive as well as wholesome. Our babies are raised scientifically with a dash of love thrown in. We are all careful of personal appearances. Do we sound like normal, well-behaved housewives? I think we are, *but* we serve liquor at parties.

It is my theory that if we mind our own business and do nothing that harms ourselves and others, there won't be many marks against us in the Book of Life.

I honestly cannot see why the fact that I serve gin rickeys or beer at a party causes me to be eternally damned. Excessive or habitual drinking I do condemn, but if a few cocktails stimulate my guests, draw them out of their shells and throw a rosy glamour over the world in general, what harm is done? Habits formed? Piffle! Anyone who acquires drinking habits from an occasional party is going astray sooner or later anyway. Please remember, I am not talking about steady drinking, but about the monthly or so parties that almost everyone I know indulges in. I do not approve of drinking to the point of intoxication. I think that is vulgar, not to mention the fact of repentance in the shape of a hang-over.

I think older people rather overwork their imaginations on the subject of parties at which they were not present. My own mother is a darling and all that, but nothing on earth could ever convince her that a party where drinks were served, which lasted all night (the party, not the drinks; they don't) wasn't the last word in deep-dyed sin. Well, I've been to many of them. Perhaps my sensibilities are all hardened, but honestly the only feeling I've ever been able to work up is, once in a while, that of extreme sleepiness.

Nancy, dear, do you too proclaim that "Lips that touch liquor shall never touch mine"? or will you catch a kiss from dat ol' sinner,

February 12, 1932   TIPPITY WICKET

* * *

I CAUGHT the kiss from my li'l "ol' sinner," "Tippity Wicket." It was sweet. It does not trouble me that lips from which it came have sipped a cocktail—though I wish she had waited till she was a little older before she began the sipping.

You say nothing on earth would convince Mother that the drinking parties and all-night parties are not advisable for young people. Is it any easier for Mother and the rest of us older folks to convince you younger ones of anything whatsoever, in spite of the fact that we would have to be very stupid indeed not to have learned something through all the years of experience that are ours? You expect to know more 25 years from now, don't you, dear? You would not be very intelligent if you did not. Do you think your knowledge and intelligence will be limited to things outside the drinking question? Do you think that Mother has learned a great deal about other things but that she is still a child when it comes to that one problem? It doesn't seem very probable to me, does it to you? Honest Injun?

Your sensibilities are not hardened. You simply see the world and its problems through eyes not yet accustomed to the light of experience and observation. You say you do not approve of drinking to the extent of intoxication. Who is going to stop the drinking at just the right point? You know, dear, that the drinking habit is one that does not decrease with experience—quite the contrary. You remember the original letter that started this discussion, signed "I Can't," told how there was no drinking at their parties; then a little later, a single cocktail or what-have-you; next, several drinks through the evening, and lastly a continued carousal. And it all grew from the one cocktail.

The monthly drinking parties might disclose to some young man the fact that intoxicants taste good. He might not wait for the next monthly party. I should not like to think that I had started even one lad down that road, should you? If you were older and your habits formed, the risk would not be so great. It isn't really just "piffle," you know, dear. It's a serious question.

Your serving gin rickeys or beer at a party does not cause you to be "eternally damned." It would be an extremist indeed who would express an idea of that kind. But there is danger in it—possible danger for someone. And who wants to take a chance—even the barest possible chance of wrecking some young person's life for the sake of a gin rickey.

You say the cocktails stimulate your guests. I cannot imagine young people in their twenties needing stimulants to make them have a good time. And that "rosy glamour" that you mention is just where the danger lies. Young people like that "rosy glamour." Some of them are going to try to experience it more frequently than at your monthly parties. That "rosy glamour" is like a siren. It lures to extreme danger.

"The marks against you in the Book of Life" is a sentimental expression. Whereas minding your own business and doing nothing that harms yourself or others is a good creed, you want to be very sure that you're not harming others. Continued cocktail parties for young people who are still forming their habits of life may leave their marks. And back of all this, little Mrs. "Tippity Wicket," is the fact that our Constitution carries a clause saying that these cocktails shall not be. It's rather nice to be law-abiding, don't you think?

Please read "Tish-ka-sha-ney's" letter in this same Column. I do not want to impress you young people with the idea that I am an arrogant objector to occasional social drinks. I am not, except nowadays it is against the law, and also I believe that young people should wait until their habits are formed.

* * *

II

Nancy darling: I'se depressed. Not just pale blue blues that an extra layer of lipstick and a dab of perfume behind my ears will cure, but the deep-dyed indigo type.

Today's my birthday. Twenty-two, Nancy, and I'm a parent, and in a few years I'll be a grandma, and once I found a grey hair. Why it seems only yesterday instead of four years ago that I tucked a newly acquired wedding license in beside a newly acquired diploma and thought I'd conquered the world. This morning I've just been remembering all my high flown ambitions and dreams. That talent they seemed to think I possessed seems to be stifled by bars of soap and cook books. There are occasions when it seems my whole life has become one mad pursuit of dirt—dirty dishes, dirty woodwork, dirty little suits. Do I sound discontented? I'm not, really. This is just one of my rare blue fits. I really have the most important job on earth, trying to bring the little Carbon Copy up to be the man his daddy is.

I think I'll put that extra dab of lipstick on after all and go downtown and buy a new hat. I'm going to pull that new hat rakishly over one eye and the first good-looking man I see I'm going to r-roll the other eye at (bet I've forgotten how), and if he looks interested, I'll scurry off like the respectable old married woman I am, but if he doesn't, I'm going home and weep and weep and weep.

Oh, but didn't "Malindy" bawl me out! Haven't had such a calling-down since I stuck a wad of gum in old Riley's (the school janitor's) pipe. I think you're sweet, anyway, "Malindy," and I wish you'd be friends.

Hello there, "Green and Gold Pajamas"! You sound like a kindred soul. My own weakness is black and scarlet.

Heaps of love to you, Nancy dear.

March 22, 1932   TIPPITY WICKET

* * *

You do not sound discontented, little Mrs. "Tippity"—just sort of a blue day. Probably by this time you are your own cheerful self again. I hope so.

Never mind about the undeveloped ambition. You did not know about the little Carbon Copy when that talent loomed so big on your horizon. And that small copy is worth every sacrifice of talent or ambition, isn't he?

Hope you got the new hat and carried out its program successfully. Come back and tell us about it.

Jasmin

* * *

DEAR NANCY BROWN: It's snowing tonight—great soft white flakes floating lazily down. My log fire crackles cheerfully and my great cushiony chair invites relaxation. Faintly, from another room I can hear the rhythmic click of Mary's high slim heels and the languorous tempo of the tango. "The Gang" is making merry here this evening, for the special purpose of keeping me out of what they call "the jitters." The blessed dears treat me as one of them despite the fact that there's not a one among them over 20. Well, I'm only 22, but it might as well be 42.

I arrived in Detroit the day of the big snow storm. What a change, after sunny Hawaii! I suppose my sudden return to that place must have seemed a little mad. I think I was mad to go back. But I doubted my own wisdom in making my first decision and wanted to be sure. Well, I found that there was nothing to do but go through with it— so here I am, divorced. Convenient place—Reno.

The consensus of Column opinion seems to be that I've made a colossal mistake. I gather from several letters that probably no other man would have married me and that I should be eternally grateful to have been so honored. It seems that I am entirely unworthy of such a noble paragon of virtue and should knock my head on his boots and consider myself very lucky to have been so honored. Neal is about the most perfect man ever. I may even say, the perfect man. But, perfect or not, I do expect faithfulness from the man I marry. Or do I deserve even that consideration, "Joanna"? But there—I mustn't lose my temper. Of course you don't know the particulars and so cannot conceive of Neal doing anything wrong. I suppose I do seem ungrateful, but I still can't see why I should feel that any man was doing me a favor in marrying me. I'm afraid I feel, on the contrary, that I'm still a highly desirable asset to any man, regardless of my "sordid" past (which, by the way, I do not regard as sordid). Why, I wouldn't trade my "sins" for all the virtues in the world! I wouldn't trade the wild young love of my bronzed young sun-god for all the conventional married bliss of a life-time. I consider that brief, heavenly episode—that one blinding glimpse of Paradise— the high spot of my life. Everything from that time till the end of my days I count as just trivial incidents. Ah, "Joanna," try to understand! How can innocence be sordid?

I want you to understand why I said I didn't want sympathy. I don't feel that I need or deserve it. Sympathy often includes pity and I'm certainly not an object of pity. You see, I think I've been singularly blessed in being permitted to know the heights of mortal ecstasy. I think every woman in the world should have envied me my wonderful child, because I think she was the most beautiful child in the world. I think my lover was perfect, and I shall never, never be disillusioned about him. I shall never see him grow bald and old, I shall never lose him to other women; he's mine, mine alone, and that's more than 90 out of every 100 women can say of their husbands!

As for Neal—well, he was a pleasant companion, interesting, but not very stimulating. Do I seem callous? I'm sure he never really loved me, nor I him, and so I can't feel any real grief at the way things have turned out. We were quite happy because we were good companions, but our relations lacked that spiritual spark that is necessary for true mating. He found it in another girl—a splendid girl who really loves him—so why should I deny him the right to seek his own personal heaven?

I can't suppress an involuntary thrill as I wonder what is ahead. When I contemplate the glorious days, months, and years ahead—

all just for living, I feel all bubbly inside, like a bottle of champagne! I'm going to grasp every new experience life offers me, and squeeze it dry. If life is just a bowl of cherries, then I'm going to eat every single one, pits and all, and to the divil with the ensuing stomach ache! With Edna Millay I say—

> "My candle burns at both ends;
> It will not last the night;
> But ah, my foes, and oh, my friends—
> It gives a lovely light!"

I've had my fling at conventionality and I find it flat. Safe, maybe, but who would choose the valley after having lived for a moment on the windswept mountain top? The stars are nearer—on the heights. My philosophy may be all wrong, but I'm going to give it a chance.

Don't worry, Nancy, Mary is going to college. She certainly is not going to accept that position in San Francisco if I can prevail upon her to do otherwise. She has talent, I know that, but she must train her head as well as her twinkling feet. Nancy, you have no idea of how the child has grown up since her sixteenth birthday. In place of the fluffy haired child who came to me, I now see a tall, slim young sprite with smooth, golden hair, like a metallic bandeau around her head, and an air of cool detachment that sometimes makes me feel *gauche!* Where these adolescents acquire such superb self-possession and poise is a mystery to me.

I must stop writing now. There's some one waiting for me in the library. Guess who—it's the sun-god's older brother. It's like old times, seeing him again.

November 20, 1932   JASMIN

* * *

GLAD to have you back with us, "Jasmin."

Of course you know best about your own private affairs, but I think you are a bit hasty and rash in your judgment of the Column

Folks' opinions of your separation from Neal. I am sure not one meant to imply the bitter thoughts that you have suggested.

I do not recall ever having heard the word "sordid" used in connection with your love for the father of your child. I believe when you are older and have seen more of life, dear, that you will change your viewpoint about many, many things. I am wondering even now if you would like to have Mary come through the same experience that you did. I am sure every woman would have loved your little Jeannine and recognized her sweetness. There is no question about that.

But you are wrong, "Jasmin," in saying that 90 out of every 100 women are disillusioned about their husbands. You make your percentage much, much too large.

Conventionality is more than just "safe," dear. It is happiness in the end. The girl who throws herself against it, and defies it, will ultimately be hurt—sometimes beyond repair. The windswept mountain top may be picturesque and romantic, but after all, it is bleak and dangerous—and even if the stars are a few feet nearer, what of it?

I am glad you are insisting upon an education for Mary before she starts her career with her twinkly feet.

*

Crumbs

Now that you're gone
I've gathered up my life,
Much as I'd gather up a tablecloth
And shake into the blue October air
The crumbs of Love.

March 18, 1932   PENELOPE

Carmene

* * *

My DEAR NANCY BROWN: Seven or eight years ago, when I was leading a sort of story book existence as the wife of a small town doctor, I used to read in your Column of the trials and tribulations of others, never dreaming that I was headed toward my own particular problem. And then all of a sudden my husband was killed, leaving me practically nothing except an adorable year-old daughter. I was an excellent stenographer, and a very kind friend procured a position for me in the office of a well known firm of attorneys.

After a time, being well acquainted in the city, I started to go about a bit and met a young man who fell madly in love with me. I liked him, enjoyed his company, etc., but never felt that I couldn't live without him. However, I guess because he was so persistent and I was lonely, we were married, and very shortly thereafter entered the Problem.

The secretary of one of the members of the firm left the city and I was given the position, at a considerable increase in salary. About the same time (two years ago) my husband lost his position and has been unemployed ever since.

As my boss does most of the trial work for the entire firm, and is in court most of the day, it follows that my office hours are more or less irregular. Whether it was because we were alone in the office so much of the time (I work nearly every night) or what it was I don't know. At any rate, we found out after a while that we were very much in love with each other. At first we tried to be casual about it, but we are both poor actors. We have discussed it from every angle. He has told his wife and she has agreed to divorce him. But herein lies the difficulty:

(1) My husband is apparently as much in love with me as ever.

(2) As I said before, he has not worked for two years, through no fault of his own, and we are dependent on my salary, which is very inadequate for our needs and for the support of my daughter in the home of my sister.

(3) The other man is wealthy and prominent in his profession, and of course I could not continue in my present position were I to marry him. He would necessarily have to have another secretary. I have always been under the impression that if husbands will desert one wife, they will another. What assurance have I that our affair would not be duplicated with his next secretary? (You should hear his argument on that.)

On the other hand, I am crazy about him, it would kill me not to be able to see him, and the present situation cannot continue much longer.

Don't tell me to get another job. In the first place, we couldn't begin to live on the $15 or $20 I could make elsewhere, and it seems to be absolutely impossible for my husband to find anything to do.

What shall I do? Don't think too unkindly of me. I really am trying to do what is right. Whose happiness is more important—my husband's or mine?

I have told the other man that I am asking your advice and we have agreed to abide by your decision. He says he used to know you.

Distractedly yours,

February 25, 1932
CARMENE

* * *

THE problem does not narrow down to so small a compass as your happiness and your husband's. There is the other man's wife—and there is your child. You do not say whether the man has any children. If he has, their happiness is to be considered. When these children grow older, they will understand, Mrs. "Carmene." Your little girl will ask uncomfortable questions. She will lose a certain something in her thoughts of Mother, thoughts that mothers do not like little daughters to lose.

You are very casual in disposing of the other man's wife with the simple remark that she has "agreed to divorce him." I have a suspicion there is something back of those few words that is not far from tragedy. I should not like to think that I was building my happiness on the wreckage of two homes, and the heart-break of two other people.

Look ahead into the future. After the first glamour of romance has faded, and you have settled down to everyday life, you are going to find the same humdrum conditions, the same misunderstandings, that exist in every married life.

This other man is going to have the same faults that exist in most men, and one that is not found in every man—disloyalty. The fact that you love each other, to my mind, is not excuse enough to divorce your present mates.

You say it will kill you not to be able to see him. It really would not, you know. Women live through worse things than that, though in all conscience that is bad enough.

The fact that your income is necessary for the support of yourself and your little girl and your husband, make a serious complication. I can see how it would be difficult to give up your position.

Here is my suggestion—that you stay where you are, refuse to work nights at any time, and when it is necessary to be with this other man, be in the room with someone else, always. I realize that you will have to be almost superhuman—both of you, but I can see no other way. If you can find another position, I advise you to take it by all means.

Green and Gold Pajamas

* * *

DEAREST NANCY: May another young wife just bursting with happiness be taken into your family? Say yes, Nancy, please do.

Hubby and I have been married three and one-half years and are happy together. We are happier as the days roll by. We have a little son almost two years of age, who is as sweet as little boys come, I am sure. Our little home is cozily furnished, with radio and many other "extras" that young couples do not always own. Hubby has his own business. We are buying it, so we try to spend as little as possible to get it paid up quicker and thus save money.

This is my question: What is the least amount of money we could live on a month? You understand we could have more for our own use in running the house, for he is doing very well, but the discount is so great we want to take advantage of it.

We pay $30 per month rent, and it is a very nice place, for our home, and we have a room rented at $4 per week. The light, gas and heat we supply ourselves. We have no debts other than the one mentioned. Both of us have to dress fairly well in his line of work. We do not buy many clothes but buy good quality when we do. This is a terrible mixup to give you to work with, but could you make out a budget for us? I almost forgot we pay $1 a month for magazines and 50 cents a week to the church.

Hubby's work keeps him away from home every evening, but I have found a grand way of spending them alone. Of course, I have to spend them all right at home and keep watch over my sleeping child. Nancy, how my friends would laugh if they knew what I did and thought while alone. I'm afraid they would be digging into the lives of my forefathers to find a trace of insanity—but, Nancy, I love this game I play; it really *is* a game. I have always had a terrible desire to be a lady of leisure—guess I'm simply lazy. I work awfully hard all morning. I even get up early so I can finish my work and play my game. After my work is finished it is usually about one o'clock in the afternoon. Then Sonny and I play. We then (baby helps me) cook Daddy a dinner that will make him smile. After the meal is over, baby is tucked in bed and I am alone. Then do I enjoy myself!

I have some green and gold satin pajamas, green mules, and long green earrings, and I get all fixed up in these. I have long hair, it's curly and soft of a gold color, and I just fix it behind my ears and let it hang down my back. Then I make a pot of tea—we have a very pretty tea set and a lovely coffee table—tea off a coffee table, is that the right thing to do? I then lie on the davenport and with my tea, radio and books, Nancy, I have a heavenly time. This is a secret —I even have a long cigaret holder and when listening to beautiful music I smoke occasionally. When I am reading and listening to music in such comfort, I simply haven't time to be lonely.

Hubby comes home about ten o'clock, asks if I was lonesome and explains it will not be for always that I will have to spend my evenings alone. Of course, I'll be happy when we can spend them together, but it makes me giggle to think I found a way of spending happy evenings alone. I study some, too, Nancy, as I feel as if I need to badly, for I didn't quite finish high school and Hubby went to college and is naturally clever to boot. Sometimes I wonder how he happened to pick me for his wife. Everybody says I am a good housekeeper, cook and mother, but other than that I think I am rather dumb.

Well, Nancy, my Hubby has been home a long while now, so I'll have to say good night. I'll sign what I am clad in now.

February 26, 1932   GREEN AND GOLD PAJAMAS

[120]

THAT is a good way of spending your evenings alone happily, dear girl—an original way, and as excellent as it is original.

Some day when that dear husband wants to give you an especially nice gift, I would suggest another suit of pajamas. You can play your game still better if you have two. An extra suit will add variety and charm.

Why he chose you as a wife is no mystery to me. A good house-keeper, a good cook, a good mother, and with initiative to find pleasure in evenings spent alone while husband is working, are reasons enough for the choice.

You ask me for a budget, but you did not tell me your income. However, since you ask your question in the form, "How small a sum can we live on?" I may be able to help you.

I am not giving you the minimum figures, because I judge from your letter that extreme economy is not necessary.

Here are the items as I have made them out for a small expenditure for three people; Savings,—; insurance, $8; rent, $30; food, $30; clothing, $25; operating, $18; advancement, $14; total, $125.00.

Operating includes, as nearly as I can judge without your income, heat, $7; light and gas, $5; upkeep of house, $3; telephone, $3; miscellaneous,—.

Advancement includes church and charities, $2; newspapers and magazines, $2; amusement, $4; vacation, $4; incidentals, $2; total, $14.

You see I have left the savings item blank. Whatever you have left after your expenses are paid, can go into that. Also the miscellaneous item must be filled in from your own judgment. It is usually a fair-sized figure.

Another Kim

* * *

I

MY DEAREST NANCY: I feel most remorseful at not having acknowledged all the messages that have come to me from you and the family, but you would be surprised how busy one can be just getting married and settling a house!

"Just" getting married! Doesn't that sound as if I *had* been all my life? Well, I wish some one would tell me what I ever did before! Apparently I led a life that had absolutely no meaning to it, since so little of it seems to have been important enough to remain in my mind. I am so very happy, Nancy.

Dear, dear "Holiday," your letter meant so much to me. It made me feel that no matter what comes to me, I still have your friendship and your interest, and that you know you have my love. Add Kate O'Brien's "Without My Cloak," and Beatrice Tunstall's "The Shiny Night" to your list of beloved books. You can't afford to miss either of them.

"Anne of Dixie," my dear, your Christmas letter headed the list for me. I carry it in my purse. Thank you for your good wishes. Don't let the book go—you have such a depth of understanding and interest in people to draw from. You can do so much, if you give of that wealth.

"Largo," "Connecticut Yankee"—all of you who sent me your love and congratulations—I can only say, so inadequately, thank you. It went very deeply into my heart to know that you cared so much. I am so very happy that it just doesn't go into words. If I tried to tell you it would sound stilted and affected, because words are so flat and cold to describe the warmth and brilliance of the flame that burns in my heart. Sometimes I find myself walking on tiptoe around my house for fear of disturbing an indescribable feeling of joy that seems to surround one. It is too dream-like, this security, this knowledge of Terry's love.

How on earth did you see it coming, some of you? I read of it with amazement. It had seemed so sudden, so breathtaking to me—like coming, all at once, from the shaded heart of a forest into a dazzling brilliance of sun. I don't think it will ever seem quite true.

I want so badly to break down and be utterly sticky—and describe Terry to you—that it is dreadful! There is so much beauty in his slow smile, his eyes, and his hands on the keys of the piano. I think my only disappointment lies in the fact that you who are all so dear to me don't know him.

We see Lowlee often. Grimsy and Penny are living happily together in a dear little house not far away. David is so contented and happy in his work, and Sue, and his son. And I have Terry! And so one chapter ends and another begins—and life is glorious. I have so much love for all of you.

February 28, 1932   Another Kim

* * *

We are happy in your happiness, "Kim" dear—very, very happy. We should like to know your Terry. Perhaps we shall, through you! It does not surprise me to hear how busy one may be, getting married and settling a home. There is no end to the busy-ness that that task involves. To the bride, life without her newly acquired dear one does appear meaningless. The happiness will continue, "Kim" dear, and will grow deeper and richer and stronger as the years pass.

How did we see it coming? It was quite transparent. I feel a bit of prideful conceit in saying that I prophesied it in words for you long ago. A man does not fix up a trolley that shall trundle hot cocoa hopping along through the trees at night for a girl, or a basket full of fluffy kitten in the daytime, or a score of other little things that the "Man-Next-Door" used to do for you, unless that man is interested in the girl.

Did you read the letter written by one of our members two or three weeks ago, asking permission to use your story for a magazine or a book? I gave my permission. Inasmuch as your signature protects you from recognition, I thought you would not mind. In fact, I do not see why you would mind anyway. It seems to me quite an honor.

* * *

II

MY DEAREST NANCY: Back again after three months of utter solitude, during which time I lost complete track of all the doings of the Column Family because there was no paper, I think, within a hundred miles.

We had the most glorious trip, Terry and I, that two people could ever hope to take. Clear up into the North Country, miles beyond any thing or any person, just us and a canoe, and two books! And I don't mind saying that the thing that gave us the most trouble was the selection of those two books. It was all we felt that we should spare the room for, and we knew that very likely our reading time would be limited—one can't do much by fire light, after one has paddled all day—and we did so want to make our reading count. So after much discussion and rejection and selection we decided on "The Epic of America" and Christopher Morley's "John Mistletoe," and we've been glad ever since! They were exactly the right two.

I wish I could tell you all about the places we went to and the things we did, and the loveliness we saw. All of it was beautiful, but so much of it beggars description that to even think about it makes my heart ache a little. There was one walk, through a lowland, with purple cliffs high on one side, and the still brown lake on the other; and everywhere one looked, soft maples in every shade of autumn red from scarlet to mahogany, against the deepening green of the pine.

It doesn't go into words, such beauty, but you feel it just at the back of your throat.

There were nights when columns of mist rose up from the water, and because it was so still they stood like pillars, ghostly, unbelievable, and you pushed your canoe through them and felt them wet against your face, and suddenly the big rock in front of your tent loomed up so that only a quick twist of the paddle saved you from the everlasting disgrace of a scraped keel.

Or you slipped off the same big rock and swam through the mists, under the moon, out and out across the lake. And once, while we swam, a storm came up and our eyes were blinded with the lightning, and the rain came teeming down on our heads.

My bed was so near the water that in the morning when I wakened I would lie and watch the water creatures swimming within reach of my hand. And as September drew to a close wild ducks came in close to the shore and swam past me, not three feet away.

We pitched tents part of the time, and then for a month we stayed in a trapper's cabin—a small, crude, brown hut in the midst of the forest, as still as only forests can be with their incessant throbbing noise.

There we read aloud our books, before a small tin stove that threw out a prodigious heat, so that often we warmed our toes and kept the door open to save ourselves from roasting!

It was something to have done—something I will never forget nor lose the beauty of, and to have taken it with Terry, who is that rare soul with the gift of silence, but a silence that bespeaks an appreciation that is almost a communication—well, I will spare you my superlatives! For only superlatives will fit such perfection.

And now to get back into the swing of things. I don't know exactly yet what the discussion about churches is all about. I know that I am glad to be back again where I can go to hear my favorite minister, who always seems to be shaking his finger right at me, and telling me the things I need most to know; and I am glad to be watching the great painted doors that cover the organ pipes swing open with the first throbbing notes—but in the back of my mind is the glory of those trees, and the peace of the silent woods, and I can't help but feel, and not humbly but exultantly, that I know about God, and that He is real, and simple, and good.

Grimsy is with me for a while—always, if I can make her stay—and sends you her love. And so does Terry—he is perfect, Nancy! But both of them put together can't equal mine, which you know you always have.

October 17, 1932   ANOTHER KIM

* * *

THANK you, "Kim" dear. Thanks to Grimsy and Terry, too, please.

What a lovely, lovely honeymoon you had! It will be something rarely beautiful for you to remember the rest of your days.

I know where your lovely church is, and the doors of the pipe organ that swing open when the music begins. I have never attended service there, but I intend to, soon—and probably often. Having become acquainted with the lovely church, I want **to** know the minister, too.

Just a Man

* * *

I

DEAR NANCY BROWN: Happiness? That's all I've ever had since we were married. The thrill when the preacher said: "I pronounce you man and wife" (she was 16 and I was 22)—Golly! And six months ago that little girl of mine gave birth to a tiny boy. I don't believe there is another thrill or emotion in the world that could possibly compare with what I felt when Mr. Doc said I could see her—and there she lay, so sweet and smiling. You know, it seemed as if I were in close relationship with God. And now my happiness is complete. It's contentment. As I write this, that golden girl of mine is lying flat on her stomach reading, her tiny heels kicking together. Baby is sleeping peacefully. Everything quiet and serene. There's only one thing I want. Just to live long enough to show that lovable wife how *much* I love her.

March 8, 1932   JUST A MAN

* * *

YOU were in close relationship with God, dear man, as you stood beside your wife's bedside immediately after the birth of your little son—about as close to God as I guess is given human beings to be.

You'll show your wife this letter, won't you? She will love and treasure it always.

* * *

II

DEAR NANCY BROWN: I promised to stay away for a lengthier time but I want to come back and tell my childhood story. Besides, you told me to come back when the baby had its third tooth—well, the

[127]

little rascal has six. Going strong, eh? He'll be a year old this July.

I'm an orphan, and Nancy, I believe that word—the mere suggestion—is a story in itself. I never knew who my parents were, and to this day they are a mystery. The orphanage is the only home I knew till I was twelve years old. Every time anyone would come to adopt a child I would scowl horribly—talk from the corner of my mouth —and display a terrible temper. I received many scoldings, you may be sure, but they didn't phase me.

One day a little girl was brought to the home. Her mother had died and her father had put her there to stay while he went on a trip to South America for his company. She was the sweetest little six-year-old that ever breathed. I can remember yet how she came up to me and said, "Ooh, what pretty hair!" (My hair is fiery red!) From then on, I was her slave, and for six months that little queen played tyrant. Then one day the Matron told me to try to be nice to our next callers, as I was getting too old to be kept in the home. Well, the next couple adopted me. They were wonderful to me, but I never forgave them for taking me away from my "queen."

My foster parents discovered I had dancing feet and a likable voice, so they had instructions given to me. I danced at entertainments, clubs, etc., then on to the stage. Then one night—my twenty-first birthday to be exact—I was standing in the wings waiting to put on my act, when I noticed a tiny little figure in gold metallic tights, leaning up against a prop. Her back was turned, but I felt queer. It seemed as if it were a matter of life and death—I had to see that face. I walked over and carelessly (?) bumped into the prop. She turned and I knew that the little dancer billed as the "Golden Girl" was my little queen of the orphanage. She just gasped "Brick!" and came silently into my arms.

Queer? Fairy tale? Sure it does seem queer and like a story book but "truth is often stranger than fiction." My cue for my act came

[128]

then and I went on. I danced with winged feet and sang with a happy heart because I had found my queen! Later, watching her tapping and clogging, I knew the queen was a sure hit. Those tiny feet gave the music the correct time. Even the orchestra seemed to play with additional pep. Later I learned her father had remarried and his wife had seen Sunny's talent.

For a year we trouped together. I had added comedy to my singing and dancing. I would stand there and talk about my "paw" and "maw"—slur them, make them laughing objects, and did the public like it? I'll say they did! My comedy was a necessity. Please don't get the impression I was ridiculing my foster parents for I wasn't. They enjoyed it as much as I, even found, or originated, wise cracks for me to use, as they in no way resembled the fictitious creatures I painted nightly to the audience. Then one night, Sunny and I were in the wings when I received a telegram, saying that Mr. and Mrs. McD—— had died in an accident, on the way to the theatre. At the same time the orchestra gave me my cue. What could I do? Only what any other trouper would do, go out in front of that audience, dance and sing, and crack jokes about "Paw" and "Maw."

That night, Nancy Brown, it seemed they screamed with laughter —mocking laughter. How I hated them—how I longed to scream and yell at them, to stop that infernal roaring and screaming—how I damned them and when tears began streaming down my cheeks— they went crazy! They were blurred to me—just gaping faces, cavernous pits which issued hellish sounds. They thought my tears were a part of the act. They sat there and laughed while my heart was breaking. A soul in hell was amusing them, but all they saw was a clown "putting it over."

Then to cap it all, as I came off the stage a fat promoter met me and wanted to sign me up. "My act was great," etc. Through tears I saw his silly mouth and somehow his mouth and my fist connected.

I can just remember a voice supposed to be mine, laughing and crying, "They're dead—they're dead!" I've never been on the stage since. Sunny, my queen, and I were married three months later, but I never look back at that night but that I shudder. No human being ever suffered so much before, I believe.

Some woman recently wrote to you and said that if her son ever came home drunk, she would consider him disgraced. I can't quite conceive any mother thinking it a disgrace for her son to be human. The wife and I discussed it and we decided that if our son ever came home drunk we'd put him to bed and wait till he was sober. When he was, we'd laugh and say, "Well, another lesson learned, eh?" Boys, or girls are rather sensitive, and if they thought we considered them disgraceful or shameless—they'd conceal their hurt by continuing and flaunting it in our face. Somewhere I once read that children don't need strict discipline—just worthy examples, and Sunny and I have both decided to dedicate our lives to being a clean and good example for our boy.

August 1, 1932   JUST A MAN

* * *

How wonderfully interesting and unusual is the story of your life, "Just a Man." It would make an outstanding plot for a book or a play. How much better we understand our Column Folks, with the insight we have into the stories of their childhood.

I agree with your idea of not making a lad's first experience in intoxication too important a matter. But I would not treat it laughingly. That first experience, if continued, *would* lead to disgrace, wouldn't it? I would be sure the lad understood that.

Thank you for telling us your story.

Arrow

* * *

DEAR NANCY BROWN: This topic "Honey Lea" started ("Dutch treat") has peculiar interest for me. It was the subject of much discussion in my "gang" a few years back—1925-27 (not a depression-emergency measure, but regular fare).

The attitude of your answer amused me, too. My reaction, after logical thinking, was just the reverse (then as well as now). Why, for any logical reason on earth, should a man bear all the expenses, except that it is customary? But first let me tell a story.

Bennie and his brother were trying to start up a business of their own, which required a car. They had little ready money. They took turns with using the car on Sundays.

Bennie wanted to make a certain trip with his girl, Jean, one Sunday, but figured he couldn't afford it unless Jean would pack a picnic lunch. That is surely a usual and frequent arrangement, is it not, for outings? So far, so good, then. Jean readily agreed to attend to the lunch.

It so happened that Jean didn't care much about picnic lunches (especially if the day should be rainy). She very much preferred dining in a quiet tea room with good service. She figured that fried chicken, with all the fixings, made an excellent picnic lunch (for those who like picnics). She also figured that it would by no means be a cheap lunch; and that it would take considerable preparation, and preparing lunches wasn't in her line, either.

Knowing that her friend's desire was to have her enjoy the trip as much as possible, she inquired about and learned the name of a good tea room in a town they would pass through. She phoned and made reservations for two fried chicken lunches at about a certain time.

Now, to blankly say that they dined out and the girl paid the bill does sound a bit bold. But if it was easier and more pleasant for her to have someone to prepare and serve the lunch, for which she was responsible, why in Heaven's name shouldn't she?

As to logic, what is the origin of the custom? Are circumstances such that it should be continued?

It is a far cry from the days of utterly dependent women, trained in housewifely duties, living under the paternal roof until a husband was found, to the utterly independent, self-supporting business woman of today (non-depression times), earning as much as many of the men she knows. In the dependent days a woman had absolutely no money, so had to be "taken" by a man. But occasions for incurring expense were far fewer and less costly in proportion to income then than now. As woman's need has been overcome by her economic independence, so has the need for this custom. It is only the economic balance of which I speak. Though the sexes have changed some customs, they are still fundamentally the same, so that the man must still protect, escort, etc.

From another angle: If boys and girls always paid their own way, the boy would plan a budget whereby he would lay aside a small amount for that home he will have to provide some day. The pastime of gold-digging would be impossible. Boys and girls might enjoy many pleasures together and find it just as logical as the girls' providing picnic lunches always seems to have been. Later, as boys become men, and begin to look for their ideal woman they would have something back of them when they found "her." It wouldn't be then that for years he had spent all on girls now gone and forgotten, and the one he cares most about he can do least for. He must ask her to wait, and then they must both scrimp and save and take the cheapest form of entertainment, all because it cost him too much all along the way.

Truly, there is a real need for reform in the financial situation.
March 9, 1932   ARROW

* * *

YES, Miss "Arrow," there is need for reform in the financial situation. You'll find no one to argue with you on that subject. However, it's not a very constructive statement. How to bring about the reform would be the helpful feature.

You feel quite strongly about the "Dutch treat" business, don't you? Quite emphatic, in fact. I understand your viewpoint in regard to the instance of the girl ordering the picnic dinner at the tea room and paying for it, instead of going to the trouble to put it up herself at home, but I can't help but think the boy did not feel so comfortable about it. Most boys would feel very embarrassed to enter a tea room with a girl and have the girl pay for the meal afterwards. I grant that it was easier and more pleasant for the girl, but I do feel that ordering the lunch and paying for it instead of putting it up at home was the act that makes just the difference between tact and embarrassing bluntness.

You ask why, for any logical reason, a man should bear all the expenses of amusement, beyond the fact that it is "customary." And yet the fact that it is customary is just the answer. A custom that has been established through centuries of civilization and culture is difficult to disregard and pretty apt to be right, even at that. Logic? Well, you did not state your premises and conclusion. You must do that, you know, in order to justify your claim to logic.

Yes, indeed, it is "a far cry from the days of utterly dependent women"—farther back than I can remember. I have had no experience with that condition. As far back as I can recall, women have been self-supporting and their lives were not governed by the one idea of discovering a husband to care for them. Women of my day—

[133]

even my youthful day—were just as independent as you girls of modern times. Even if conditions are different, Miss "Arrow," we of your mother's day have not lain in a stupor on a dusty shelf through all the march of progress. Perhaps we have kept abreast of it, even. Perhaps we have even gained knowledge through all the years, and perhaps our experience has brought us wisdom, even as you expect you will gain wisdom in the years to come.

I was surprised at your statement that though the sexes have changed some customs, you agree that those of modern times are fundamentally the same, and that man is still the escort and protector, etc. What does the "etc." include? They *are* still fundamentally the same. The girl still wants privileges rather than rights. She still enjoys the protecting attitude from the man, still appreciates his paying for the entertainment that they enjoy together, and is still willing to give up expensive entertainment for simple when he is unable to pay for it, rather than to cause him the embarrassment of paying for it herself.

*

My Christmas Wish

I wish that I, this day, could be
Just six—and stand at Mother's knee,
And see the love gleam in her eyes,
And watch her feign complete surprise
At how old Santa knew each thing
That I had wanted him to bring.
That child-like trust, its faith divine
I cherish yet; they still are mine.
And so, in life's swift race I pause
To long—today—for Santa Claus.

December 24, 1928   ISABEL

Guillermo

* * *

Nᴀɴᴄʏ ʙʀᴏᴡɴ: No, I won't say "dear." And I thought you were a friend of man—biologically speaking! My faith is shattered; here, all these months I have rushed madly to the door, beating my wife by a mere fraction, in order to be the first to read "Experience." And I've always admired you for your straightforwardness; your frankness and kindness, and the clearness with which you went to the bottom of problems. All is over; I'm going to drink of the waters of Lethe and forget you.

In replying to "Nobody's Mom" who went shopping and felt guilty because she thought she had spent too much, you actually go on record as being in favor of buying sprees for women—and this, when I have only, and just, convinced my wife that she ought to be careful; ought to control herself, her wild desires, and keep that darn monthly bill at—down to normal; and just when she had almost agreed, herself!

Shame on you! Disrupting families in this way. My whole Sunday is spoiled now, for I must start over once more from scratch and try to convince "the wife" (how she hates that expression!) that you're nothing but a woman and subject to all the frailties of nature. Oh, of course, she's still willing to swear by you, but why shouldn't she? You've knocked all my very best and most powerful arguments into a cocked hat, and you've broken up one happy family, at least.

But, after all is said and done, I, me, myself, have done just what you recommend. Once when I was out of work, and down in the depths, I actually bought a watch and spent $125 for it; and another time, to the tune of $45, got myself a beautiful ring. And I spent idle hours admiring these things and was glad I had them.

Oh, well,—what's the use! I wish I could dislike you for the "bee you have deposited in the *chapeau*," but I 'spose I'll go on reading your Column and appreciating your good qualities.

March 11, 1932   GUILLERMO

* * *

THANK you for that last kind paragraph, "Guillermo." I was cast down—very far down—by your refusal to address me with the prefix "Dear" and denying me as a friend. But now at the last line of your letter I draw a sigh of relief. And when you confessed to the $125 watch and the $45 ring, when you were out of work, well I felt that you were a congenial soul. I do not mean that I would do the same rash deed—I should like to, but I might not have the courage of my convictions as you had, or else my down-East-Yankee-thrift background would not permit me.

Perhaps in the mellowed mood, indicated by the last paragraph, you'll go a little farther and deliver my message to your wife—that nothing—nothing—can drive away the blues as efficiently as a shopping spree.

*

Life's Lesson

Life is a game of give and of take,
 Each of us giving less than we make.
We get out of life just what we give.
 This lesson learned—you'll know how to live.
I have a wish for each member here—
 Peace and Good Will and a Happy New Year.

December 31, 1931   PUDDIE

Beni-Dick

* * *

DEAR NANCY AND COLUMN FOLKS: May I come in? Thanks! I am urgently in need of self-expression. I feel somewhat like a man in the cage at Loches, in which one could not stand upright or lie at ease, and so was done to death slowly by constraint.

Suppose I begin with my garret. It's rough and unfinished. In the winter it's unbearably cold, in the summer intolerably hot; and sometimes when the wild winds moan and howl in the night, the shingles lift allowing the snow to sift through and form little mounds in the cracks and corners. But withal, I take a certain amount of pride in possessing it, for it is my refuge, my stronghold to which I can retreat—and dream—and work. Then I am happy! I walk in company of de Maupassant, Kipling, Verlaine and hosts of others.

Shall I describe my work bench? It's an abandoned library table of "ante bellum" vintage, but strong and serviceable. A lamp sits in one corner (slightly dusty), two ash trays which should be emptied —A lapse of time has ensued—I've been having tea and toast. To go on—a black onyx ink stand is pushed to one side, filled at times, but now encrusted with corroded ink of an earlier period. Above, and before me hangs a lithograph by one Angelo Bianca, called "The Quadrille," and all around is a mass of scribbled paper in wild confusion.

My chair is a straight backed, fragile affair that has certainly seen better days and will not last for many more, judging by the assortment of squeaks and groans it emits whenever I move.

May I voice a faint whisper concerning our modern literature? Our prose is really all that matters. The rhymesters and verse makers, pale, shallow, insipid, delight in manufacturing weird, fantastical designs that no self-respecting singer would acknowledge; with the possible exception of a few.

But with the novel we have blossomed and flourished! "A Farewell to Arms" is a classic, though the author is ridiculously physical. Thornton Wilder is excellent reading, but hopelessly out of step with his romanticism in this day of realism. We are indeed in some age—if not golden, then a near substitute, with our brilliant nebulae of Dreisers, Cathers, Lewises and Hemingways. Enough of that ranting!

A word about "La Honda"—someone whom, from the personality gleaned by reading, I would love to know. And "Jade," too, who was my Column favorite, but who is now amongst the missing. Have I stayed too long, Miss Nancy? I know I have. Forgive me? Thanks.

March 13, 1932   BENI-DICK

* * *

You did not stay a bit too long, "Beni-Dick." (Please notice I changed your name because we have a "Benedict" in the Column, and I was afraid the two names would become confused. All right?) I enjoyed your letter very much—enjoyed picturing that garret, with you in company with your beloved books, or busy at your work bench. It all sounds typically masculine, with its dust and unemptied ash trays. Did you make the tea and toast? You did not tell us what is on that mass of scribbled papers that is "all around" in "wild confusion." Please do, it sounds interesting.

I have an idea you are going to bring down an avalanche of protests on your unsuspecting head because of your opinion of modern verse makers. I agree with you in regard to some, but not all, no indeed. And I emphatically disagree that "prose is really all that matters." There is much—very much—too much—of our modern prose that does not matter at all, but there is much that matters a lot, too.

Mary

* * *

My dear, dear Nancy: I'm supposed to be studying *mes leçons*, *chérie, mais malédiction!* Who wants to study lessons? Not little Mary, I'm sure. Emphatically not little Mary. You see, I'm not going to high school any more. I stay home and a be-spectacled tutor has the unwelcome task of beating knowledge into my head. *Le Docteur* says I've got "nerves," or something; and he's determined to put back 10 or 15 pounds I so laboriously danced off my frame. Result, no school, no dancing lessons, and no parties. But sh! As long as there's a kick left in Mary, she'll never turn down a party.

Speaking of parties—have you ever been in a penthouse, Nancita? Sis and I were invited to a week-end party in Chicago recently, and our host has a ten-room ultra modernistic penthouse. It's absolutely gorgeous, marvelous, swelegant! And did we have fun! My first taste of real metropolitan whoopee, and I was so thrilled. I met a real movie star, friend of mine host, who happened to be in Chi at the time. And also a well-known modern sculptor.

I danced six times with the movie star, and I earnestly hope he never discovered how my knees were knocking together. Long have I adored him from afar, and to actually be dancing with him and on the receiving end of some perfectly grand compliments, left me limp. That was one thrill I'll never forget. And now home, and lousy lessons, and "nerves," and cod liver oil. Phooey!

I see where the perennial favorite, the petting question, is once more in the limelight. And I rise to remark mildly, "What's all the shootin' for?" Why all the hullabaloo? To me petting is a matter of personal taste, and not morality. A really fastidious person knows when a little kiss is not amiss, and when it is simply not the thing to do. Anyone who goes around petting promiscuously is merely guilty of an unforgivable breach of good taste. That type of person probably is careless about everything else pertaining to personal conduct.

If I have an awful crush on an adorable boy and he is simply ga-ga about me, I think I have a perfect right to let him pet me a little. But mark you well, Nancy, I mean just that—"a little petting" —and not undue familiarities. And I certainly don't feel the least bit soiled afterwards. I can count all the boys who ever kissed me, on the fingers of one hand. Believe you me, my big moment Freddie begged long and earnestly, for five long months, before he had the privilege of kissing me goodnight, and he certainly appreciated it by then!

We (the gang) had a grand party the other night. We called it a "Guess Who" party. Everyone came representing some famous (or infamous) character. Try it some time, In-Betweens, it's fun. My Freddie got the prize for the best characterization with the least "make-up." He merely carried a keyhole, which he peered through *a la* monocle. His conversation was liberally sprinkled with such classic expressions as "middle-aisle it," "Reno-vating," "blessed event," and "swelegant." *Voila*, Mrs. Winchell's bad little boy Walter. The funniest was Max, who enveloped himself in a sheet and silence. Behind him trotted his pet collie with a whiskbroom tied beneath his chin. Mahatma Gandhi and his goat! Later, when we all went out to a not-far-distant roadhouse, they wouldn't let the Mahatma bring his "goat" in till we threatened to go on to a competitor nearby. The manager weakened, and Gandhi and the goat strode majestically across the dance floor to the vast amusement of the other patrons.

It was a grand party, marred by only one distasteful occurrence. A newcomer to our gang sang a risqué version of a popular song.

Well, when he finished there was an ominous silence in place of the loud guffaws he expected. And then the enraged boys in the gang seized the offender and administered a good old-fashioned punishment. They washed the laddie's foul mouth with a good strong soap! He howled and kicked and blew bubbles, but finally apologized. I don't believe he'll repeat the mistake. One of the rules of our gang is that there shall be no coarseness. Anyone who persists is promptly cold-shouldered.

"Paradox," have you deserted me? Hasn't anybody got a welcome for poor "Mary?" I wanna be liked, but nobody says: "Hello, Mary."

Well, it's time for my owl-eyed purveyor of learning, the prissy old dear. Some day I'm going to muss up his hair, and see if he's really human. He hasn't smiled since he's been coming here and his face must hurt like heck. Maybe if I were to tickle his ribs—Ah! Another repressed desire! Love,

March 23, 1932   MARY

* * *

IF I published all the "Hello, Marys" that were sent to you, child, you would be in such a state of elation that "Jasmin" would have trouble in repressing you. I cannot imagine, however, how it could be possible that none of the greetings crept in.

Your gang sounds pretty good to me.

Petting as you define it, Mary, is the kind that belongs to right-thinking human nature. You are a wise, understanding little girl. I do not like to hear about the necessity for the tutor and the doctor and the cod-liver oil. Better turn down a party or two than lose your health. You have heard that before, haven't you? I only wish I could make you believe it before you learn the truth of it by bitter experience.

[141]

Showers

* * *

M<small>Y</small> DEAR NANCY: Here I am with a couple of man-sized problems.
Nancy, my first baby was 15 years old on St. Patrick's Day, and if
I do say so myself he is a big lovely boy. He is in the 10-B grade,
Senior High, and is all set on being an aviator, so my husband said
when he is through "Hi" he will put him through an aviation course
at Cass Tech. That, however, is apart from the subject.

As I said, he is just 15, and I am without experience as to what is
expected in the line of money for a boy of that age.

There is no transportation, as the high school is just about five
minutes' walk from our home, and wet days I drive him over.

Up to now there have been a few cents for pencils and writing
pads, books being furnished, so there is no expense really, there.

He does not attend dances and school parties as he does not care
for the company of girls—thinks they are too giggly—but figures
strongly in all boys' activities, base ball, foot ball, basket ball, gym,
swimming, fishing, etc., and is captain of two ball teams at school.

I buy all of his clothes, subject, now, to his approval.

He does spend quite a bit on airplane construction parts, which he
assembles and makes to fly—must have 50 now. He buys the kits,
then Saturday afternoon he and his particular boy chum go to a
show close by.

Every Friday night his father takes him to a local boxing match
(that's why I'm alone tonight), just the two of them, and they enjoy
it so much. They each take a pocket full of peanuts or pop corn to
munch and I suppose they behave like two kids. When I'm along,
it seems as though I am a damper to the hilarious feelings, they are
so proper, and that is one reason I like for them both to have that

one night together. It is an entertainment that I could not enjoy but they do, and seem on that evening to "unlax." When they come home about 10 o'clock, I have a nice little hot-dog lunch to cap the "he-man" night out.

For the past year, Nancy, Son has earned 40 cents each week doing a bit of work for a neighbor. He did not care to accept the money at first and said it was a pleasure. But she, being older, I suppose, knew that the kid would soon get tired and so insisted on 40 cents payment, and you can easily imagine that he has come to depend on his pay day.

So I think you have it, Nancy. We supply the cash for whatever he may need at any time. There are no school and lunch or transportation expenses and his regular money is 40 cents a week. Now what should we give him? And what should he be expected to do with it? I forgot to say that he has a bank account dating from the time he was born, but we do not allow him to draw, and indeed he has never wanted to, so I don't know why I say we "do not allow."

That disposes of Problem No. 1. The next is more difficult—at least I think so. As you know, Nancy, I was born and brought up in England in a very, very, straight-laced home.

Until I came to America 10 years ago, I had never seen a deck of cards, had never been to a show other than opera, and only since coming here have I listened to dance music. I played bridge and enjoyed some lighter form of show, but still do hold to my early training in the line of the question of right and wrong. To me quite a number of the modern, shall I say modes, are an absolute sin, but while I want my boys trained with a generous sprinkling of these ways, I do not want to go too far, though I realize they live in a faster age and country than mine.

Nancy, I don't know if I can make myself understood. I am 16 years older than my 15-year-old lad, meaning that I was married when only one year older than he, so I'm not too old to sympathize with youth. I want them to have all the joy and pleasure that life affords, but in a good clean way. I don't want them to find pleasure in drinking; oh, I want them to know there is happiness, joy, and pleasure in other ways. It would kill me, Nancy, to see one of my sons brought home—to quote one Column mother—"plastered." I'd rather lay them to rest now while they are as God made them, than see them live to believe they only live when disgustingly drunk. Can you help me, Nancy? If you had a growing lad who promised to justify your pride and adoration, a lad as popular and well-liked as mine is, what should you do from now on, in the belief that you were surely going the only way to insure him always being the clean, lovable kid that he is now?

I realize mothers have duties, but just how would you go about making him want to stay good and clean, the way he is now?

We never serve any kind of drink in our home, Nancy. We seem to have a good time without it, but will he always think so? Or when he does go out in mixed company, as he is sure to do in another few years, well, what will he want to do, Nancy? I have three boys, 16, 6 and 1 years old, so the subject is vitally interesting and important to me.

My husband says he never did see as wonderful a mother as I, but up to now they have been babies, and it is my natural element, but from 15 on I do feel incompetent.

Oldest son has the basement practically to himself, gym corner, pool table and work bench. There is a crowd of boys and they all know they are welcome and seem to like to come. I never see such a bunch of boys in any other home.

Sometimes after being in the basement for an hour or two they will come up into the kitchen and make fudge, or just whatever takes their fancy, sometimes a wienie roast, and I am always happy to leave anything I am doing and help them. Son is quite a radio artist by this time, and he and those of the other boys who play instruments come here. I play the piano for them and they play their own instruments. Sometimes six or eight of them in my living room, and most always they bring their new pieces of music to have me try over for them to give them an idea. Well Nancy, all those little things have just been my method of training, and making my home to them what it should be, but I feel as they grow older there will be other more elaborate methods and I want you to tell me just what they are.

Thank you, dear Nancy.

March 31, 1932   SHOWERS

P.S.: Mrs. Leslie did promise to write me on the subject "The Heart of a Little Boy," because I reminded her that girls haven't all the hearts. I've watched patiently in her little corner for two years and I'm still patient.

* * *

I ENJOYED every bit of your letter, "Showers."

Seems to me the methods that you have used for 15 years have produced good results. Why not continue them? Surely, there is no better way of bringing up children to be the fine young men and women that we want them to be than to present them with high ideals and examples in the home. That's what your children have had and are having, dear "Showers." Only just recently I read in a very fine book the statement of a man saying that the first 15 years of a child's life would establish his future. If that is true, and I believe it is, you have no cause to worry, have you?

There is one point in your letter, though, that I cannot help but feel is a bit exaggerated. It is what you said about the way you would feel if your boy came home under the influence of drink. I am sure you did not mean literally what you said, or perhaps I understood it too literally. I could not help but think that most every man has at some time or another in his life the experience of having drunk too freely of intoxicants. If that comes into your boy's life, and he should come home to you in that condition, I should not like to have you feel that he was on the road to destruction. Better, dear "Showers," to recognize it as an unpleasant incident in the boy's life, but one that need not be taken too seriously. We deplore children playing hooky from school, but we do not consider it too serious a matter.

I recall an experience of a young man who was out with other young men one evening and came home "plastered," to use the expression of our Columnite. His mother wept and mourned and felt just as you said you would feel. The boy did not say much, but finally remarked: "Well, Mother, every boy has to have this experience once. You need not worry, it will never happen to me again" —and it never did. So you see the mother had her unhappiness for nothing. The incident did not affect the boy's future in any way except to make him know that there was no pleasure in intoxication. That story gave me a new slant on the subject, and I believe it will you. We hope no such thing will ever happen to your lad, but if it does, you'll remember this tale that I have told you, won't you? It may save you a heartache. You have already made him want to stay clean and good, as you suggest. He'll not change.

Now about the allowance for son. The regulation allowance for a high school student who must pay for his transportation and lunches and buy his pencils and other school accessories seems to be settled at $2.50, if one can afford it, or he will be able to get by with $2, if necessary. Since your boy has neither lunches nor transportation and has not yet reached the girl age and stage, I should think $1 a week would be enough. Out of that he can buy his ice cream, or whatever boys like, his small school supplies and the contraptions he needs in carrying out his airplane experiments.

I remember a letter that came to the Column some years ago from a mother who said that when her son reached the age of 15 or 16, I forget which, she and the lad's father decided to give him an allowance that should cover all his expenses, including his clothes, and let him do his own buying. They started a checking account for him which taught him how to handle business of that kind. He consulted them when he wished to buy anything expensive and they advised him. It worked out very well. The boy was also supposed to keep up a savings account out of the allowance. I do not remember what the allowance was, though I have a dim recollection that it might have been $25 a month. That included every expense the boy was supposed to have.

Mrs. Leslie says she has never forgotten the editorial about the heart of the little boy, but has not had the time to give it the thought she feels that it requires. But she will some day.

Thanks for letting me use your letter.

*

Trudgin' Along

Just to trudge along at the break o' day
And kick up the dust o' the old highway,
Just to be merry and laughin' and gay,
And go happy and carefree upon my way!
Just to hike up the road with a joyous song,
Though the way be hard and the road be long,
And to give my best no matter what's wrong—
That's what I want, just trudgin' along.

August 12, 1931   PUSS IN BOOTS

Manito

* * *

DEAR NANCY: It was "Beni-Dick" who inspired me to write; I want to visit him in that garret room of his, and watch him work at that abandoned library table. I can't sit down, though, for he only mentioned one chair. Perhaps I can get a peek at the papers that are scattered about the table.

I have a leaning toward writing, myself; in it I am lost to the existing world. Is there any greater fascination than seeing a plot take shape as the sheets are torn from the typewriter in ecstasy; than meeting face to face a beloved character from your own imagination, or a letter from a publisher saying that your MSS. will be published on a certain date? To me there is nothing more engrossing than to feel the "writing mood" coming on; yes, I am like that. I haven't reached the stage where I can sit down at any time and tear off a story or article at will. Have been chided several times for this and told to try and force myself to write. It's no use, however. When I do, the result of the effort is so much bunk. I am on the right side of 25 yet, so I guess I still have time to mend my ways.

"Beni-Dick," there is no better place in the whole world ('less it be under a tree high on a hill-top, or ensconced on a mossy mound deep in the solitude of a hemlock swamp) to write and dream than under a garret roof! Here one seems vast distances away from the everyday world. Here is that necessary adjunct to the thinker— silence. Here one may commune with himself and settle those little perplexities which are constantly cropping up. Here, too, when one is tired of writing, there is the companionship of those books you mentioned. I quite agree with you that prose of today is more important than verse, but I find some poetry very good.

But to go on with your workshop, or should I say studio? I like to hear the voice of the rain which seems so near in such a place, although at times I get desperately lonesome listening to it. But there is something soothing about the sound of a steady downpour as it drives against the windowpane and runs joyously down the roof. A few years ago I lived a few blocks south of the Book Tower and would sit for hours at my window watching the lights blinking through the swirling rain.

"Blue Feather" is an ardent rain-worshipper as well as I. When a thunder storm approaches, we have one thought—to get out in it! For hours we walk or drive and drink in the beauty of the winding sheets of water as they drift across the river valley made famous by Hiawatha. There are few scenes to compare with the panorama of swampland and hardwoods stretched for miles at one's feet, with the orange and gold of the horizon reflected in the mauve and deep blue of the wavering mists over distant hills. I have been with "Blue Feather" on many trips in quest of beauty in our North Country. One does not have to look far up here. Each forest glade and shimmering lake is soul-filling, not only with what the eyes encounter today, but with the priceless lore of the vanished Indian and the hardy Jesuits and voyageurs.

"Blue Feather" does not like to break the communion with Nature by word of mouth. I have seen her sit for hours contemplating the glory of a sunset through the arches of Pictured Rocks, the angry roar of Superior's waves as they rolled in at Grand Marais, or the quiet sweep of waters which stretch across to Les Cheneaux. Her room, as she described it some time ago, is a haven of rest where she retreats to write of the wonders of her Northwoods.

"Blue Feather" and I were invited to a Coast Guard station last fall. The station is situated on Superior, noted for its horrible temperament. Some thirty miles of uncertain road had to be negotiated before we could get there. It was nine o'clock when we started out in "Blue Feather's" Tin Woman. And raining cats and dogs. I think this was the only time I didn't like the rain. The roads were swimming with water and every few feet the car sank to the hubs in slippery clay and mud. It was dark as Stygia.

It took over three hours to reach that bluff that overlooks the Coast Guard station and Superior. The wind shrieked and howled in unabated fury; it was impossible to hear conversation at close range, and walking upright against the blast of the storm was almost impossible. It was a welcome relief when three Coast Guardsmen had pulled us into their attractive rooms over the boathouse! But the feast that they had prepared for us more than compensated for the difficulties we had passed through—a bowl piled high with various fruits, hot biscuits over which was poured a delicious gravy of rabbit stew, baked squash golden from the oven, baked potatoes, coffee, and pumpkin pie. It took a poet to gather and cook that meal and I, for one, will be eternally grateful!

Northwoods, April 3, 1932   MANITO

* * *

THAT was a thrilling adventure with a happy ending—that visit to the Coast Guard station, "Manito." To have "Blue Feather" as a companion would put the perfecting touch to the experience.

"Beni-Dick's" garret sounds intriguing indeed—but I can't keep the thought of spiders and mice from my mind.

I agree with you that silence is a necessary adjunct to best thinking. However, it is not a bad idea to learn, as newspapermen must, to think even in the midst of countless noises, big and little.

I can imagine that "Blue Feather" would enjoy silent communion with Nature. Please tell her I am looking for a letter from her.

Wavering

* * *

DEAR NANCY BROWN: I have been reading your Column for years with the greatest interest. May I join it now? I have a problem that is very real to me. I have been in the States three months, after spending four years in Europe studying voice with one of the greatest masters. I am returning in two weeks to continue indefinitely. Music is bound up in my life. I couldn't live without it.

While studying in Europe, I met a man who loves me and I love him. We belong to each other and we know it. It is not a mad romance, but a sane facing of facts. He is poor and following a profession that will never bring him much income and I love him for sticking to it. His work is a vital part of his life as mine is of mine. We would be mere puppets without them. Therefore we can not be married. We do not wish marriage. But why, dear Nancy, can we not live together in unconventional Europe?

My head, which has always until now been very level, tells me to do one thing and my heart another. I've had a strict, conventional bringing up and am old enough to be able to decide questions sensibly, but here I am, wavering.

A brilliant future has been promised me. I may never have it. I shall not be disappointed if I do not have great success. But I do not wish to spend my life washing dishes and planning budget meals and living within four narrow walls.

Perhaps you will say I am not in love, that I am thinking only of myself, but if you say that, you are wrong. I am thinking, too, of the man I love. He would be only burdened with a wife. But I want to live. Nancy, I want to be myself. And he does not ask me to do this thing. If I do it, it will be my choice.

Am I weak in character and a traitor to the ideals that have been instilled into me or am I too much of a coward to answer my heart and let convention go by the board? Give me your counsel soon, dear Nancy, before I go. I need it badly.

April 8, 1932   WAVERING

* * *

IT IS not merely a matter of convention, dear woman. It is more than that—far more. It is a matter of vital, moral importance to you.

You ask why you may not live with the man you love, without marriage, in "unconventional Europe." There are many reasons why. First and foremost, there are the ideals learned at your mother's knee—ideals that your mother culled from the rugged laws of morals and ethics that Moses carved out of the rock. That's one reason. Then there's another. You do not want to belong to the class from whom good women draw aside, and observe with questioning eyes.

And there's still another reason: The children who might come from such a union—you know what the life of a child born under such conditions is like. 'Tis the child that pays, and pays, and pays—and you would pay, suffering for the child's suffering. The man? Well, he is protected by the double standard. Wrong? Of course, everyone knows that. Nevertheless, it has existed for ages and will probably continue to exist as long as there are men and women. And the woman is foolish indeed who throws herself against its walls of granite.

You would not be happy with the man you love, living in the fashion you contemplate, brought up as you have been.

Yes, and there's still another reason that I have not mentioned. Consideration of Mother and Father. If they are living, I'm sure you could not bring such misery to their last days as the knowledge that you were living immorally would cause them. If they are not living, such a step on your part would be the greatest act of disloyalty to their memory.

Immorality is a harsh word; and one I do not like to use with reference to your problem, but I am doing so in the hope that it may shock you into a realization of what your rash act would mean if you carried it out. I am sure you would not deliberately choose to enroll under its banner.

I cannot see that the marriage ceremony would make such a great difference to either your life or the man's. It would place you above criticism, and your children would be safe in the security of a father's name. If you are a mature woman, as I think you are, you must have learned from observation and reading and from other sources that the man who agrees to such conditions of living, almost without exception, tires of the woman who has put herself in the questionable position. Moreover, the man who loves a woman unselfishly will never permit her to so compromise herself.

Many years ago, when the Column was still young, one of our favorite Columnites who signed herself "Bob-o'-Link" asked me the same question you are asking. She decided in favor of her early ideals, and she and her "Terry" have been happily married with a legitimate child, for many years. I have not heard from her for quite some time. Perhaps she will see this letter and write to you of the arguments that led her to decide as she did.

Don't do it, dear woman—don't do it. Either marry the man or else let there be nothing but friendship between you.

Muddled

* * *

DEAR NANCY BROWN: Is it selfish of me to bother you with my problem when there are so many who write to you in desperation? If so, I'll understand; if not, will you please listen? It's about myself.

I'm one of these uncertain people, don't seem to have any definite opinion on any subject, don't know whether I believe in the Bible or not, whether I believe in so-called loose morals or not. In other words, I guess I've no mind of my own. Usually there are two sides to every problem, but instead of defending one side whole-heartedly, I either don't know which to agree with, or agree with both. Now does that mean anything?

Another thing, one day I love only my husband, have eyes for nobody other than him, the next day I imagine I'd like to have other men friends, sort of be a "woman of affairs," don't you know. And yet people call me sweet and good-natured. None who know me would dream that I am troubled with the question of "morals," I'm certain, simply because I've always led a clean, wholesome life. Had the usual amount of good times and boy friends and now at 19, am happily married. But this little problem sure bothers me, and being very moody, I cry often. Summing it all up, religion is what I need.

Can you please understand this letter at all, Nancy? Please, please, try. You see I don't know what I believe. I'm quite certain there is a God. I have the habit of always saying my prayers, tired or not. And yet the Bible—it's so hard for me to grasp its meaning. How could such impossible things ever have happened? When I hear a minister over the radio preaching his sermon, my first impulse is not to listen; then if I do, it somehow doesn't sound sincere. How does one know what to believe when there are so many different theories, so many different religions, so many who openly disagree as to the Bible stories? I've discussed this with many, but no one satisfies me. The usual argument they present is, Why do so many educated men and women attend church, accept it as it is, without question, etc.?

I haven't attended church for seven years, simply because I do not enjoy it. Is that so terrible? And I just do not like hymns. I realize that religion is to help us to lead better lives, and the funny thing is, it really helps many. I'm truly glad it does. But for myself, I'd rather have a more practical, shall I say, religion, not so spiritual, not to have men tell of things that happened so many thousands of years back. How do we know these things really did occur?

Oh gosh, Nancy, this thing is driving me crazy. I guess one could write on and on and never reach the end. Won't you try to suggest something that will help me? I know I would have a much clearer understanding of life if this one little thing were fixed up.

Should a woman have a few "affairs" before marriage, so as to know what to expect, sort of have a full life?

April 17, 1932   MUDDLED

* * *

OLDER people than you are muddled, trying to puzzle out the religious problem, dear. The more one puzzles, the more muddled one becomes. Here's what I would do if I were you, I would say to myself: "I am going to do whatever I have to do, just the best I can do it. I am going to bring all the happiness to those around me that I can possibly bring. I believe in God, and my soul bows in reverence to the good, the true, and the beautiful, all of which are a part of God."

I would not try to puzzle out the why and the wherefore of the Bible stories that are troubling you. One does not know how the grass grows, or why the flowers bloom, but one knows they do. I would let that suffice as explanation for the puzzling questions.

[155]

As you grow older, you will find your religious views changing, and that is nothing to worry about. It is simply adjusting one's creeds to the subtle, daily development of human life. What does it matter whether you know if the events in the Bible really occurred? Like many other people, you are taking your religious questions and problems too seriously. Just let them slide for the present.

Church-going is a good habit. If you could find a church where you enjoyed the sermons, or perhaps the music even if you do not like hymns, it would be well. Personally, I am very fond of hymns. Do you know that the very finest music that has ever been composed in all the world has been written around religious and love themes?

Not very long ago, I was talking with a young man—young, though probably 20 years older than you. He said the reason he did not attend church as regularly as he used to was because they never sang the old hymns any more. He liked "Rescue the Perishing," and "Bringing in the Sheaves," and others of the same kind.

I do not think you need worry about your morals, either, even if the dawn of certain days finds you with a hidden yearning to be a "woman of affairs." I don't believe the "affairs" would be very wicked. Maybe it keeps your husband guessing a bit, too, and that isn't a bad idea.

"Should a woman have a few affairs before marriage?" Depends upon your meaning of "affairs." Clean romance and love? Then of course. They are among the pleasant things of life.

Don't worry. Just go right on being the good little girl that you are, and you will find the religious problems will solve themselves in time. I do not mean by that, that you will be able definitely to say, "I believe this and that," and set down your creed with mathematical precision—Oh, no! You will learn to accept your belief in all its moods and tenses, and know that it is right.

Richard De Bury

* * *

DEAR NANCY: I had my mind made up to write you my "tale of woe" over a week ago when out of a clear sky came "Muddled's" letter in the Column. She was 19, married, and "in a fog" as to the truth and authenticity of the Bible stories. You gave her your usual good, common-sense, conservative answer, but I'm afraid little "Muddled" is in as much of a "haze" as ever.

Curiously enough, I was going to write on the same subject, but my story starts where she leaves off.

When I was 19, I was pretty much in the same frame of mind, although I "got that way" when I was about 17. I went to our minister, whom I greatly admired—and still do—and asked him to give me something concrete as to the truth of the Bible material. He could deal in nothing but abstractions, and finally said: "You will just have to have faith." I interviewed others and always I received the same unsatisfactory answer. I had been in college a year when I was 17, and was then following a resolve to find out for myself what the facts were, during my college career. I am now 25 and will wear the cap and gown here at the University in June. I have had eight years (there was time out to gain finances) in which to look into the situation, and what have I found? Nothing but more and more reason to suspect the existence of everything religious except God himself.

I have studied the history of the Christian church quite thoroughly, from the earliest Roman fathers—Ambrose, Hilary, etc.—down to the Fifteenth Century. St. Augustine, the Gregories, Thomas Aquinas, and all the rest have been studied, along with the history (and the literature in part) of the entire Western European world. I am unable to find any reason to believe, other than that the Christian people, requiring, like all other people, some stabilizing influence against the uncertainties of the world, were at the time of the inception of Christianity peculiarly ripe to receive such a body of doctrine. For at least the first ten centuries of the Christian era, the validity of documents and physical phenomena was never questioned. Witness the long list of supposed miracles that were believed to be absolutely legitimate.

My tale of woe, then, is that my college career has put me more and more in the dark. The church, with its dogma and ritual, appears to be built on fairy tales. I need spiritual comfort as everyone does, but how can I have faith in the authenticity of Christianity any more than that I have a million dollars in my billfold at this moment?

I am not malicious or intolerant. I believe that God gave me a mind to use and that he will not punish me if I have missed the truth. Perhaps through the great and wholesome influence of your Column, some authority in the church may be moved to attempt to point the way to "Muddled" and myself, and to others whose numbers I feel to be legion.

So many ask you about going to college, Nancy. Tell them that it is a great and worth while experience, though some might be happier without it.

Have you read "Philobiblon?" Then you are personally acquainted with

May 8, 1932   RICHARD DE BURY

* * *

AN assured belief in God is a pretty good foundation for religion, "Richard." You need have no cause for worry if you hold fast to that one established item of faith.

The comparison of a faith in Christianity to faith in having a million dollars in your billfold is not quite legitimate. You *know* the money is not in your billfold, but you are not quite sure that Christianity does not exist as it is pictured by the New Testament.

I agree with you entirely that God gave us minds with which to think, and certainly there will be no punishment coming even if we make mistakes in our thinking. Moreover, the word "God" itself implies love, and love does not include punishment for honest mistakes. Many a lad—and many a lass—is muddled about his religious beliefs at your age. It is part of life that one always encounters at the boundary line between youth and maturity. There is no cause for worry.

Most certainly the question whether the miracles actually happened need not be a cause of mental anguish. One does not have to decide that question, anyway, so there's little use in being troubled about it.

Modern college study of science is quite sure to disturb the faith of one's childhood, but out of the haze and bewilderment will gradually emerge a finer, stronger faith that will be the comforting, stabilizing influence against life's uncertainties, that is, as you suggest, a necessity to most mortals.

*

Snowflakes

When I see snowflakes,
Then I think that God
Must find the whitest clouds,
And break and scatter them in
Fragments from the skies,
To make a blanket for the sleeping earth.

June 1, 1929   RED

Madelon

* * *

DEAR NANCY: Wonder if you've any faint idea of the tremendous scope of the Column influence. Oh sure, you say, you have. But you don't know the half of it. It goes all over the world! It's—it's breath-taking!

I'm one of the "girls," 30 now, but one of them in that I'm still wishing for the white cottage and flagged walk, tulip bed and a tree at Christmas time. Being, by taking three deep breaths and squaring the shoulders before making "contacts," a more or less cheerful soul, I have "company" now and then. And I've struggled through all the loneliness most girls experience who lack that certain some-thing, that *savoir faire* that makes some popular while others just aren't among those present. Having come philosophically to the point where I assure myself cheerfully, outwardly at least, that I "don't care," I'm gradually getting a little attention. But nothing to brag about. The few—very few!—suitors I've had weren't any-thing you'd take even with a sprig of parsley and a gold platter thrown in. If I could just stop falling in love with the high class ones, it wouldn't be so bad.

What I meant to say when I started this monologue is: I think women are responsible for some of the men as they are today, the discourtesy and the drinking, I mean. You didn't know there was anything wrong with 'em? Well, there isn't—much. But I like the older ones best. Or is it that they are mostly married and therefore "ungettable?" Or do the wives add a certain polish that makes them so much nicer and more comfortable?

Yep, aren't men the pains in the neck—but don't we wimmin like to be the hot water bottles and mustard plasters?

One "err" the sexes have in common: The girls think they're heaven's gift to man—his salvation, soothing syrup, cute little trinket and pocket piece, and the one thing he can't do without; the men *know* they are heaven's gift to women. If they'd take the chips off their shoulders and get busy being useful and helpful to one another, what a nice sociable time would be had by all.

Had to take this typewriter in lieu of wages on the only job I've had in nearly a year. Well, I don't have to feed it.

And the double spacer "ain't" so I had to remember hard at each shift. So there! But—I should have confiscated 75c for a new ribbon for you, shouldn't I?

"Goofy" is my most fav-o-rite favorite. "Jawn" was. But he quit. Darn him. 'Member long time ago when he was convalescing from a sickness and looked out the window and saw the new buds on the trees in the springtime on which the rain had frozen and I think he called them molasses covered popcorn—or something like that? Anyway, my scrapbook of his letters is all gone, due to the zeal of a former roommate.

But imagine going to a ball game with "Goofy!" Wouldn't that be your idea of a Working Girl's Sunday at Coney—Family Reunion—Heart Full to Bursting—and All-Happy-Tired-Out-Feeling idea of a good time! His girl is one Lucky Lady.

Well, this is silly and taking up a valuable lady's valuable time. Sorry.

April 24, 1932   Madelon

* * *

It wasn't a bit silly, "Madelon." I enjoyed it very much and had more than one chuckle out of it.

Of course you're wishing for the white cottage, and the flagged walk, and the tulip bed. What girl isn't? And 30 isn't so old, you know, dear, as to make the wishes for happiness impossible. I'd keep right on with the outward "don't care" appearance. For perverse reasons, perversity in girls does seem to attract masculine attention. I'm sure you will have plenty of sympathizers in not wanting the men who are interested in you, and wanting those who are not. 'Tis human nature, especially girl nature.

I agree with you that women are responsible to a great extent for what men are today—or any day. But whatever they are, we like them—as a whole—don't we? You remember what the old lady said: "There's no living with 'em and no living without 'em." I agree also, that we enjoy the rôles of "hot water bottles and mustard plasters."

You were a good girl to double space for me and the typewriter ribbon was all right—nice and clear.

Come again.

*

A Friend Indeed!

(*To* "*Wayfarer*")

"Your cheek is silken as a fairy's wing," he said.
　"It is as fragrant as an opening rose."
　(I'm glad I bought that scented powder, friend!)

"Your hair is a soft sea of precious gold; deep
　greenish gold reposes in the hollows; bright
　liquid yellow metal rides the crests."
　(It was worth the price of a finger-wave, my friend!)

October 6, 1929　　　　　　　　　　　　　Penelope

Stone Cabin

* * *

DEAREST NANCY: You didn't offer me one word of greeting when I called to see you, after an absence of two years, but I know you will let me come in again to pay this tribute to a singularly happy and beautiful childhood.

I wish that every person in the world could look back upon such warm, sunny years as were those that wove for me a fabric of memory so fine and enduring that I can take it out today and wind it about my fingers like webs of scented old lace.

There was a friendly, colonnaded old house (my father's birthplace) set comfortably on a hilltop just outside of San Francisco. It was loveliest on autumn afternoons, when the eucalyptus and pepper trees showered the roof with twirls of yellow and brown, and the sun, flaring across the water, set its dozens of western panes afire. But always, no matter the season, there was about it that atmosphere of peace and well-being that belongs to all mellowed, seasoned things. Generous lawns stretched away on three sides, and to the south, backed against the house, was an old walled garden, dim and heavenly sweet, with pastel drifts of bloom along the walks and in the corners.

It was here that we (my two brothers, two orphaned cousins and myself), played in summer when the sun was too hot for comfort elsewhere, and here every afternoon was served our supper of bread 'n' butter and jam and milk. In the center was an old fountain which looms high in my memory because of the sound spanking I received when I was about four, for walking into it on a Sunday morning after I had been carefully dressed for church.

There were grape arbors, vegetable gardens, orchards, stables and paddocks dropping down the slope at the back of the house, and in their own small paddock nearest our play yard were always two or three Shetlands. There was a doll's house in the fork of a great tree, and see-saws, sand piles, slides and a "flying jenny" scattered here and there. Over all was the blue, blue sky and the stiff, rackety breeze from the bay.

There was our fragile little grandmother, some of whose graciousness I hope we absorbed, who so fully and lovingly undertook the task of mothering us when our own mother had to go away. There was our grandfather, always rosy and smiling and disheveled as if he had just come in out of a high wind, and our grave, judicial, handsome father.

And there was "Nu'Sella" (Nurse Ella), black faced, snowy aproned and beloved, who coddled us and spanked us and mended us through a succession of beautiful years. "West Virginian," how well I understand your grief upon the death of your black mammy. My grandmother was a Virginian, and her black folks were one of her first considerations. Nurse Ella had gone out with her to California when she went as a bride in '59, had nursed our father in his infancy, and 33 years later, when our mother died, she took over our turbulent selves with the same faithful tenderness that had always distinguished her. She passed away at the age of 93, as deeply grieved and as tenderly laid to rest as one of the family.

Then there was "John Ike," blackest and most fascinating of story-tellers, who was ever pleased to have us break in on his eternal raking and digging and spraying with our demands for entertainment. He would interrupt a sing-song narrative a dozen times to shout, "Git out o' dat water, chile!" as some impolite listener strayed away to meddle with the hose, and return to his story without once altering the lazy smile on his huge mouth. Peace to his soul. I know that today he is plodding about in some sunny corner of heaven, with a string of insistent cherubs trailing after him.

Marching with us up the years was a procession of pets: dogs, cats, rabbits, parrots, turtles, mice, ponies, and heaven knows what else. One of my most imposing photographs is that in which I (at about two) am seated upon the back of "Wee Boy," our tiniest Shetland, with my fat little feet sticking straight out before me.

Every year in summer we were allowed to give a party for the children of the village which surrounded our grandfather's manufacturing plant. They came, happily, those scrubbed and shining little Portuguese and Mexicans, each one carrying a fistful of wild-flowers "for make the freend-ship grow more beau-tee-ful like the blos-soom." And such a time as we would have! There were mountains of ice cream and fields of tall layer cakes. There were popcorn balls and suckers, lemonade and melons, pop-crackers and funny hats. And once an indulgent uncle sent out from the city a stranded vaudeville troupe, which included among other fascinations a trained bear and dog act. That was a red-letter year!

During our first years a governess came out each September and remained until May, to teach us, but later we went to school in the city. I can see us now, flying along the road through streamers of fog, or showers of thin, yellow sunlight, behind Franz and Diana, our grandmother's carriage horses. A little later there was an automobile, the first the family had owned, and were we magnificent then! We roared up to the curb, looking like smug little toads, no doubt, while our schoolmates stood on the sidewalk and gaped. If there was sufficient time, old Ben would sometimes put us out and load up the car with some of our acquaintances and whirl them around the block three or four times before the bell rang.

It was a beautiful, beautiful time, Nancy, and it has made me happy to recall it. The old house has been replaced with a more modern structure (to my regret) but the patio surrounds what was once the walled garden, and the old fountain has been preserved. My father spends much of his time there, and it is still home to all of us. The stables are now garages, but the arbors and paddocks and gardens are the same—even the Shetlands are there (others, of course) with a bevy of youngsters (my small nephews and nieces) forever swarming over them.

Don't forget to tell us about your childhood, Nancy. Write us a long letter and head the Column with it on a Sunday when you have lots of space, won't you?

I love you heaps, Nancy, but I am afraid that your jewels and flowers and travelers and friends of this, and that and the other have caused you to forget your humble little Stone Cabin. Have you read "A Victorian Village," by Reese? You will love it. Huxley's "Brave New World" will irritate you unspeakably, but if you can overcome that, you will find it thoroughly amusing.

Bye—

April 29, 1932   STONE CABIN

* * *

FORGET you, "Stone Cabin"? Not for one minute! I think it rather hurts me that you should suggest anything so unthought of. You have never called at Column House that you have not been received immediately. As nearly as I can recall now, the last letter was received around Christmas time. If you have written since then, I have not received it. Any time in the future that you do not find a letter you have sent me in the Column, please know that there has been a mistake, somewhere, and that I certainly have not forgotten you.

What beautiful, beautiful childhood memories you have! Your story of them tells us more about "Stone Cabin" than mere words offer. But I don't think it is quite fair not to tell us the titles of your books. We want to add them to our Column book shelf. Please!

[166]

My own childhood? One of our In-Betweens asked me some time ago to write it. Perhaps—some day, when there is a lull in the Column demands. Thank you for wanting it.

* * *

<h1 style="text-align:center">II</h1>

DEAR NANCY BROWN: A special wish for your happiness this Christmastide, dear Nancy. I have been sitting on the steps of Column House, over there by the juniper bush, since October, just watching the procession come and go. Expect to be here until March, and hope that some of my old friends remember me, so that I may feel free to come in the house.

My idea of happiness? Just this . . . a fine and durable companion-ship with one man, the sort that would never fade, shrink or ravel . . . enough of success that my banner of pride may never quite trail in the dust, and enough of failure that I may not be smug . . . the cocktail of play, the meat of work, and the dessert of love always upon my life's table . . . smoke above my chimney when the dusk falls, and a whistle at my door when the steak is broiling and the coffee bubbles . . . a wreath of not-too-sweet virtues to hang in the window of my old age, with the red taper of one superb old folly shining in the center.

December 24, 1931   STONE CABIN

Douglas

* * *

Dᴇᴀʀ ꜰʀɪᴇɴᴅ: As you see, I have moved, and probably before I write again shall move another time. I gave up the apartment about five or six weeks ago, just before I went south—for my health. Suppose you're wondering how come I came back so soon. Nope, I'm not "cured" yet, but felt that I had to get back. Hence the hotel room.

It all came about like this: I went to Chicago and points west on a business trip, in February. Dad wondered why I didn't return, when I stayed much longer than he knew it would take to take care of the few business matters in hand. So after several urgent wires from him I confessed that I was ill—in a small town in Illinois—the return of an old trouble. I realized that he would fuss around more or less when he knew I was ill, so I gathered courage enough to return to town. Soon as I arrived, he gave one look at me and pushed me off to his physician, who, in turn, shoved me southward. I returned in time to get the latest edition of Tʜᴇ Dᴇᴛʀᴏɪᴛ Nᴇᴡꜱ with your broadcast in it. May I, at this time, offer sincere, if late, congratulations?

Monday I am to take my place in the firm as junior partner. Somehow, there is something flat in that announcement. I have often thought what a thrill I would get when I could write and tell you that simple little statement. Will you think me immodest if I say that I have worked very hard these six months that I have been on probation? And now that I have attained my desired goal, something seems to be lacking. It is indescribable, rather indefinite, and yet there seems to be something missing, which I cannot define. Not my health—it will come back in time, it always has before—but truly I do not know what it is.

[168]

Perhaps you will think it is because I have reached my goal and have nothing for which to work now. But, my dear, you are wrong if you think that—I have much work yet to do. The days before me stretch out in endless monotony. I hate to think of all the weeks, months, even years that I must go on doing the same things day after day, year after year. Work, eat, sleep, play a bit—what does it all mean after all?

This isn't just an outburst from the mood of the moment. I have felt this way for weeks, but thought that it would change, when I became junior partner, but I feel no differently. Maybe I should go out and get tight, but then, on the other hand, maybe I'd better keep my promise to you, Nancy, and to my Column mother—"Mother's Career."

And now, goodnight, Nancy, but not goodbye. You will be pestered by me again, sometime.

One Lonely Evening, May 1, 1932   DOUGLAS

* * *

GLAD you did not make it "goodbye," Douglas. I like "goodnight" a heap better.

Let me offer you my sincere congratulations for the new office that you have earned. That's splendid. The something that seems lacking will appear after you assume the duties of your office and begin to feel the honor of your position. I know you have worked hard these six months, and my hat is off to you.

I do not think that your work is over, now that you have reached your goal. Quite the contrary. You have only accomplished the position where your real work begins. You'll enjoy that work, "Douglas," as you have never enjoyed dancing or play of any kind in your life.

Not so very long ago, I heard a man who holds a very high executive position say that he never had so much fun in his life as he has had in the few years he has been at that desk of his—and he has worked hard, too. That's where the pleasure came in. My work, "Douglas"—I would not exchange it for any pleasure that could be offered me; in fact, no pleasure could be as pleasurable. I should enjoy a bit more leisure time, to be sure, but the steady, absorbing work is the outstanding happiness of my life.

A few years ago, with conditions different, I grant I had a different viewpoint, too. And yet always, always, whatever work has been mine, I have enjoyed—real, genuine, enthusiastic enjoyment, and that is what you will feel, lad, when you have reached your stride.

"What does it all mean, this working, eating, sleeping, playing, and so forth?" Why, it means life. And that's your responsibility right now, "Douglas." Whether you make of it a disgruntled failure or a joyful success is up to you.

In the years to come, when you are nearing the sunset trail, you do not want to look back over a misspent life. Therefore, lad, open your young eyes to the joy and happiness of work and living. There will be trouble and sorrow, of course—to be met like the good soldier you are—and the happiness always follows.

I guess maybe you'd better keep your promise to me—and I guess maybe you intend to, all the time, and are just trying to "get a rise" out of me!

Please come back soon and "pester" us some more. We like it.

Above all, *Take care of your health.*

Del Rose Husband

* * *

I

DEAR NANCY: I don't know how to begin but my wife she is sick in bed. She has been since March. My wife Del Rose she ist from Spain and has been here in this country for one year but she has not her first papers my wife she tells me they will send her back with out me. I have all my papers. Nancy, Del Rose reads your paper every night she is educated in her own country she plays a piano beautiful and sings like a bird. She is beautiful and her people are rich in Spain they keep writing to her and tell her to come home and they will forgive her for marrying me. I make only forty dollars a week and went too night school until the baby was on the way. Then I think my place is with my wife. Sometimes I think I loose my mind with those letters coming trying to take her away from me. Nancy, I work hard every day and I love my wife. I could not live without her. I think she thinks she will not live through the birth of our child. What shall I do? I think my wife is only five feet and weighs only eighty-nine right now. Nancy, answer as soon as you can to my letter. Can I come back and tell you what our baby is and how everything is going?

May 12, 1932   DEL ROSE HUSBAND

My wife she just said she loves "Little Brown Girl" and her "Daddy Long Legs" and "Blossom" and you Nancy.

* * *

I SHOULD not be disturbed about Del Rose's fear, dear man. Many a young wife feels the same way before her first baby comes. You tell her there is nothing to fear—that it is just one of the natural things

[171]

of life, like breathing. And if there is a period of pain it will soon be over, and she must think of the joy of holding that little pink baby in her arms—all her own. One of the men writers to our Column, who signed "Just a Man," said he knew, when he held his first baby in his arms, what it meant to feel close to God.

Never mind if Del Rose is little. Sometimes the little folks stand trials better than the bigger ones. It is your task to keep up her courage and reassure her. Tell her to think how many millions of babies are born each year and how very, very small is the proportion of mothers who do not come back. There are thousands and thousands of people walking our streets every day, and only a few meet with fatal accidents. It is just the same with mothers and their new babies.

Please tell Del Rose that there is no danger of her being sent back to Spain, simply because she has not taken out her first papers. Tell her, too, that she must stay contentedly with you, and some day you can both go back to her Spain and take the little new Spanish-American with you.

I am glad she loves me. It is very sweet. Thank you.

* * *

II

DEAR NANCY: Just a few lines to let you know I am a daddy twice. My sons arrived—one weighs four pounds and six ounces and the other five pound. My little Del Rose is all smiles although she is very sick. She said it was worth all she went through. Isnt that mother love Nancy? They will not bring the babys to her so she can see them both they are perfect but oh so tiny. The only reason they let me see them so soon is to tell my wife they are perfect—she would not believe them. I am glad "Just a Man's" wife is about to be a mother again and am so sorry that their little son was taken from them. But Nancy, I would rather have both of my son taken from me than to have Del Rose taken away from me. I felt like "Just a Man" when I first look at my babys. What will I feel like when I hold them. Nancy, I would rather not have any more children than to see Del Rose go through what she did. I was by her side till the doctors made me get out she beg them to let me stay but they wouldn't. My Del Rose had no mother to be with her for she is in Spain and she has no sisters then they wouldnt let me stay I cant understand this country and there ways. Well Nancy I would not bother you know more only I thought you would like to know about my little Del Rose. Nancy say a pray for her

   June 3, 1932   DEL ROSE HUSBAND

* * *

INDEED we did want to know about Del Rose and those babies, dear man. We are happy with you and send you our best congratulations. The reason the doctors did not let you stay with Del Rose was because they feared your emotion and excitement would be harmful to her. You would not want that, would you? Even though it was all difficult for little Del Rose, she has probably forgotten all about it by this time and is happy only in the knowledge of her babies.

What will you feel like when you hold those little sons of yours for the first time? No words can describe the holy emotion. "Just a Man" came closest to it when he said he felt very near to God.

You will come back and tell us more about the babies and Del Rose, won't you?

Half Crazy

* * *

DEAR NANCY BROWN: I just listened to Jesse Crawford playing
"My Mom"—it certainly did dig in deep! You see, Nancy, my
Mom's gone—and so, in my trouble and loneliness I come to you—
My Mom.

I'm facing a bitter future—blindness—at 25. Everything I've
planned has collapsed. I can't even see a break coming. I also lost the
only girl I really loved—I guess I was too fast with my tongue—
but everything's gone wrong lately, so I imagine she was just one
of those bad breaks.

Poison is putting out the light, together with three months of in-
somnia. If any one wants to know what a young man in his early
twenties thinks about, upon approaching blindness, I can tell 'em.
It's horrible. All the friends I've enjoyed so much have left me, because in my grief I've said things I didn't mean, but was driven to it.
Now I've learned the bitter truth. I guess they'll see why I did it.

Just one more week, Nancy—then curtain. I've been called a
quitter, a mess, and a failure, but, by Golly, I've got pride and when
it does come I'm going to fight all the harder. A girl has no use for a
blind young man, I guess, so I shall be deprived of that particular
pleasure. Very soon. Gee, it would be a great satisfaction to have
some nice young lady say something nice to me before I go. I mean
just that, Nancy. I've already looked over the river front. I won't be
able to read your answer soon and if you would print this as soon as
possible it would be a great thrill to find someone who still knows
how to say nice things—I've forgotten what they sound like. It's
so lonely here now.

Oh I guess I've said too much, so I'd better sign off. Would you do me this one favor—My Mom. Gosh, a few kind words do help, don't they? I think I would stand it a lot easier if somebody really did care.

June 25, 1932   HALF CRAZY

* * *

SOMEBODY does care, son—somebody cares very much. I care, just heaps and heaps. It made me proud that you chose me for your "Mom." "Moms" always care about their sons, don't they? And there will be a lot of other folks who will care, too, when they read your letter. And there is somebody in particular, whom I am going to tell you about, right now—somebody whose story you will appreciate and will take to heart, and that will encourage you so much, there will be no talk of the "curtain" a week from now.

The story is about one of our young assistant prosecuting attorneys, Ned Smith, whom I have known for several years. I called him up and asked him if I might tell you about him, and he said "Yes." So here is the story:

Mr. Smith lost his eyesight and became totally blind when he was a lad in his teens. He went through all these terrible mental experiences that you are suffering now—and then he had a good think and decided, with the help and encouragement of his friends, that the loss of one of his senses was not going to ruin his life.

He wanted to become an attorney. He continued his high school work, the boys reading his lessons to him. He entered the University of Michigan and graduated from the law course, by the same method. Always, always there was a friendly boy companion to read his lessons to him. After his graduation, he entered our prosecuting attorney's office as one of the assistants, and is there now.

He, too, had a girl who meant all the world to him. He hesitated about asking her to share his life, even as you are hesitating. Then he decided to ask the question and leave the answer to the girl. They

[175]

have been happy together for several years now and there is a little three-year-old daughter to complete their happiness.

Now doesn't that story bring you courage? And there is even more to it for you. Mr. Smith said he should be glad to have you come down to the office (Police Headquarters, Clinton and Beaubien) and talk with him. I wish you would go at once, son. Tell him you are the lad about whom I called him. He will know. And I am sure you will come away from that talk with him much happier and with a different outlook on life. You will go, won't you?

And now about those friends whom you have estranged with bitter words that you did not mean. Write to them, my boy, and tell them that you did not mean the discourteous words you spoke, and tell them why they were spoken. They will understand.

You say you have been called a quitter, and other names. Maybe the people who spoke them did not mean them any more than you meant what you said to your friends in your desperation and your bitterness. Maybe those who spoke so unkindly to you have their troubles, too, and their words were as impulsive as yours. Your experience will make you understanding of such conditions.

Here is another, possibility, too. Doctors sometimes make mistakes—even the best of doctors, like all other mortals!

Maybe your doctor has made a mistaken diagnosis. I would refuse to give up hope. Try to quiet your mind. Try, oh, so hard, with the thoughts of the one you love best and of the things that interest you most. When you lie down to rest, try to make your mind a blank, or fill it with thoughts of what you would like to be, instead of with bitterness. In time, you will find the priceless sleep coming to you. I would ask the doctor for a sedative, too. I would protect those eyes in every possible way.

Here is a very simple little act that I find helps wearied eyes, very much. Place both hands over them, tightly, so that no light is admitted, and sit quietly for a few minutes. You will be surprised to see how rested your eyes are when you open them again. It is just like using your arm constantly—like beating up a cake, to use a house-wife's illustration—and stopping to rest once in a while.

Go to that girl whom you love and talk it all out with her. You will find her ready and tender in her understanding and sympathy.

P.S.: The little secretary lady who takes my dictation stopped long enough in her short-hand to tell me this story: She knew of a woman who had no money whatsoever and who was almost totally blind. She met an understanding person who referred her to one of our big hospitals. The physicians at the hospital said that since she had not entirely lost her sight, they could restore it, at least partially. And they did. Now doesn't that help, too?

*

To Nancy Brown

A book of letters gathered through the years,
Cross sections, black on white, of scores of lives;
Husbands and lovers, mothers, maids and wives,
Caging in words their vital joys and fears.

Penning to one, whose certain sympathy
Is more than gold or frankincense or myrrh,
Their bitter griefs; or pouring out to her
Their too full spirits' lyric rhapsody.

A book of letters? May it well not be
A Book of Life, compiled exquisitely?

May 1, 1932   MEREDITH

A Connecticut Yankee

* * *

I

Hᴇʟʟᴏ ɴᴀɴᴄʏ ʙ.: "The thing that goes the farthest,
Toward making life worthwhile,
That costs the least and does the most,
Is just a pleasant smile."
—W. D. Nesbit.

Now, then, how's that for poettery? That's the kind I like.

My heartfelt sympathy to "Largo." 'Tis sure sad to lose a pet. I know 'cause Mike, my big yaller cat of which I was very fond, met the same fate as "Largo's" dog.

I do not know who did it, but it wasn't unexpected. Mike was in love, and like all other he-things, when love entered his heart caution left his head, and the fool cat picked a super-highway for his tryst. After several drivers nearly wrecked their cars driving around him, one came along who didn't like cats, and that's that.

Does "Beni-Dick" or anyone else want a spider for his garret? I have plenty of all sorts and sizes, from the head of a pin up to a door knob. Most of 'em are in the garden, for I guess they know I don't like spiders.

Nancy, I don't like to talk about the depression but I just want to ask you have you noticed how it has knocked the high hat off a lot of folks? Yes siree, that's one good thing that has come out of the hard times, folks are getting human again.

You know, I don't think I will write you about my past childhood. I'll just wait a few more weeks, then write you about my second childhood. Yep, I think I'm nearly, if not actually in it. Well, anyone who will go out in a cow pasture on a hot sunny day and whack a little white ball around till they ache in every joint and are so sunburned they fairly sizzle, must be senile and childish.

Now I've gotta go do a murder. 'Twill be murder by the wholesale, too. Mr. and Mrs. Aphis and all their little family are about to die, or at least I hope they are, for if they don't I won't have any garden left. I hate to kill things, even pests, and always do I apologize to them before I swat 'em or squirt the pizen on 'em. So you see what a tender hearted pusson I be.

"Pen," you said it, and if they ever drag in any form of mathematics we will go down to oblivion together, for figgering sure gives me a pain in the neck. So here's hoping the Column never turns mathematical.

July 15, 1932   A CONNECTICUT YANKEE

* * *

THE Column will have to find a new editor when it goes mathematical, "Connecticut Yankee."

Maybe you have discovered the real reason for the depression. It is, indeed, not conducive to the wearing of high hats.

Sorry about Mike. He didn't show very good judgment, did he? Reminds me of the story of the cow that stood on the railroad track when the engine was coming. The farmer said he admired her courage but he didn't think much of her judgment!

I want that past childhood. Never mind about the second one— we'll wait for that.

* * *

II

YES SIREE, NANCY B.: You are right. We are thankful? Well, if we ain't, we should be. Thankful that things ain't worse than they be, if for nothing else.

[179]

Now I haven't much money, but after checking up my blessings I find I have much to give thanks for. F'rinstance! I am sound in limb, if not in wind, and I am feeling quite salubrious. Ha! Thar's a ten gallon word for ye.

There are so many people so much worse off than I am that I actually feel that I am lucky. For although our income has practically ceased, we are not suffering for the bare necessities of life, as many are. So until that does happen, I can't be termed as "Gallant."

Honestly, it makes me feel so sorta shamed like, when I read all the nice opinions the Column Folks have of me, for I really am not the nice sort of person they think I be. I am really a cantankerous sort of critter and I can be so churlish it would make your hair stand on end, or curl up at least. Mean! Say, I can be so mean that Old Bill Sykes would seem an angel compared to me. And am I thankful that there are some folks who think me the sort of person I would like to be? Golly! I'm so grateful to you folks for your good opinions that I am actually trying to live up to them. And I am getting so sort of sweet and patient that I have Sir Boss worried to a frazzle and he keeps asking me if I feel sick or sumpin'.

Printed November 26, 1932   A CONNECTICUT YANKEE

* * *

I SHOULDN'T wonder, "Connecticut Yankee," if the adjective "gallant" fits you even now.

I was interested—very much so—in the paragraph in your letter that speaks of the regard in which Column Folks hold you. I do not, even in the faintest degree, believe that you are a "cantankerous critter," but I have often thought of the psychological influence of the Column upon us all. We feel a certain obligation to try, at least, to live up to the opinion that the Column has of us, don't we? That very effort makes us more nearly like the personality that we have built for ourselves, through our Column writing.

I am hoping you had a pleasant Thanksgiving. Thanks for the good wishes that you sent to us.

[EDITOR'S NOTE: *This was "Connecticut Yankee's" last letter to the Column, written shortly before she died.*]

*

In Memoriam

(*For our beloved "Connecticut Yankee"*)

We shall remember,
Thro' all weary days,
Her cheerful ways.
We shall recall
Summer and Winter, Spring and Fall—
Thro' long nights—sleepless,
Tortured of unrest.
We shall remember best
Her gaillard manner,
Her undiminished crest—
Her and her good "Sir Boss"—
Her priceless words, "Fight nice."

Oh, we shall mourn her loss,
And miss such gay advice.
Nothing can quite suffice to fill her place,
She, who with fun and wit,
Who with such kindly grace
Would always make "the best of it."
So, thro' all nights and days
We shall remember,
Ever, in "Yankee" phrase,
Her lovin', laughter ways.

December 25, 1932   CUP O' TEA

Spots

* * *

M<small>Y DEAR NANCY, AND ALL</small>: I decided to indicate my independence
—if any—by the pleasant task of jotting down a few random notes
from the past twelve months. Do you mind?

A year ago today I was staff announcer at a Denver radio station
—with two additional specialty programs (one a singing quarter
hour, the other a comedy monologistic political current events under
the apt heading "The Loose Nut"). Forsaking it for the age of com-
mercialism I, as it were, girded up my loins and paraphrasing the
olden cry of "On to Berlin" with "On to Texas," went thither to
seek my fortune.

Evidently someone else sought my fortune more successfully, for
even in Texas I could not Garner it. Followed days of worry and
effort and extreme heat until I finally worked myself up from nothing to a state of extreme poverty, a faint upon the street, four days
in a Dallas hospital (remind me to write "Adventures in Aphasia"—
it should rank with De Quincy), returning consciousness and home
for a few weeks' rest, via McAlester, Tulsa, Joplin, Springfield,
St. Louis and Chicago.

A theater job in San Antonio—house closed in one week due to
labor's refusal to accept wage-scale. Charming place the Alamo City;
no prettier sight in the U. S. than that peaceful S'Antone River me-
andering its serpentine route under a myriad of pretty little bridges.

Have to speak Spanish to read the city map. . . . More soldiers
than I have seen in 15 years . . . Christmas in S'Antone . . . Ditto
New Year's . . . and how dry it wasn't. . . . The land of the spree
and the home of the slave . . . A telegram . . . "Come to Denver"
. . . Hooray!

Off via Del Rio, Langtry (the erstwhile home of Judge Roy Bean, the Law west of the Pecos), Alpine, Marfa and Van Horn to El Paso ... a visit *en passant* to Chihuahua ... Elephant Butte Dam ... a night at Hatch, N. M. ... dinner with Mickey Gallagher ... "Welcome Home; whatever became of," etc., etc., *ad infinitum*. ... How the old place has changed! Ed. Wellington still remembers the dinner party I gave, doing all the cooking and the serving ... even remembers the menu ... can I help it if I'm clever?

Quaint old Santa Fé ... Glorieta Pass ... La Bajada Hill removed from the highway ... well, it was a dangerous hill. ... To think that so great a work as "Ben Hur" emanated from the odd old palace of governors in Santa Fé. ... A night with my old pal, Togo Patterson, at Pecos ... Las Vegas (happy memories) ... Raton Pass ... that bleak, endless five miles north from Wagon Mound ... I like Trinidad ... it looks so "old-world." Hustling Pueblo and Colorado Springs.

Heigh ho! back in Denver. ... What! The job is in Seattle? ... Tsk-tsk ... five weeks of delay ... order to move ... Cheyenne ... Rawlins ... old Fort Bridger ... Rock Springs, the oddest shaped town in U. S. ... Evanston, and the Yellow Peril becomes a panic ... every other door is labeled Sling Mud Hi or Low Flung Hooey or Hung Far Low, or what have you ... Ogden ... stuck in the snow, west of Evanston ... beautiful Webber Canyon ... the Devil's Slide ... ugly towns in eastern Utah, in strange contrast to beautiful Salt Lake City ... the trip from Ogden to Pocatello by the light of a great full moon ... Boise ... the inability of the road to choose between Idaho and Oregon—in and out three or four times ... on to Pendleton—ride 'em cowboy ... Umatilla. ... The Dalles at dawning ... no more beautiful and awe-inspiring sight than the Columbia River Highway down to Portland ... Multnomah Falls ... the serene majesty of Mt. Hood ... a lovely trip to Seattle . . . only thirty days to Alaska. . . . Sorry, but I was close anyhow.

Back to Portland . . . ten weeks in the Rose City . . . great country out there . . . roses and rhododendrons (wish it was daisies, easier to spell) . . . Terwiliger Boulevard—a trip to Astoria . . . now I know what became of the Scandinavian rights . . . they're all in Astoria . . . Salem, Eugene, Medford, Roseburg, Ashland and Grant's Pass . . . over the Siskiyou range . . . Yreka . . . Sacramento, and do I like that town! . . . Stockton . . . the San Joaquin Valley to Bakersfield and over the Ridge Route to Los Angeles . . . Santa Monica beach . . . I'm the man who didn't try to crash a studio or get into pictures . . . Cajon Pass . . . the Mojave Desert . . . Death Valley in summer (evil-doers there would find Hades a welcome relief) . . . seeing the highest point in the United States from the lowest point (Mt. Whitney and Death Valley).

Las Vegas, Nev., and the thermometer bulging at the top . . . gets so hot out there that once a gunny sack of popping corn popped, and a gust of wind blew it into the air and the station agent thought it was a blizzard and froze to death. . . . Funny-named towns in southern Utah—Moab, Nephi, Lehi, Kanab, Paragonah, Parawan, Panguitch, Manti and Provo . . . the drab monotony of eastern Utah . . . and northwest Colorado . . . Steamboat Springs . . . Turkey Creek Canyon . . . Denver again . . . three inches of rain in an hour in Phillipsburg, Kansas . . . Kansas mud . . . and why is St. Joseph (and all Missouri cities) naturally dirty? . . . The sun never sets on British territory (nor shines in St. Louis) . . . Hannibal, Mo., shades of Mark Twain . . . and so home again!

So, now I'm a little older, a little more bald, a little more stupid—and the well-known *joie de vivre* is not veeving so well . . . possibly your book will help me to recover my lost youth. (Has anyone seen my wheel chair?) . . . Grandpa wishes to r'ar back and relax—and reminisce . . . the good, old days! . . . maybe I'm wrong, but despite all our vaunted progress I think we may truthfully bemoan "the good old days" . . . eh?

Well, let's just mention a few ghostly echoes of the days agone before it became smart to be cruel, blasé, unfeeling, emotionless, and—curse the word—sophisticated. . . . I'll trade 50 "blessed events," an armload of Eugene O'Neills, a carload of Constance Bennetts, several assorted Walter Winchells and a whole collection of Sharkey-Schmeling fights for one "Hearts of Oak," old Pop Geers, or an illustrated song slide in the naive days . . . on with the Parade of the Past . . . a hot Tom-and-Jerry . . . Eddie Leonard's "Roly Boly Eyes" . . . Tinker to Evers to Chance . . . Hoyt's "Trip to Chinatown" . . . fifteen acts for 10–20–30 at the Grand in Pittsburgh . . . Dan Patch . . . nickel car fares . . . "Ragged Robin" . . . an old-fashioned waltz . . . conversations that don't embrace prohibition, biological phenomena, or a dirty story . . . correct grammar without bringing its user insults . . . Bert Williams singing "I'm gonna quit, Satiddy" . . . John L. Sullivan, Peter Jackson and Joe Gans (and none of them ever reported a Democratic convention or read a Greek play) . . . no need to pick advertising hooey out of every song, story, joke, picture or orchestration . . . ads for barroom articles, perhaps, but not for bathroom articles . . . rackets meant noises . . . muscling-in was confined to Little Egypt . . . taxidermists instead of taxi dancers . . . the Castles, "Honest Hearts and Home-spun Shirts"—"Turn to the Right"—"The Squaw Man"— "Raffles," Olga Nethersole, Kyrle Bellew, William Faversham, "Cash Hawkins," William S. Hart, Hans Wagner, Nap Rucker . . . Police Gazettes, but no Hooey, Bunk, Paris Nights, Artists Models, Art Studies, Hot Dawg, filth, etc. . . . dime novels about Nick Carter and Frank Merriwell and Buffalo Bill, for surreptitious, if innocuous reading—but no racketeers, gun molls, Ace High, etc.

O tempora, O mores!

Still, it's not so bad . . . one can always ignore the things that are revolting . . . but one cannot, alas, always see the things one used to see . . . which seems to be an unchangeable law of life . . . and one more law can't hurt as much.

This is really a good deal of a washout as a letter—and its only claim to a place in the sun is the patriarchal status of its author (further proof that youth should be served) . . . not much like the one I sent you from Las Vegas in '26, or the one from Boston in '22, or the Christmas letter of '22 (or thereabouts). But you had better humor my senility and print this—to give me a thrill at breaking out into print again after all these years.

August 7, 1932   SPOTS

* * *

OH, "Spots," what a splendid letter! Full of adventure, and thrills, and reminiscence, and travel, and wit, and humor, and oh, everything that's just like our "Spots" of some eight or nine years ago.

I laugh at your suggestions of senility and "bygone days," when I consider that you must be close to 30!

I lived in the past with your list of plays and players. Not all were familiar to me, but most of them were. How well I knew "The Grand" at Pittsburgh. It did not used to be a "ten-twenty-thirt" house, but one of the best theaters in the city—at one time, legitimate; at another, vaudeville for the Keith circuit; then the high priced movies; and lastly, the low priced show.

Vivo

* * *

DEAR NANCY BROWN: What would you do if you were the mother of sons and daughters of high school and college age, who possessed this new "viewpoint"? Would you sit calmly by and allow them to "experiment," because it is their "right as individuals"? Could you see your fine, clean, young son degenerate to a level somewhat lower than that of a beast? Could you see your sweet little daughter drag herself through the mire of these "experiments"? Of course I know you couldn't. I remember your wise counsel of "June."

But isn't there something that can be done about it? Are we mothers and fathers so helpless, or are we just cowards, afraid of being called "old-fashioned" because we believe in a Supreme Being and a certain commandment?

For doesn't the root of the trouble lie here? In spite of all the hue and cry about prohibition (and I am not a prohibitionist), I think the real trouble lies in the teachings of our high schools and colleges where our children are taught to "think," which in most cases means discarding the teachings of parents and church, to follow, sheep-like, the radical teachings of M.A.'s and Ph.D.'s whose degrees have, apparently, bestowed upon them the power to peer beyond the grave. "Eat, drink and be merry" is the creed expounded in our modern institutions of learning. Do you believe in God, you are medieval. Do you observe the commandment, "Thou shalt not commit adultery," you are hopelessly out of date.

I know whereof I speak, for although I am the mother of children of high school and college age, I am also a college student. And I want to testify that invariably at the mention of any religious belief (and you may be sure the tone is intended to beget laughter), a titter goes about the classroom. "I do not believe we have a soul in the sense in which the term is generally used," was the statement made by a professor of psychology, and he went on to elaborate that when one is dead he is dead.

Another went farther and said that he saw no reason why one should not "experiment" if he so wished—this statement, too, in more elegant phrasing.

Now, how can impressionable young people listen to such statements day by day by men whom they are taught to regard as models of wisdom and knowledge, and not have much, if not all of it, sink in and displace the old teachings? "As long as you do not invade the rights of others," is a stock phrase among them. Have parents no right to happiness and peace of mind? Has a possible child (and there are thousands of them in spite of the widespread knowledge of birth control methods) no right to a name and a father and a home?

Try to dispute one of his precious radical points of view with a learned doctor and what happens? He heaps such ridicule upon your degreeless head that you are disinclined to engage in further argument.

So we run panic stricken from this juggernaut of modern teaching and allow it to crush our children.

I wonder if those men ever heard the warning: "It were well for him if a millstone were hanged about his neck, and he were thrown into the sea, rather than that he should cause one of these little ones to stumble." Of course they have, but it doesn't mean anything. The Bible is merely an excellent piece of literature.

Perhaps I cannot view this subject as dispassionately as I should. I am too deeply concerned. But I do think mothers and fathers ought to wake up to the perils confronting their children. After all, ours is the grief, ours the shame, and ninety-nine times out of a hundred, ours the blame, even by these same sophisticated youngsters, when the penalty due to the infraction of the moral code must be suffered, which moral code at such times assumes astonishing reality.

I want my children to go to high school and college, but I do not want them to come back to me atheists and free-love disciples.

August 12, 1932   Vivo

* * *

I AGREE with you entirely in your opinion of these moral "experiments" which some young people think it their privilege to try today. I do not know what I should do if I were faced with the problem of bringing up a daughter—or even a son—during these times of extremist viewpoints. It would, indeed, be difficult to continue in the middle of the road, between our creeds of right and wrong, which the young people and the ultra-liberal ones of today term old-fashioned. Colleges are contradicting home teachings. The young people, between the two, do not know which to believe, but moved by the fear of appearing out-of-date, are inclined to adopt their professors' teachings. Mothers and fathers must concede and compromise, and must expect but very little in return.

The only answer, to my mind, is thought on the part of the parents—sane, steady, never-ceasing, intelligent thought.

One must be able to meet these young people's arguments with practical answers—spiritual reasons have no appeal.

And in all this discussion and all the concern about it, I do believe that these "experimental" conditions are not as prevalent as they appear at first consideration. The youngsters' pet slogan, "I must live my own life," may possibly be met by the appeal you offer— that they cannot separate themselves from mothers and fathers and families. I have heard that argument given to young people who were expounding their "individual life" theories, and have not seen one whom it did not reach, and whose argument was not shaken by the simplicity of the appeal.

[189]

Friend of the Poets

* * *

DEAR NANCY: I suppose you often wonder why some people write to you. Me, for instance—for long ago I have worn out my welcome, and you and the people who were interested have served as a "breaking point" that adjusted me to a life of rather unbroken solitude and somber recollections—when alone, man is always somber and always sincere. As a writer I aim to preserve this healthy equanimity of mind.

Who am I to continue?

Well, for one thing, I have avoided being anything but a character. It has made me shallow, perhaps, and that I don't like, but it has made me warmly received and mentioned and loved more than I expected or really deserved. I am not having any misgivings, you see, but I see my place. And maybe you don't like it. Maybe you think I'm just a punk.

I've got the good old American jitters today.

This typewriter needs fixing because it has just finished the rewriting of my last novel for the sixth time. It has taken me three years and for the last three months my publishers have been hovering over it in a welter of indecision, juggling its fate.

It's a swell book. I think it's the best thing I've ever done. And I've worked so hard that I've spent the night crying in exquisite pain. And I feel like I'm hungry all the time. But I can't eat a thing and am down to a funny hundred and thirty pounds.

It's an American novel—my last one was just a burlesque of America. But this one is America. And it probably won't get published.   As to this letter—I side-tracked a bit up there.

I want you to know that I have thoughts on all the questions in the Column. Something you said in the "Vivo" argument annoyed me terribly. You said something about that youth should be content to sit back and not experiment, that nobody ever got anywhere that way, that it was better for youth to accept the judgments and experiences of age—in other words, show the old tribal wisdom that reeks of feudalism, slavery, custom.

But I'm not mad any more. You didn't mean that, really. You said it because 90 per cent of the people who read the Column believe that. You want to be believed in—but I know something else now. You really didn't mean that. You have a mind. Something you said about churches showed me that. I was amazed by your practical, open, truth-finding gesture. What kind of woman are you? A pretty damn fine woman. I'm proud to have you for a foster mother.

Don't you see the shift? You're surprised that M. R. Rinehart takes an ultra-modern view on "Vivo's" subject. She does, because now she is beginning to think for herself. Her writings have made her a mouth-piece and a bank account. Now she can say what she thinks. You are in her position. You can be a mouth-piece—about your bank account I don't know a thing. But it is a truism that man feels all his emotions through his pocketbook. In the present upheaval he has begun to doubt and question his world and its institutions. It's a shame, and it's sickening—but everything comes from one source, even man's own most chivalrous and inspiring thoughts —man's greed.

Bernard Shaw has so well expressed in his preface to "Misalliance" what I believe to be the rights of youth that I must refer you to it if you wish to learn my views. It is essentially that all progress is achieved by painful trial and error process. We learn very little except by *experience*—the very heading of your Column.

As to churches, I would study them as you are doing. I would try to determine, if they have any value, what that value is. Or if they are valueless, then like all outworn institutions, they should be done away with. Like you, I'm no Bible hugger, but I admire the tenets of Jesus, the factual, practical policies of loving fellow men, of casting out greed, lust and fear. The churches do little of this I think. They perpetuate nothing but their own narrow beliefs and desires. (By the way, I dare you to read "The Profits of Religion," by Upton Sinclair—all of it, especially the last chapter. Another thing I'd like to recommend is "Call Home the Heart," by Fielding Burke, a good novel.)

You asked for suggestions about Christmas. Why not a questionnaire? Here's mine, modeled on one THE LITTLE REVIEW sent out for its swan-song number:

1. Do you believe yourself a reasonable being in an unreasonable world or vice-versa?

2. What do you like best about yourself?

3. What do you dislike most?

4. If not yourself, who would you rather be, or if yourself, what would you prefer to do, if what you are already doing does not interest you?

5. What keeps you going on, living, existing from day to day? Why don't you commit suicide?

6. What do you consider the most valuable thing you ever learned?

7. If you were given an extra hour of leisure every day how would you spend it?

8. Briefly, what do you believe? What would you call your philosophy of life?

We'll start out with *you*. You answer them.

With sincere affection,

October 9, 1932   FRIEND OF THE POETS

THERE is so much in your letter to answer, "Friend of the Poets," that I think I shall begin at the beginning and run right through it.

I was surprised that you were surprised at a "personal interest" in my answer to your last letter. Of course there was a "personal interest." Am I not your Column mother? Mothers of any kind always have a personal interest in sons.

I do not wonder why some people write to me. That's what I am here for—to be written to.

Certainly you have never worn out your welcome. I wonder how you arrived at that conclusion? Surely nothing has been said in the Column that would lead you to feel unwelcome. Quite the contrary, your letters always have a special interest for the Column Folks.

"Who are you to continue?" Just one of our most beloved Column writers. Isn't that enough?

I do not know what you mean by saying "I see my place." Your place is right with us—an honored, loved place. Certainly I do not think you are a "punk." Whatever put such an idea into your head? Probably those American jitters—which I hope have worn off by this time, and taken with them all those foolish notions about not being wanted.

I am excited about the American novel you are finishing. Is it the same one for which you asked the Column to mention subjects? I remember I suggested that you write a novel of home and home life. I have thought about it several times through the years and wondered if you had given up the writing. I am glad that you like your book, son. The writer knows better than anyone else, I believe, whether his writings are worth while.

But I am very much opposed to that "funny 130 pounds," and the fact that you are not able to eat. That's not good. Not even the best book that you have ever written will compensate for the breaking down of your health. You know that yourself—you are an

[193]

intelligent man. Why continue to take chances of losing your most valuable possession?

I am sorry you were annoyed at anything I said in the "Vivo"-and-Mary-Roberts-Rinehart discussion. I do not think you quoted me exactly; at least, not enough to carry my real meaning. I am sure I never said that youth in general should be content to sit back and not experiment. If that is what I said, the experiment was applied to one certain line. You know that, don't you? Applied to that line, I maintain every word I said. I doubt if you would want a daughter or a mother or a sister of your own to try moral experiments such as were discussed in Mrs. Rinehart's famous article. One writer said "Mrs. Rinehart has no daughter. If she had, she would have written differently."

Aside from the undesirability of the experiments themselves, the possible results to innocent victims are too grave to consider the experiments right, by any code whatever.

If you had read the thousands of letters that have come to me through the years that I have had this Column, from girls who have tried the youthful experiments and are paying the price while their partners in the experiments go free, or if you had met those girls, desperate with shame and disgrace, ready with poison or gun to end it all, I am sure you would never again uphold this special form of so-called "progress of youth."

If these youthful experimenters were honest in their beliefs, they would not feel the shame that they do, when their experiments are to be made known to the world. Any experiment that must be covered up and kept hidden, you may be very sure is not an honest experiment or a good one.

I do not think that a mother's natural attitude of protecting her child from experiments that she knows will bring only wretchedness, reeks of feudalism or slavery.

I meant every word I said on this subject, but my belief did not, in the sense that you quoted, include all kinds of experiments.

Perhaps it is because I have a mind that I can see that similar escapades that swashbuckle under the title of "modern experiments" are neither wise nor right.

You ask what kind of woman I am, and then profanely answer it yourself! Thanks. I am proud to be the foster mother.

Do you not think if one has a mouthpiece, as you suggest, that one should use it very, very carefully and conscientiously and conservatively? I do. Please know, beyond the shadow of a doubt, that my opinions are not expressed simply to conform with 90 per cent of my Column readers. My opinions are mine and expressed sincerely. I am not hampered editorially.

Also please do not think I am "scolding." Sometimes when I have been very much in earnest and expressed my opinion very seriously, I have been accused of scolding. I do not mean it that way. If you and I were here talking this matter over together, you would not feel in any way that I was finding fault. I know. Please try to read what I have said in the manner that it would have been spoken.

I did not realize that I was studying the churches. Perhaps I have been, subconsciously. My creed, if so severe a word may be applied to my undefinable beliefs, has shaped itself through my years of life and experience. I am not applying it to any church as a standard. I have adopted what seems logical and right to me, and satisfies me spiritually. And everyone must have the same privilege, mustn't he?

I smiled a bit at your creed that admires the tenets of Jesus, the policies of loving fellow men, or casting out greed and *lust*—and yet advocates modern moral experiments!

No need to "dare" me to read "The Profits of Religion," by Upton Sinclair. I shall be glad to read it when I have time; also Fielding Burke's novel, which I have never read.

The questionnaire for Christmas offers suggestions. We had a questionnaire one year and it was very popular and successful. Some of your questions are a bit serious for holiday discussion—and some of them are just right. I'll save my answers to them, for possible use at Christmas time.

Am I not to know anything about the book when it appears? Mothers like to know what their sons are doing—even foster mothers.

*

Look, Love and Leave

It took the trillium seven years to grow
　　To this perfection. Would you pick it off and throw
The waxen flower to be trampled down
　　To lose its beauty, wither, and grow brown?

The lovely blossoms which we see in Spring
　　Are not a chance and casual happening;
They are the culmination of a plan
　　Man couldn't form—but God and Nature can.

The Johnny-jump-ups in the emerald grass
　　Delight the eye of countless folk who pass;
The dancing daisies, too, are elfin fair;
　　The fragile ferns, the lovely maiden-hair.

All these are crowning glories of their kind,
　　And we appeal to those who, fair of mind,
Will let old Mother Nature's magic weave
　　These dainty things, so "Look, and love, then leave."

May 14, 1932　　　　　　　　　　　　　　　　　NORTHWOODS

The Lace Maker

* * *

DEAR NANCY BROWN: Is it too late for a childhood letter? I have always read and enjoyed your Column, but since these letters have been appearing, I've had an undeniable urge to participate in the reminiscences.

In the spring of about 1899 on a twilight evening, a girl sat with her mother on the shady porch of a rambling old house, talking. Shyly, the girl offered two letters to her mother to read—one bore a postmark of a week before, the other was ready to be mailed in reply, to her sweetheart. The first letter was a question, the other its answer, that she would marry him.

The little mother's heart was heavy, because the man her daughter loved was a widower, with two little boys, an invalid sister, and a dear old mother, all living with him and being supported by him—and he was a young preacher, with apparently little prospect of ever struggling beyond his heavy obstacles. But the mother knew her daughter, and told her if she had considered all the disadvantages of such a marriage, and still wanted to marry the young minister, they had her blessing.

The young preacher and the girl who became his wife were my parents. During every year of their married life they became better friends, closer companions, and more in love with each other. Nancy, that is the most blessed heritage that parents can give their children; that background of love, security, and a peaceful, happy home. We were seven, and the two boys of the first marriage made nine children, but we never knew until we were almost grown that the two boys were not our full brothers, and they loved our mother with a devotion as strong as our own.

Oh, dear, when I think back to those childhood days, I laugh out loud with the crowding, happy memories. Such rollicking happy times under the big trees in front of the old parsonage of the little southern town. Our house and yard was the center for all the youngsters of the neighborhood, because we had such good times, and mother was glad to have us there.

There were big shallow pans of cold sweet milk always in the refrigerator, and barrels of apples or bunches of bananas and crates of oranges in the basement.

With a family like ours, we went into things on a wholesale scale —we bought flour by the barrel, sugar by the hundred pound sack, cereal by the 24-box carton and everything else in proportion. I imagine managing our family, keeping the children clothed, schooled, fed and religioned, was a job that no one other than my mother could have done. And there were hand made dresses for the girls, with lots of dainty embroidery, hand smocking, and fine lace, rolled and whipped on, all done by Mother. How she had time to do such things, and still be president of the missionary society, teacher in the Sunday School, prime moving spirit of the Epworth League, and wife to Father, I still don't know.

There were lots of things we couldn't do because we were a preacher's children, but there were other things that more than compensated. A minister's family is sort of public property, but it is also loved and appreciated accordingly. When I was tiny, and wore pink-checked gingham pinafores, I would make my morning rounds of the neighbors' houses, and come back laden with varied tributes. My tiny pockets would produce melted chocolates, wilting rose-buds, and bright bits of ribbon. And my hands would be full of fat red tomatoes still dewy from the garden.

At Christmas time the church members would send in turkeys, huge baskets of fruit and presents galore.

That Father was successful was inevitable, the way he lived, believed, worked and loved. I remember one little incident that happened when I was about four years old. We were being transferred to the "First Church" of a big city—the best appointment the conference had to offer, and we were leaving a small town where Father was the loved leading minister. After the furniture was all out of the house except one bed which was to stay there, and Mother had shooed the movers out, we all knelt around that bed, and Mother and Father both prayed that the move would be for the best, that Father would mean much to the new church, that we children would help all we could, and that none of us would ever think too much of the things of this world. I remember peeping, while they were praying, and seeing a flap of wallpaper hanging from the ceiling and I thought, "If not liking torn wallpaper is worldly, then I'm a lost soul."

When any of us had a birthday, there was great celebration. At the breakfast table, there would be presents from each member of the family piled around the plate of the lucky one—most of them were from the ten-cent store, it is true, but what mattered that?

At Christmas there was Santa Claus, who put fruits, nuts, candy, raisins, and one small package in each stocking, which we investigated the first thing in the morning. After that came a gala breakfast; then the crowning excitement of the day, the glowing Christmas tree, with all the presents piled around its foot. We'd each claim a big chair in the living room, or a corner, and sit there while Father called out the names on the packages, and everybody would watch breathlessly while each package was opened. Then much hugging, squealing, and occasionally a shiny tear that would splash on silvery paper or red ribbon from pure joy.

Easter was another holiday. There would be a decorated breakfast table, with little bunnies and green nests here and there, and a small needed gift for each member of the family; a summer nightie, a hair ribbon, or a longed-for jack-knife would be enough to cause many happy exclamations, and to weld us more closely and joyously into a family.

Father taught us thrift by encouraging us to open savings accounts with him. He had a separate page for each of us in his big account book. He gave us ten per cent interest on all we saved and we would use the interest to buy birthday presents and Christmas gifts, while the "capital" remained untouched and growing.

Once Mother and I started a business venture by buying baby chicks, raising them to the laying stage, then selling the eggs to the family larder. But someone stole the chickens! We always had two or three cows for family use and my brothers used to feed the cows, milk them, and sell the milk to Mother and the neighbors.

Father used to laugh a lot about one business "deal" the boys put over on him. Someone gave Father a little baby pig and since we lived out in the suburbs where we could keep it, Father gave it to one of the boys to raise. He fed it on scraps from the table, then when it was grown, had it butchered and sold it back to Father for twenty cents a pound!

Father always had a big garden, and the children had to help; many were the hours we spent collecting potato bugs, picking them off the vines, spraying the delicate tomato plants, and later picking the beans and cutting the stalks of okra off the tall sticky bushes.

Mother was interested in our schools and once or twice a year she would have a big dinner for our teachers and the principal. There would be vegetables from the garden, fried chicken, great silver pitchers of cold milk, and of iced tea, and home made ice cream, frozen in one of the old "cranking" freezers, at which we took turns, and yelled to "lick the dasher." And when brother graduated from college and won the Rhodes scholarship to Oxford University in

England, there was a big dinner for his whole class with us younger ones peeping enviously through the door.

Another thing I don't know is, how they managed to give us the education they did. We all went through high school and college, and those of us who wanted it were sent through professional school or university. We're all grown now and the youngest boy is graduating from college next year, but as a family we are as close together as in the days when we played and fought beneath the big magnolia trees in the front yard.

When we were away at school, Mother would write to us regularly, and she had to keep a written schedule of when she wrote to whom, so none of us would be skipped. That would have been tragedy, because her letters were, and still are, things very precious and full of her. During examinations, or other times of stress, she would write us illustrated letters that were so cute I used to share mine with friends.

Oldest brother is now a professor in a university, oldest sister is practicing medicine in a southern city, the next boy is a minister in the same city, one girl does social work in her spare time from her married life, another girl has been a teacher and is marrying this fall, still another boy is doing construction engineering, and so on.

When Father died a few years ago two colleges had memorial services for him, and his work will live forever. As for Mother, she is still as active as any of her children, this summer having charge of two girls' camps, and sponsoring work for the Goodwill Industries in the South, and above all being a perfect mother and grandmother.

When I was ready to go away to college, Father gave me a Bible with this inscription which he had written on the fly-leaf: "May it be said of you, as of one of old, 'The King's daughter is all glorious within'." What better thing could a Father do for his child than give her that to live by?

I know this is many times too long, but when I got started remembering, there was no end. I'm just stopping in the middle. And, anyhow, it isn't as long as it appears, because I double-spaced to save your eyes—you need 'em.

August 14, 1932 THE LACE MAKER

* * *

I READ the pages of your childhood story in utter absorption, "Lace Maker." No tale of fiction could be more interesting than the story of simple home life that you tell of in your preacher father's big family.

That gift that Father gave you when you entered college—what better banner for living could he offer you!

I hope you noticed that last Wednesday I called the attention of our In-Betweens to your letter. I want each and every one of them to read it.

*

Thanksgiving

I thank Thee, Lord, for life and health,
For all I own of earthly wealth;
I thank Thee more for faith and hope,
My soul's own gifts which help me cope
With all the aches and pains of life
And climb beyond this worldly strife.
I thank Thee much for what I do;
For friends who prove their friendship true.
I thank Thee for the grace to see
That I still owe my thanks to Thee!

November 24, 1932 OLD-FASHIONED

Douchka

∗ ∗ ∗

I

DEAR NANCY: This is my first visit to your Column House, Nancy;
but I am one of your oldest silent members. I read the first Experience Column, April 19, 1919, and liked it so well that I've seldom
missed it, since.

You may not think my problem important, but I am so afraid of
making the wrong decision that I'd like your opinion.

I am 33 years old, a widow; I have a stepson almost 29 and three
children of my own; two boys, 14 and 12, and a daughter 5. My stepson has asked me to marry him, has asked me at least once a week
for the past year and a half, and he insists that I must make a definite
decision. He is in the East now, and expects to return soon. He says,
too, that if I don't decide, or if I refuse, he intends closing his office
here and building a new practice in another city. I know him well
enough to know that he means what he says. I *positively* do not want
him to leave Detroit.

If you are to understand the situation, it will be necessary to give
you a sort of "case history" of the last fifteen years. Don't sigh; I'll
make it as brief as possible.

Fifteen years ago last February I was very ill. Our family physician was in the South, and Mother called a doctor recommended by
a friend. Long before he had me out of bed I was wild about him.
He was tall and slim, he had brown hair and gray eyes, and I thought
him the handsomest man I'd ever seen. I had plenty of boy friends,
so it wasn't a case of falling in love with the first man handy. He was
older and very "professional," so I thought he wasn't interested in
me. A bad cough that hung on after I was up and around took me to

his office several times, and on one of these visits he kissed me; he said that he had not intended to, and that he was sorry. Then he told me he had loved me for a long time, and that my age was the only thing that kept him from asking me to marry him.

There isn't time to tell you about my short romance, tonight, but it was far from smooth. Everyone said that it wouldn't, in fact it couldn't last. Even Dan thought me too young to know my own mind. You see, that day he kissed me for the first time was a month before my eighteenth birthday, and Dan was almost 35. He had a son 13½; his wife had been dead nine years, and Tim, the boy, had been shifted from one relative to another for five years. About four years before, Dan had hired a housekeeper and made a home for Tim, but the housekeepers didn't like Tim, and Tim didn't like them. Dan had seven housekeepers in four years.

We were married a week after I was 18, and 22 days later Dan sailed for France; he served as a physician with the United States forces during the war. I was too young to worry much about being in sole charge of a house and a hard-to-manage 13-year-old boy; at that, I believe I understood him better than an older person would have.

Tim liked me, yet I felt that he was disappointed in me. I have four brothers of my own, and I know boys, so I found that he didn't want a big sister; he wanted someone to take his mother's place, someone he could tell things to and kiss goodnight. I did my best; I kissed him goodnight, I answered questions his father should have answered, I fished and swam and hiked with him. I let him have his friends in on his fourteenth birthday—the first party he'd ever had. I talked with his teachers, and helped him with his home work. When Dan came home, he was more than pleased with the improvement in Tim, and a little ashamed when I told him that he could have done the same thing if he had shown an interest. Tim called me

"Mother" until the summer before his twenty-second birthday, but has never called me that since then. He says that he discovered how he felt about me that summer.

After Tim graduated from medical college and had served his year as a hospital interne, he went into his father's office and, of course, lived here with us. I noticed that he seemed to have lost interest in girls, and that he always used my first name, but I didn't know why.

My marriage was a very happy one; I never felt the difference in our ages, and I don't believe that Dan did. I am hot-headed and Dan was just the opposite. When I got mad, he'd laugh and muss my hair, or kid me. It made me furious; but I could not fight alone, so I gradually gained better control of myself. I am not anywhere near as quick-tempered as I was, but even yet I have to watch myself. I sometimes think that we were too happy. The three children came, and I was expecting my fourth baby in a few months, when we had an automobile accident and Dan was killed. That was three and a half years ago.

We were on our way home from a concert. We stopped for a red light and I moved closer to him and put my head against his shoulder. It was snowing hard; Dan said something about nobody being able to see, kissed me, and said, "Tired, sweetheart?" He never spoke again. Half way across the intersection Dan saw that a car, coming from our right, was not stopping. He turned in an effort to run parallel with the other car, but it crashed into us. Just as our car went over, Dan turned my face to his shoulder and held his hat against my head. Dan died on the way to the hospital, but I was not seriously injured. I was badly bruised, had a few minor cuts, and was very ill from the shock, but I hadn't a scratch on my face.

It was Tim who told me that Dan was dead; Tim who asked me if I realized that I'd lost my baby. I had forgotten about the baby. I don't know what I would have done without Tim, the next few months. He took charge of the house, the children, and of me. He settled my business affairs, talked with insurance adjusters, and read the paper that I signed. I still depend on him a great deal, and he takes care of most of my business transactions.

Tim didn't tell me how he felt about me until New Year, 1931. I went to a New Year's Eve party with a bachelor friend. When I got home later, or rather earlier than Tim thought I should, I found him waiting up for me, as angry as my father might have been, years ago. He said a lot, and so did I. Finally, I told him it was none of his business what I did, and that I was going to bed.

I went over to kiss him goodnight, as I had done every night for years. He asked me how much I cared about him. I laughed, reminded him of all the devotion I'd heaped on him in his youth, and that I'd taken such good care of him when he had mumps that I got them myself. Instead of answering, he pulled me down on his lap and kissed me; not the nice affectionate kisses he'd been giving me so long. I didn't like it, and told him so; he said that he had to do something to make me realize he was not a boy, even a grown-up one, and that he loved me; said, too, that every time I began acting "maternal" toward him he intended kissing me again. He did it, too.

It has been months now since I've felt "maternal" (as he calls it) about him. All spring and summer I've let him "make love" to me, and I have liked it, but I can't make up my mind about marrying him.

I keep feeling that it would not work out; that it would not be fair to Tim. I'm not worrying about myself; I care enough to marry him, and not be sorry. But I am older; I *have* been married, and to a man I loved intensely. My children are doubly dear to me because they are Dan's children, too. I can't give Tim the same intense love that I gave his father, and I'm afraid if I marry him he will realize all this in time, and be unhappy.

[206]

What do you think, Nancy? Do you think I could marry him and make him happy? I will appreciate your advice very much.

Affectionately,

September 5, 1932

DOUCHKA

* * *

IF THE few years difference in your ages is the only objection to your marriage, Mrs. "Douchka," I see no reason why Tim should not become your husband. He sounds good to me. And you certainly know him.

I am wishing you happiness.

* * *

II

NANCY DEAR: When I read your vacation notice, the day after I mailed my letter, I gave up hope of receiving help from you. As it was, I read your answer just 35 minutes before Tim drove into the yard. I appreciate your kindness in giving me space in the first after-vacation Column.

After reading my letter and your answer in the Column, I feel that I did not make clear just what worries me. It isn't so much the difference in our ages, as the difference in the love I felt for Dan, and the love I am capable of giving Tim; as the strangeness of marrying him after the mother-and-son sort of relationship that existed for years. I'm not even sure that knowing each so well is an asset. Tim doesn't want to wait; says the longer I think about it, the more uncertain I'll be. So now, with the wedding only 73 hours away, I find myself full of "doubts."

All of my family, except my 16-year-old kid sister, disapprove, emphatically. We drove out to tell Tim's grandmother (Dan's mother) a few days ago. I never dreaded anything so in all my life;

but she was lovely about it. She asked us to be married there, and we accepted. For some unknown reason, I don't want the wedding here, and I can't ask Mother and Dad to have it, feeling as they do.

I talked with my children, last Sunday, and they are pleased. My sons are exact opposites. Dan, Jr., has his father's steady disposition, and Billy my more or less uncertain one. Billy hugged and kissed me, and said that it would be "swell;" Dan, Jr., that he thought it would be nice, if I felt quite sure that I'd be happy married to Tim. He sounded so grown-up! Patty doesn't care one way or the other, as long as she has Tim here, to spoil her.

We have decided, after a few days at Tim's summer cottage, to drive north, to see my little 78-year-old, half-French, half-Russian grandmother. Because I have inherited her name, looks, temperament, and talent—dancing—I am often taken for a foreigner, but I'm not. The other three grandparents are all Americans; two of them had ancestors on the Mayflower.

I have wanted to write you, many times, during the Column's 13 years of existence. But I knew that my meager ability could not compete with the interesting, and even brilliant letters your family write.

Wasn't it "Blossom" who felt Tom's education so superior to her own? I know how she feels; I worried myself sick, at first. But after a few years of being the only degreeless member of Dan's particular set, I didn't mind quite so much. You see, Dan not only graduated from U. of M. Medical, but had done extensive post graduate work, as well. Now I'm marrying another university graduate, and I didn't even finish high school! It was during my senior year that Dan brought me through pneumonia, and I didn't go back after my illness. I've always been sorry.

All through high school I loved every subject that comes under the head of mathematics, and I had an uncanny memory for history dates (I told you that so you'd not think me entirely dumb), but I was a thorn in the flesh of my English teachers. I simply could not spell. And while I knew all of the rules perfectly, heaven only knew where the commas went. Dan improved my spelling considerably, for he not only refused to spell words for me, but insisted that I look them up in the dictionary, myself. He wasn't disagreeable, or anything like that; we used to laugh about it, but he knew that it was the only way I'd learn.

As the mother of two adolescent boys, I have been keenly interested in the discussion about moral experiments. I know, as you say, that a little knowledge is apt to be dangerous, but I can not feel that "repression" would help. My mother was of the "hush" variety, so I found other sources of information.

When our boys began asking questions, we decided that while we would not advance unsolicited information, we would answer all questions with the truth, telling them enough to satisfy them at the time. Shortly before Dan's death, he had a long serious talk with Dan, Jr., and a few weeks ago Tim had a similar talk with Billy. They have the health side of sex knowledge, and so far, I've not had cause to regret their frank training.

Nancy! Oh Nancy! Did you get this far? Never meant to write so long. I'm sorry.

Thank you for the "good wishes;" I may need 'em.

September 17, 1932   DOUCHKA

P.S.: May I be a member? Please, and I'll buy a new ribbon, to save your poor eyes.

* * *

PERHAPS by this time, Mrs. "Douchka," you and Tim are spending your honeymoon days along the St. Lawrence. Our wishes for happiness follow you. I believe that the former "mother-and-son" sort of relationship will adjust itself, without trouble, to new conditions.

[209]

I agree with you that when children begin asking questions about the story of life, it is time to give them truthful, intelligent answers. But I am wondering if there is not a happy medium between the modern sophistication and the repression of former generations? I believe there is, and I do think no one will deny that the "little knowledge" that present day youth has of the subject—and thinks it is the whole knowledge—is dangerous.

You are already a member. The typewriter ribbon was quite all right. Thank you.

*

Rebellion

Smiling fields to me are calling,
Coaxing me out in the sun.
"Come, the leaves will soon be falling"—
But . . . the dusting should be done!

Berries sweet grow in the marshes,
Water lilies fringe the lake,
Winding roads are so beguiling—
But . . . I ought to bake a cake!

What if I should hide the duster,
Bake the cake a cooler day,
And by lake and field and highway
Spend a happy, carefree day?

Waters cool await my coming,
Peace I'll find beneath a tree;
Days so filled with toil and striving
Surely were not meant for me.

August 9, 1931   KATCHIE

Cathy

* * *

I

Dear nancy: If you could see me now you would laugh—and I should chime in with you at my own expense.

I'm in the bathtub luxuriating in a baking soda bath, with one of my bedroom pictures serving as desk and lunch tray, while I write my problem to you and "soak" in comfort.

The folks are out—Dad at his club and Mother entertaining a sick friend. I am, however, trusted on my honor to stay at home quietly after my terribly prolonged round of fun with temperature at 93 degrees.

I'm 18. I played three sets of tennis—swift tennis, swam an hour, scrapped a while with Bill, my brother, danced, and played another set of tennis. Mother is furious. Dad lectured about my "supreme foolishness," credits me with no sense at all—and thinks he can get away with it. In an hour, if Bill doesn't get back, I am going out for a drive with the kids. Have to teach Dad respect for his young daughter.

Nancy, it (my problem) happened last night. I'm terribly worried about it, not because I did it, but because if Dad hears about it, as he is sure to, I'm sunk—utterly and beyond retrieving. I was allowed to go to a birthday party—a girl chum's—given at her aunt's home. I was to call Dad when it was over, and he was to have taxied me home. But much to my surprise a dear boy whom I used to know and who had moved away, happened to be there. We struck up a new friendship and at ten o'clock he dared me to call Dad and tell him Ruth's uncle would fetch me home later and not to stay up for me. Nancy, I did.

It was fun and a glorious night. Instead of riding around, we danced for a while at a roadhouse, drank a little, and hardly before we realized it, a waiter reminded us it was two o'clock, and closing time.

Gee, Nancy, I thought then of Dad and Mother. They would probably not even admit me by the time we reached home. After I had fussed a while, gotten my wraps, I was shakingly scared—and sick. Don laughed and tried to lighten things; offered to get a room some place for me. Ruth entered my mind; so after ordering Don to take me there, I called softly till she finally croaked, "What—you?" Well, Don dropped me there and I stayed all night. Dad had called by phone and by person, she said. Scared, I called him and told him I had been ill and to a doctor, during that interval, and afterwards came to stay with Ruth.

He simply said, "All right," and today he's frightfully cross. What shall I do, Nancy? Lately he threatened to whip me, but I turned suddenly sweet. Do you think he will, this time? Help me, please!

September 16, 1931   CATHY

P.S.: I'm 18 and I'm too old to whip—please say "Yes." Maybe I'll show Dad this! I wish you were my folks till this is over.

* * *

PRETTY poor cricket, wasn't it, "Cathy"? I'm afraid I should not be much help to you if I were your folks "until this is over."

You are too old to whip—yes. Daddy probably did not mean his threat when he uttered it. I wonder what you would suggest as consistent punishment for yourself for the deceit and the late hours with Don. An 18-year-old girl at a roadhouse with a lad at two o'clock in the morning, dancing and drinking and telling her friends she is with a girl friend, is not so good, now is it? Even an 18-year-old would recognize that it is not playing fair and square. And to continue the wrong-doing by the fabrication of having been ill and at a doctor's—well, I would not do *that* again, if I were you. Seems to me a pretty poor way to repay a good Mother and Dad.

Your letter sounds as if they allowed you everything possible for the happiness of a girl—a car, dances, parties, swimming and probably other pleasures that you did not mention which fathers and mothers plan for their daughters.

I am sorry you said you were worried—not because of the deceiving, but because of what Dad might do when he hears of it. That does not sound good, little girl. I do not really believe you are like that. Don't you see that such things destroy Mother's and Dad's confidence in you? In time they will not trust you at all. And that is not a happy condition between parents and daughters. Besides, girls who take no heed of Mother's and Dad's wishes almost always regret it afterwards.

If you have not already come to terms with Dad about this affair, I believe I would screw my courage to the sticking point, go to him and tell him that you did not tell him the truth the other night, and that you know you were not playing fair with him. Tell him you are sorry and promise him you will not do it again.

I wonder how you would feel if Mother and Dad should deceive you as you have deceived them. You think about it, dear, and see if you cannot understand.

* * *

II

'Lo, NANCY "MOMS": Real sweet of you to be my "Moms" for a while. Going to need you lots 'n' lots during the winter, I know.

Been dangerously good lately, however, mostly because of a physical let-down. The silly, serious doctor pronounced it too much hilarious excitement and lack of sleep. First time since the archaic infancy of mine I've been sick, and it's disgusting because only see what I'm going to miss—a hike and roast, a coveted Sunday night supper, a meeting of the little club of which I'm president, and to-night another movie and drive with the boy friend. Makes me mighty mad, and moody, too, Nancy.

Miss mother, too, though I 'spect that is natural. A funny, chatty letter came today, bearing her Arizona town postmark. "Moms" is settled and comfortable for her winter's stay.

This p. m. my chum, Ruth, came in to see me, but only for a wickedly curtailed chat. Dad chased her out much too soon.

Tomorrow is Daddy's birthday (46! just think!) and Bill is having friends in for dinner to celebrate. Only going to be there by proxy—Ruth is playing hostess—so it isn't going to do me any particular good, is it, Nancy Moms?

Don calls every few hours, which is surprisingly sweet of him. He's still in high, but uses every vacant phone thereabouts and, too, every Canadian nickel. He's coming up to see me some evening, too, when Dad is safely out. Have to do this underhanded, you see, Nancy, 'cause Daddy thinks it would hurt me to have him call. Imagine! Guess I'm never going to be "a good sport" like "Caroline," because I'm more dashingly constituted, and besides, maybe she hasn't auburn hair that is quite red, and the fighting disposish that's included.

October 28, 1931   CATHY

* * *

'Lo, Daughter. I am sorry you are ill—I gather from your letter, quite ill. Otherwise Ruth would not be playing hostess at Dad's birthday party. Also, you would not stay home from all those wonderful attractions if you were at all able to go.

"Physical let-down" does not sound very good to me. Better do just as the doctor tells you. There is not much "hilarity" in being sick, you know. Besides, just at this time you do not want to cause any worrisome news to be sent to Mother. If you should be seriously ill, she would have to know and would return at once.

Another thing, Daughter, I receive more letters than I can tell you from girls who are not strong and yet persist in overdoing socially, staying up nights, losing sleep and rest, and making too heavy a drain on the small reserve strength that they have. Sometimes, "Cathy," girls who persist in too much hilarity pay a heavy, heavy price in the form of tuberculosis. If you ever read anything about our sanatoriums around here you will know that they are altogether too well filled with girls who would not listen to the demands of their bodies for rest and normal living.

I would do whatever Dad says about the boy friend, too. I do not like doing things "underhanded," do you? I would rather not do them than do them that way. And I would rather my little Column daughter would not do them than to have to stoop to do them in any way of which she should be ashamed.

Now write me again soon and tell me that you are taking heed of the doctor's and Daddy's concern about you.

* * *

III

HI "MOMS"! Ship Ahoy! I'm up, and in veritable seventh heaven 'cause I'm downstairs. Even the rooms seem magically concerned about your "Cathy." There are fresh drapes, a snapping fire in the fireplace, a newly done portrait of Mother looking so wistfully at us, and a cozy corner for me and my convalescence-to-be.

Daddy, the grandparents and I dined together and talked endlessly, even endearingly about Mother, the kids, clothes, my "bill of

[215]

fare" and what's got to be a glorious future. Setbacks shoot us that much farther ahead anyway, don't they, Moms, dear? It pains Dad terribly because of all this. He is unearthly kind to me but—"Cathy" beware!—with health and pep coming the whole show will be spoiled, because moderately probably I shall want to do things again, and he will want me to rest eternally. Being sick is so provincial, anyway.

Billy is playing basketball tonight, and without Mother, it's—well, different. Dad tries to be kind, Grandma and Grandpa entertaining, Girl-Friend runs in often, but they flatly refuse to have Don call. Nancy Moms, I yearn for him constantly, but aren't most romances tragedies? You see, Don drinks, wisecracks indiscriminately, smokes endlessly, goes to questionable places, until Dad's verdict is that he is too much of a natural education to Billy and me. He thinks he is a "blockhead." Well, what of it—aren't there sermons in stones?

I must see Don even if it means secretly. That isn't willfulness or being melodramatic—it's only that I'd love to, and will if there isn't a single logical argument to the contrary. It would be all right to take French leave some afternoon, wouldn't it, and call around there, although Grandma disagrees?

Oh, yes, Grandma has heard of Eastport—been there, in fact. It's nice, isn't it, that we're all natives of 'way back east?

Feel "fine, thank you" today—but here comes my malted milk—so bye, Moms, dear.

Tubs of love,
February 17, 1932   CATHY

* * *

YES, it is very nice that we are all from 'way down east, "Cathy." Makes us seem closer, doesn't it? I cannot tell you how happy I am to know that you are better and able to be downstairs, dining with the family.

Now about meeting Don. There are plenty of "logical arguments to the contrary," but you are not willing to receive them. You are like the old lady who was willing to be convinced but she would like to see the one who could convince her. However, let's talk it over.

In the first place, isn't there an element of sneakiness in going out to meet Don when Dad and Grandma are away? I cannot connect sneakiness with you, child. I do not *want* to connect it with you.

Second, you have been very ill and are still only a convalescent. A set-back right now might mean a return to bed—perhaps a relapse, and relapses, you know, dear, are not things to be played with. I am sure you would not take even the barest chance of risking further sickness, perhaps even your life, for the sake of sneaking out to see Don.

Third, Father has had enough to bear without having to learn that you are deceiving him in something so vital. You will not add anything to his hurt, will you?

Fourth, from your description, Don does not sound exactly like the kind of young man I should choose for my Column daughter to have for a boon companion. He drinks and frequents questionable places. Well, I should prefer different company for my little girl.

Sermons in stones? The poet says there are—but he never met Don.

I shall feel badly, "Cathy," if you carry out your foolish threat to take French leave some afternoon and meet Don. Stay in and rest and get well for college, next fall. That is your job right now.

The Brown Bird

* * *

My Dear Column Lady: A line from Whitman comes to mind:
"Logic and sermons never convince;
   The damp of the night drives deeper into my soul."
What sublime truth for some of us!

This brings me to the real reason for my letter. Why do people—
other people (I am a very regular attendant)—attend church services? What do they expect of such a service? What part of the service means most to them, the worship period or the sermon? What
kind of sermon helps most? This discussion I mean to be quite
apart from reasons which might be given for the existence of the
church as an institution.

September 18, 1932   THE BROWN BIRD

* * *

You suggest an interesting subject for discussion, "Brown Bird"
—why people attend church service and what they specially like in
it. It is a timely subject for the Column, where the religious views
of the ultra-moderns are being considered.

I put your question to several people of different doctrines, with
these results:

One man replied that he enjoyed going to church and attended
frequently. It did not matter much what the creed of the church,
was—he enjoyed the atmosphere; said he felt better—a better man
—when he came out. He did not like the sermon, as he expressed it,
"that preached hell-fire" and that told him what a sinner he was, or
asked for money. The regular collection was all right with him, but
an appeal for finances offended his sense of what was fitting to the

pulpit. He liked the old hymns, too—"Shall We Gather at the River?", "Jesus, Lover of My Soul," "Rescue the Perishing," and others of that type.

Another man, the son of a minister, replied very seriously—very seriously, indeed—to my questions. He said he was forced to go to Sunday school and church throughout his boyhood and was educated for the ministry, though he had no inclination for it. As a result, he never attends church services now. But if he did go, a fine, sensible sermon, free from doctrinal prejudices, would be the attraction. Also, the old hymns, such as "How Firm a Foundation," and "Holy, Holy, Holy," moved him most.

One of the girls said she did not attend church regularly because she did not have time. There were so many things to do on Sunday! But when she did attend, she liked a sermon that would give her something to think about afterward—something that would benefit her—a sermon of the philosophical type. The ceremonial part of the service had no appeal, but she liked sacred music of any kind.

Two other girls replied that the special appeal of church-going, to them, was the ceremony or the liturgy.

A fourth girl said she liked the sermon, providing it was a good one, with strains of something practical in it. She specially liked the responsive reading.

One man's reason for attending church occasionally (only occasionally) was because his son wanted him to. He did not care for the music at all, and only rarely would a sermon appeal to him, because he said many ministers preached as if to an audience of twelve-year-olds. However, he wanted his boy to go and learn all the church side of the subject. Later, college would give him the scientific side.

Two other men who were asked what they would like best in a church service, if they attended (which they didn't), answered in chorus, "Atmosphere." One of them did not like the sermons because he did not believe that the preacher could speak with authority on the subject, and because, as a rule, the music was "awful." The other man did not care for the music and did not approve of the sermons because, for the most part, he felt they were not on a high plane of thought.

The last man interviewed said that he went to Sunday school and church regularly all through his boyhood, and would like to go now if he could find a minister who would preach a practical sermon—one that would be of real service to him in living. He said also he felt better after going to church.

Personally, in attending church I enjoy most the hush, the sense of "peace that passeth understanding," that pervades a church, whether it be a country meeting house or a city cathedral. I, too, feel better—more at peace with the world—after leaving a service. I enjoy the sermon that includes a strain of both spiritual and practical, and I like the fine old hymns and music—hymns like "Abide With Me," "Lead, Kindly Light," "There Is a Green Hill Far Away," and countless others—not one of which I can recall at this instant.

I am hoping our Column Folks will respond generously to your questions. Perhaps the churches may even find suggestions among the answers.

*

'Cinquain'
(For "Wee Dundonian")
Stars are but the liquid gold, of notes
Far flung from Angels' throats;
Becoming, of their own exquisite sweetness,
Crystallized.

Cup o' Tea

Soldier Sam

* * *

DEAR NANCY BROWN: Do you know the meaning of the term "ridge runner"? It is used in certain sections of the South to apply to the "sorry folk" otherwise designated as "pore white trash."

My earliest memory is a resentment amounting to real anger that I belonged to such a family of shiftless, lazy people. I especially envied the only son of the leading family of the community, a boy four years my junior and whom we shall call John. We presented a real contrast, John and I, he with his bright little face, perfect manners and neat, clean clothes, and I, an overgrown, slouching, ragged, tough guy who was two grades behind John. And because I envied him and his life and all that it stood for, I hated him bitterly and used every opportunity to make life difficult for him—not an especially hard task for the school bully who could lick several Johns with one hand.

The crisis came one day when I was 15. I had done something especially outrageous and the lady teacher (courageous soul) had decided the future discipline depended upon punishing me. There was only one known method of punishment down there in those days, so she sent John out to the hickory tree in the school yard for a good-sized limb. She never did have an opportunity to use it for I ended my school days by walking out and never going back. Strangely enough, my resentment was all centered on John and I swore revenge.

During the next month or two I kept away from the village, but in June there was a wedding at the church and my curiosity took me to the church where I joined a crowd just outside the open door. As the people inside the church were coming out after the ceremony I caught sight of John, resplendent in a new suit. I became conscious for the first time of my own hill billy appearance: my ragged, outgrown, dirty overalls, my shock of matted hair, my bare feet. I saw red for a moment and darted at him, aiming straight for his jugular vein with the big hunting knife I always carried. Someone jostled me and I dropped the knife and while women fainted and screamed, their men folks seized me and began to take the reins off their horses. They were going to take the law in their own hands and hang me then and there.

I am not sure yet how it happened that their plans were frustrated, but at any rate the sheriff soon came and took me off to jail and a short time afterward I was sent to the reform school.

There I was fortunate enough to meet a man who was truly one of democracy's aristocrats and one of God's own noblemen. He showed me that I was harming myself far more than any one else in harboring such destructive thoughts, so when my term was finished, I went back home, resolving to give myself as well as the other fellow a fair deal.

Small chance for living down my reputation there. No one would give me even half a chance. There seemed to be only one place for an uneducated tough guy so I went there—to the army. I was in service for a long time before the World War, most of the time in foreign territory, that is, Alaska, the Philippines, Cuba.

Then came the World War and one of the peculiar parts of my story. While on the front I suddenly, for the second time in my life, saw red, and while in that savage mood I made history by cleaning up three of the enemy's machine gun nests and capturing a large number of prisoners. I received so many medals for this act of bravery that when I go out on dress parade I always feel like a well-stocked hardware store on legs. Funny, though, isn't it, that the first time I tried to kill one boy I was almost hanged for it, and I'm not saying that wasn't exactly what I deserved, and the next time I turned to a savage and really succeeded in killing several men, I should become an international hero for it. Which all, perhaps, leads to the conclusion that Sherman was right.

On account of my service out of the U. S. itself, I was retired shortly after the war with full honors and a pension that is enough for a person of my simple needs.

Lately I have been overcome with a genuine nostalgia. I want to go back to the beautiful hills where I spent my boyhood, build a comfortable little house and live there in comfort and contentment the rest of my days. I don't care what else the house contains just so it has a fireplace, a big bookcase and a radio. But here is the problem: To the folks down there, I am still the blood-thirsty bully who tried to kill little John. My war record is of secondary importance to them, and of my real accomplishments, well, they probably couldn't see those at all. For the part of my life of which I am really proud is that part which has come after my retirement. I have learned to read, write, and talk like a gentleman. I have learned to appreciate art, music and literature. I have learned to live.

Please don't advise me to go back and prove my worthiness to the people of my boyhood home. I haven't any desire to prove myself a hero thus and I don't want their friendship. I much prefer that of Shakespeare and Mendelssohn. But one can't be entirely a hermit and the few casual contacts I make I would prefer, of course, to be pleasant ones. I would rather my neighbors would know nothing whatever of my past life but on the other hand I want to build my house on that certain "Inspiration Point" I have always known and loved.

September 19, 1931   SOLDIER SAM

A WONDERFULLY interesting life story you have, Soldier Sam. We should like to know more of it. What you have accomplished in the few years since the war is almost miraculous. Only supreme, inborn ambition, backed by a strong spirit and a good mind, could have accomplished so much.

I am wondering if other hills of the South in a different locality—perhaps not too far away—might not cure the nostalgia. That could be readily accomplished. Although you might not find the "Inspiration Point" of your childhood, you might find something that would substitute.

But you are still a young man. It seems as if you should not retire from active life yet. There is a place in the world for a man who is capable of accomplishing what you have achieved in the past few years. My suggestion would be to have a home in the hills in which to vacation for a part of each year, and the balance of the time spend in active life in whatever line pleases you.

I wish that John might see this letter of yours. He might understand. Please come again. You belong with the Column Folks now, you know.

*

Philosophy

> I want a breeze across my face,
> Flowers and trees and an open space;
> I want to see the sunset's glow
> And rest at ease where the rivers flow;
> But I must stay in the city street,
> List to the tread of a million feet.
> Yet I'll be happy and I'll be gay,
> For if I can't go, I'll have to stay!

May 29, 1932   PUSS IN BOOTS

Goofy

***

Dear nancy: The story of a childhood? Well, why not? I feel like reminiscing; besides, it's raining, and I guess that helps.

A few years spent as by most anyone else—a swimming hole, tramps in the woods, the collecting of different kinds of birds' eggs; corn roasts, a scrap or two at school; a few teachers that just didn't know anything; being a southpaw on the school nine; fishing, sailing, horseback riding; breaking an arm a couple of times, a boil now and then, and looking at girls as merely necessary evils.

Then Dad died. I was 13, so I started selling papers. Not so lucrative, so I took a job in a furniture factory and learned that was no way to make a living. Then, shortly, Mother died, and the neighbors talked of putting me in the Home, where all little boys wore the same kind of clothes. After the funeral I left everything—afraid of the Home—and hit up the railroad tracks. Lying on the incline and watching the wheels go by—taking people places, and from places; being fascinated by the thought of "places." Then I hung around a section gang. They gave me sandwiches. I swiped apples.

Finally hopped a freight; arrived at some town next day with a good appetite and nothing for it. Slept in the town park, back by the fence and under the pine trees. Talked the boss of a livery stable into letting me wash buggies at 10 cents per; slept in the hay loft; sold papers; got into a scrap with the locals for copping the best spots.

Hopped another freight and rode all night, watching the poles and stars go by. Landed in another town and talked a grocer into letting me rearrange his canned goods. Made a good job of it and he gave me a dollar—the most I'd had up to then. Met a boy friend, Chuck, who proved to be the best pal I've ever had. Talked the dry goods man into letting me break up his crates for firewood; another half dollar—and was I wealthy!

Out with the harvesters to western Canada. Slept on the prairies; gophers running over us; getting a bit tougher each day, and learning that a glib tongue and a steady line, mingled with common sense, helped plenty.

Up to a lumber camp in northern Quebec with a bunch of huskies. Had a fight in a "gang royale" with a rival camp, Chuck and I circling the fringe, popping the enemy as they staggered out of the mêlée, and shoving our own gang back in; finally being clipped and going out like a Democrat after election. It was a tough gang. We got tired of beans and salt pork, so hit out.

Arrived at a small town and checked in at the hotel. Chuck went out and shortly returned with a couple dozen small bottles, a bag of marbles and a quart of vinegar. I made a crack about a back-to-childhood movement, but the young chap had a good idea. We sold four marbles in a small bottle of vinegar to the natives as chemically treated and scientifically manufactured anti-explosive balls, to be placed in their coal-oil lamps. We sold them at 50 cents per, or whatever we thought we could get. Left town next day, as we felt the men folks didn't like us.

Shipped on a boat out of Seattle and learned we were on a sealing hunt, which is nix with law and order. Couldn't stand hearing the seals cry as we hit them and couldn't stand skinning them and throwing them overboard after. We quit. The captain got tough, so we skipped when we landed the cargo somewhere in Canada, hit for the interior and got lost in the mountains for four days. Caught trout in the brooks with our hands. Got a job as nursemaid to a flock of sheep. No like, so choo-choo to the U. S.

Took over a city slicker in a crooked poker game in Salt Lake.

Cowboys in Oklahoma. Not enough excitement. The road again. Hit for a jungle back in the woods. A tough looking lug sitting brushing a stick back and forth in the fire; a dopey kid, but plenty tough—Jack Dempsey in a year and a half. To Mexico, and heard a knife buzz by my ear and stick in the wall because I was kidding the Spanish waitress, who happened to belong to someone else. Back in U. S. A job at Houston. No like. New Orleans. A rattler for the Coast. Got kicked off and loafed around for the next one. It didn't slow up much at the bend. I made it, but Chuck didn't— quite. I swung off and left him on the side of a hill—a good pal and true friend. From then on I've been the lone wolf.

You already know most of my recent doings. Have been all over the U. S., to Canada, Mexico, Europe and China—just a kid that did fairly well.

I hid a chap from the cops in "Chi"; kept him a couple of days. Not a bad lad. Bawled him out. Told him I was a fool, but I'd play a 100-to-1 shot, and gave him $20. He said he'd remember; I said, "Nuts." He saw me in Detroit a few years back. I was broke. He asked me who I was and if I remembered him. I didn't, at first. He took me over to his bank and paid off at the above odds. He had sure made good. That was when I left for China—remember?

You know about Buck, Billy and Mary, also their "Goofy, Jr.," and most of the recent developments. I've done most every kind of work—carried three union cards at one time; never worked more than six weeks at any one job and never more than six months in any year. Now I've worked steady for almost three years. I'm looked upon as being successful. The girl of my dreams has come true and I am dedicating my life to making her happy. Yet there are times when I feel terribly depressed and compressed—and I wonder if I'm really smart or just a round peg in a square hole.

But one of the smartest and luckiest things I ever did was write you from the hotel out Fort Street. I still enjoy writing you. This is too long and dry to put in the Column, Nancy, so just toss it in the basket. I enjoyed it myself. Please give my regards to all, though, and best of wishes to you.

September 25, 1932   GOOFY

* * *

IT was not too long, "Goofy," and certainly not "dry." I could not toss it into the waste basket even if I wanted to. The Column Folks will be as interested in your story as I have been.

You have done well, Son—wonderfully well. You may rightfully accept the credit that is due you. There must have been something —some fine, inner force—that kept you in the right path through the homeless childhood. The girl of your dreams is a fortunate girl, and it makes me very happy to know you feel that writing to the Column was one of your lucky moves.

*

No Regrets

Had I a chance to choose once more
    In what I do,
I know I'd act just as before—
    In loving you.

For failure now has taught me this:
    I never knew
Until you came what I would miss—
    In loving you.

July 24, 1932   OLD-FASHIONED

Hugh

* * *

DEAR NANCY BROWN: I'm lost in a maze of indecision. I wonder if you will help me get my bearings. Here is my story:

I'm a young man of 30. Six years ago I married the girl of my heart and brought her to Detroit to live. We bought our own furniture and lived in a cozy little flat and it was like heaven for five months, months I'll never forget. They were absolutely perfect.

In the sixth month, when she was carrying our baby under her heart, came the terrible tragedy that changed our lives. She was out riding in a car with a girl friend. There was an accident. The other girl was killed instantly and my pretty wife injured so badly that she has never walked since and never will for the rest of her life.

She insisted on going back to her folks. They live in a town about 70 miles from Detroit. Our pretty furniture was disposed of. I gave up the flat and took an apartment with some other fellows.

I have never missed being with her during vacations, week-ends, or holidays. Every time I have been with her, she urges me to divorce her and find someone else. She wants me to marry again and discard her. Her mother and father are at me all the time to go out and have a good time. Mother tells me I am too young to be expected to live the way I am the rest of my life, that it isn't natural, etc.

She (my wife) is financially independent of me. I tried to keep her with me, was more than willing to care for her myself, but the three of them allied against me was too much for me. They argued that she was much better to be constantly in the company of the two who loved her so much, whereas I would have to be gone all day and she would be lonely. Therefore, for her own happiness I agreed to let her live with her parents.

[229]

What hurt me worst was the cool treatment I received from her. I was stunned at the change in her. No kiss to greet me. Just a verbal salutation and that was all. I couldn't understand it, after all we had been to each other.

And now, Nancy, comes the hard part. About a year ago I met Janet. She's great, Nancy. She's everything fulfilled that my wife would have been. This last year has been a heaven and a hell. I'm happy with Janet because of her own dear self, and unhappy when away from her because of thoughts of my wife. Janet knows all about my story. Because of this there has been no talk of our feelings for each other. But it is there, unexpressed.

I care terribly for Janet and I want to tell her so and I know that she loves me. I want to marry her and set up a home and have children, and on the other hand there is—my wife.

Am I wrong to want to divorce her? Next week-end when I go to see her, the first thing she will say will be, "Have you got a girl friend yet, Hugh? Why don't you get rid of me? I'm perfectly happy here with Mom and Dad." Maybe we'll talk impersonally for a few minutes and then she'll beg to be excused, and I'll wheel her to her room. When she is gone, her father and mother will talk to me in the same vein. That's the way it has been for over five years.

Do you think I'm justified in doing anything about it or am I nothing but a cad? I'm torn between loyalty to my wife and love of Janet.

What shall it be? I want your honest opinion, and be as brutally frank as you please. Wretchedly yours,

September 30, 1932   HUGH

* * *

I WILL be frank, Hugh—but not brutal. I see no reason even for harshness. Quite the contrary. The solution of your problem involves tenderness and gentleness and oh, such a lot of thought-fulness.

I have read your letter several times and thought much about it. I will do my best to help you.

You are not a cad—far from it. Instead, you have been very loyal and very kind and very considerate of your wife, and have done your best to solve the problem, I know.

I think your wife's decision about divorce is right. I believe most any woman would feel the same, specially if she loved her husband. And your wife does love you, Hugh, in all probability. She could not destroy that love so suddenly, simply because she has been in-capacitated by an automobile accident. Because she loves you, she wants you to be happy. You are young yet. It is, as she says, natural that you should love some one else and want a home of your own, such as she is not able to give you.

I think if I were you, I should have a heart-to-heart talk with her—a very grave, very gentle, very tender talk. Ask her to tell you honestly, how much it would hurt her if you should follow her sug-gestion for the solution of your problem.

Whatever she says, Hugh, there is no doubt that the knowledge of your love for Janet will hurt her, but she is brave and good and just, and will realize that even though her life is marred so pitifully, it will not help any to hamper yours, also. From what you tell me of her, I am sure she will understand.

However great the hurt may be, time will soften it, you know. Please do not say that is just a platitude. It is, I know. But it is so surely the truth, and so important in consideration of your difficulty, that it cannot be disregarded.

I am wishing you happiness, Hugh—you and your wife—and Janet.

Will you not come back and tell us the next chapter—please?

[231]

Gingham Grandma

* * *

DEAR FRIEND NANCY BROWN: I have always considered going to church as a privilege: therefore I feel constrained to tell why.

I have recently passed the eightieth milestone on life's highway, and for all that time have been a constant attendant at church, whenever possible, and have always enjoyed it.

Why do I go? Well, first and foremost, because I love it. There are several reasons for that love. To begin with, history proves that the presence and influence of an organization of real Christians is very necessary to the existence of any well-regulated community. We have only to recall the character of frontier towns without any, to realize that. Secondly, such an organization, to be effectual, depends upon the sincerity and activity of its individual members for a continued existence. And that is where my enjoyment begins, for I was always active in the work.

At 15, I began teaching in the Bible school, a class of girls about 11 or 12 years old. A year later I took another class of girls, 14 or 15 years old, and for two years taught the two classes every Sunday, one in the morning in a mission school, and the other in the afternoon in the mother church. When I said goodby to them at leaving for school, I was crying and so were some of the girls.

When I finished school, the mission school had become an organized church, of which I was a constituent member, and from then on to my marriage I taught classes, sang in the choir, helped on programs, and entered into all the social activities. Since my marriage, I have resided in other towns far away from that church, but have always gone to church and shared in its labors to the extent of my ability.

The point I wish to stress is that while I did it from a sense of duty, I enjoyed it because I went for what I could give and not for what I could get from it.

That is one exemplification of the parable of the ten talents. We, personally, get far more from using them than from just sitting still and taking the results from the use of other people's talents.

That is my advice to anyone who wishes to get the most out of church going: take hold and help.

"Gee Dee," thee has suggested that perhaps I might be able to answer thy question in regard to prayer. My dear, it would be utter presumption on my part to try to give all God's reasons for action. If He were small enough for humanity to comprehend Him, He wouldn't be God. It would be like trying to put the oceans of the world into a pint cup. However, I can make a few suggestions, which perhaps may be helpful.

Thy remark concerning "unselfish prayer" would indicate a prayer for some one other than thyself. In the first place, no prayer is ever "unanswered," but sometimes the answer is "No." Oftentimes the "Yes" is only delayed, because God knows that the ones prayed for are perhaps not yet ready for the blessing, or maybe it might be the worst thing possible for them. God can see much farther into the future than we can. Again, perhaps thy own faith is not quite strong enough as to receiving. Read Mark 11:24. Take God at His word.

It is possible, too, that what might seem to be beneficial for one would be disastrous for someone else. Also, He may be bringing it to pass in a way totally unexpected by thee. Oh, God knows many, many things that we do not.

If thee has a copy of THE NEWS for Tuesday, Sept. 27, read "Soldier Sam's" letter. The part I like is too long to quote here, but I will give one excerpt which holds much truth:

[233]

"There is sure knowledge, instead, that 'in the beginning' every possible need was filled, every prayer answered, and that it is only through willful blindness (call it lack of faith if you will) that we do not see that the answer to our prayer is right at hand."

Above all, remember we cannot hurry God. He has Eternity to work in, and can take as long as He sees is necessary to accomplish a sure thing.

October 1, 1932 GINGHAM GRANDMA

P.S.: What a splendid thing our Column is growing to be! With loving prayer for thee and thy work,

G. G.

* * *

SUCH a gentle, sweet, tolerant letter, "Gingham Grandma."

Your faith, unshaken through all the 80 years, has broadened and grown more understanding, to include those who have deviated more or less from the original creed. I wish all of us might add sympathetically to the years as you have.

*

The Hill of Graves

(*In China*)

As I sat
With Twang Hse
High upon the hill
I asked:
"Why do you
Place your dead
Upon the hill?"

He replied:
"Evil spirits
Are fond of lingering
In such places.
Over this hill
Strong winds blow
And
They cannot tarry."

January 22, 1932 TOYO

[234]

A Pastor's Wife

* * *

DEAR NANCY BROWN: This is in reply to the question asked by "Serious": "Is dancing sin?"

It may be answered by another question. What makes dancing enjoyable? Do you dance for the music and the rhythm? Then why must you have a partner of the opposite sex?

Everyone knows there are liberties permitted on the dance floor that would under no other circumstances be considered proper.

If a stranger in your home would, after a casual introduction, hold your daughter in such close embrace as he has permission to on the dance floor, what parent would not soon show him the door?

No, there is no harm in dancing! But what a "flop" would your dance be if you were not permitted to dance with the opposite sex. There's a reason!

October 18, 1932   A PASTOR'S WIFE

* * *

I AM wondering, Mrs. "Pastor's Wife," why you are so positive of the disagreeable emotions that you ascribe to dancers. If you have danced, you will know that dancers do not think the unpleasant thoughts you suggest. If you have not danced, it is not fair for you to judge.

I have danced all my life, and I give you my word of honor that I never knew such thoughts as you suggest existed, until they were put into my mind by a pastor in a pulpit, who admitted that he had never danced in his life.

This is not spoken in any spirit of criticism of pastors in general.

Anne

* * *

Dear nancy: Why should "Holiday" not fall in love? I doubt whether there exists in all the world a man or woman who has loved just once, though but one love has been made a lasting part of the life structure. Love being the pleasantest ingredient of the cake of life, it seems too bad that the slightest deviation from the proper recipe should so surely spoil a wholesome thing and make of it an indigestible mess.

If you're in love you'll probably be a much more interesting wife, mother, writer, and what have you, for the experience. Only— don't be a silly awss and let a passing phase upset a whole life's structure. Falling in love is not sin, by Golly, Nancy, it's fun— clean fun, only it's apt to be so difficult teeter-tottering without wrinkling up one's nice, clean pinafore! Still, it can be done!

Apropos of nothing, the most ravishing sight encountered during my recent journey was a tiny baby girl but three weeks removed from Heaven, or whatever land is the natural abiding place for beauty, with curly brown fuzz for hair, a pink curlicue of a mouth, and two wide, wondering blue eyes just cognizant of a strange, new world.

There is no argument for law and order, no plea for passion kept pure, so unanswerable as the soft, sweet body of a new-born child.

What besides Life itself is the mere physical impulse to create it? How dare anyone in all the world "experiment" for the sake of thrill with an issue so magnificent, so breath-taking, so incomprehensible? My friend's wee baby exuded the very spirit and substance of a God made manifest. Passion, prosaically speaking, is neither more nor less than a creative urge—and creating is pretty serious business. As a purely sporting proposition, experimenting with physical forces for fun stacks up poorly, doesn't it?

I am no moralist, but I insist that my responsibility toward society is somewhat weightier than is that of my pet dog! The very fact that I recognize the importance of restraint, and possess the power to employ it for the benefit of generations to come, marks me as something superior to the animal kingdom where impulse reigns supreme.

As a moral issue, I have no quarrel with experimental mating. As a crime against four-square decency, I have, to the death conflict. The creative impulse was made strong necessarily; and the intelligence to use it properly must certainly have been appended in order that man might continue thereby to lift himself up and up until his animal body might be finally fitted to house the spark of the Infinite so "lamely named" a soul.

Freedom is a glorious thing. In so far as modern morals are concerned with it, they have my unbiased endorsement. But License is unthinkable, filthy, loathsome.

I do not condemn a woman who, through an unwise love, has made a mistake, Nancy. I do not condemn anybody for anything. But I pity beyond measure the very young who have been shoved out upon the high-road of life without definite instructions as to the direction in which beauty lies and worth has its dwelling place of light. The fault lies, as it will later lie with them, at the door of the two who called them out of the infinite into a finite existence.

There is a matchless beauty in holiness where life-forces are concerned, as much as there is absurdity in sanctimoniousness. Any girl who doubts that as an idealistic assertion, need only test it with any man she knows as a bald psychological fact.

Men may love loose women, but they respect straight ones. And any girl who thinks the love of the man she covets can atone for his lack of respect should try it once. If she is inherently decent and sensitive to standards, she cannot endure the torture of his scorn.

Though he may never express it, he cannot conceal it from her; she can never get away from it.

This is a space-taker, Nancy. Your

October 20, 1932   ANNE

* * *

THERE is food for thought in your letter, Anne—much food—food that is fine and digestible.

That point of human beings having been given the intelligence to use their creative instinct properly is the point that should be made outstanding to young people. Intelligence against license—that is the combat for youth, especially modern youth. I believe when our young people understand that license means a lack of intelligence, a lack of using intelligently the great creative urge that is given them, then they will see that the youthful experiments of which Mrs. Rinehart writes are anything but desirable, and show misuse of perhaps the greatest power that Nature has bestowed upon them.

The fine quality of restraint that you mention falls under the modern head of repression. However, the name matters not. The recognition of the importance of restraint as a life factor is what counts.

Neither do I "condemn anybody for anything"—with the usual exceptions.

Blossom

* * *

DEAREST NANCY, DEAREST FOLKS: My goodness, Nancy, what a lot of fine letters you've had in these childhood stories, poetry, and "why-I-go-to-church" discussions of late.

My folks were all tobacco growers, Nancy. I can just see that dear old silver-haired daddy of mine yet, out at the first breath of spring, burning and getting ready those tobacco plant beds. The white canvas covering after the bed was sowed always reminded me of "Jack Frost" on the ground in the early morning light, against the tall woods backgrounds.

Aunty Margot was always happy to pick her favorite spring dish —wild greens! She'd always added a few poke leaves to the mess from a stalk that had grown for years in the hollow of an old tree stump.

And "Tippity Wicket"—dear girl, I know all about the "white ladies" who showered the orchard ground with pink, satiny petals, and filled the air with perfume; and the white dogwood and wild plum blossoms that grew in the woods, too.

There's not a prettier sight anywhere to be found than spring-decked mountain country, Nancy, on a clear day. I've always loved rain, too, not gloomy weather, but the pitter-patter of rain on the roof when you're all tucked in snug and warm for a good night's sleep.

I feel the silent and invisible and best things in life better, more thoroughly, by going to church where I can hear love, truth, hope, faith and purity preached from the pulpit. I love to receive Holy Communion to the soft sweet strains of "Oh, Lord, I Am Not Worthy," and afterwards strive hard to make myself worthy.

[239]

Another sacred song that I love is "In the Garden." The heavenly beauty of those precious words almost takes my breath, Nancy.

Speaking of prayers and church, Nancy, I've never prayed more earnestly for anyone than I have for our "Stout Fella's" recovery. I dreamed the other night that he told me he had gotten all the way well and was soon returning to his beloved England. I tried to think my "Rosaries" for him had helped.

November 1, 1932   BLOSSOM

* * *

I, TOO, wish we might hear from "Stout Fella," "Blossom." I am worried about him.

You never told us before that your daddy was a tobacco grower, dear. And I don't believe I know what "wild greens" are, unless you mean dandelions. Neither do I know about using "poke" along with them. I know the poke weed, but did not know it was edible.

We all knew that you would love your church.

*

Promise

Last even' I saw the sunset,
Heaven's glory in its wake,
Vivid rose-tint hues that met
Their reflection in the lake.

'Twas not hard to feel that near
Was a Presence most divine,
Taking from our hearts the fear
Of our sunsets—yours and mine.

September 12, 1930   LARGO

Flower Face

* * *

Dear nancy brown: "Grease Paint's" letter has been in my mind ever since I read it. She had the urge for a theatrical career, but had children, husband and home to care for. She and I have a lot in common, and I'd like to tell her how I satisfied my desires for a stage career.

It is 7 a.m. I just finished reading the Column letters. You'll never know what they have meant to me. I save them to read early in the morning before the others are up. That is my only leisure period all day. I get up early on purpose to have it.

I was playing piano in a cheap vaudeville show in a small town when I met my present husband. After the last show I went to a cheap restaurant for a sandwich. This boy sat next to me at the counter. He was so good looking I began to talk to him. He had been to the show and liked my act. Late as it was, he took me home with him, and I played his mother's piano a couple of hours. I had a good voice for Negro songs and they liked that.

I could see his mother and sister were suspicious of me. That didn't bother me. I'm the kind that can't help putting on a show any time anywhere there is a piano, pay or no pay.

We were simply crazy about each other from the start. We were married the end of the week and I left the show.

His mother was so angry she wouldn't let him come home. He had $22 and I had $50. We came to Detroit.

He had no trade, but he got a job delivering chickens. We lived in two furnished rooms for $3 a week and it cost $3.50 for food. He made $16 a week and we actually saved money.

After a while I began to want a home of my own. The only house we could afford was a shack on the outskirts, in a subdivision. Well, we moved out there, bought second hand furniture, the bare necessities, which I painted, and fixed up the windows with cretonne.

Nancy, I have to laugh at the two poor, happy kids we were. We were thrilled to death with our home.

Well, the next thing I knew a baby was on the way. I cried all the time. I didn't feel badly. I was glad it was coming, but still I cried. At last I told my husband if I had a piano I'd feel better.

Nancy, in all these years I've never asked for a thing I didn't get. A piano seemed impossible, but he bought one, $5 down and $3 a month. We were years paying for it.

Well, I had four babies as fast as they could come. I was a terrible housekeeper, but the dirt didn't bother me and the kids as long as I could have music. I'd jerk things around tidy before my husband came home, clean up the kids and doll up myself, and he was happy.

When my last boy was two years old, I saw the names of a couple of my old pals in the ad of a downtown show. I went to see them, and asked them out to our shack. They came after the last show, and if we didn't have a good time!! They both played banjos. I played the piano all night. At 5 a.m. I got breakfast. They wanted me to join them on the road. It was a big temptation, but I couldn't leave my family. My husband will never know how I longed to go back.

But, Nancy, as my family grew older, I saw that each one had a quality of talent I could never hope to equal. When my oldest boy was four, I taught him songs and poems. He was so cute. He could clog a little, and loved to show off. His songs and recitations were the ordinary popular and comic variety; some weren't even very nice. I didn't know any better. It was the type I was used to.

When the two oldest were six and four, they sang and danced together at a school concert. I taught them myself. They brought

[242]

the house down. The school teacher came to me and said, "You have two very talented children. You should secure the best teachers you can for them." I was highly insulted. I thought I certainly could train them as well as any one. But the more I thought about it, the more I was undecided about my own ability as their teacher.

Well, we finally started the oldest boy on the piano and elocution lessons, at the conservatory. Nancy, his teachers were crazy about him, he learned so quickly. I took them in for their lessons, and always listened with both ears and mouth open. It was a revelation to me. I didn't know there were so many levels to the Arts.

Well, my youngsters will be real artists, all four of them. We can put on a good show any time in our own home, and a high-class one, too. My oldest boy is going to be a pianist. He just loves the best music. My second girl plays the violin and piano, too. My other girl dances and recites beautifully. My baby boy is the only one who seems to have inherited his mother's low tastes in art. He is the vulgar comedian, but we'll all take it out of him.

"Grease Paint," it is more fun anticipating their careers, and helping to train them. I know I couldn't be as happy on the stage myself, now I know my limitations, but my children will be real artists. Love to you, Nancy.

November 8, 1932   FLOWER FACE

* * *

SUCH an interesting letter! The suggestion to "Grease Paint," that she find outlet for her dramatic urge in her children, will help, I believe.

You are justly proud of your talented little flock. Maybe that little four-year-old's "low comedy" is only a foundation for fine comedian work in the future.

The urge for the stage is strong within you, but the pull of the little hands is stronger, isn't it?

Quite Elderly Person

* * *

I

Nancy brown: In casting about for an excuse for writing this letter, I can only find one that will hold water—the fact that I like your Column and its people. I like the things of which your members write, and I like the replies which you give them. They certainly cover the range of human experience and human emotions. I don't always agree with the opinions given, but I'm not what you would call a "good agreer."

I don't seem to have any problems. I have found that if you turn a problem the other side up and take a good look at that side, the problem usually "unproblems" itself. Nor have I any troubles. It is true that I am "broke" financially, and that I am not in very good shape physically—or perhaps I should say "mechanically." There is nothing the matter with my "works," but locomotion is difficult and sometimes painful. However, I can drive, and do much. Anyway, the difficulties mentioned are so common that there is no use fussing about them.

Your family are all so delightfully human that I could spend an evening in front of the fireplace with any one of them. If I may, I would like to speak of and to some of them here.

I am sorry that we no longer hear from "Slim of the Hills"—a lot of man there. I'd take the trail with him any time.

Regarding "Sad Old Man." Why, the whimsical old fraud, he's the unsaddest thing I ever heard of. Man, about one hundred miles north of Nancy Brown's infant forest there is a log cabin with a stone fireplace, and on the mantel are some church warden pipes and a can of fine mixture (God bless James Barrie). Anyway,

Man, perhaps some day you and I can sit in front of that fireplace and smoke and talk, or maybe smoke and not talk.

Was it "Jawn" who wouldn't write unless he could publish in the Atlantic Monthly? Mister, as we would say in the Merchant Marine, if you can write in such fashion as to reach the hearts of men, it matters not at all in what language it is couched or through what medium it is given to them.

Speaking of "Stone Cabin," we should rename her "Fidelis." Women of her kind help us to keep our faith in human nature.

"Kim"—"Kim" the valiant and the lovable. Any man would be proud to have her as his daughter.

"June"—brilliant woman and clever writer; but much disillusionment coming to her.

"Wind Along the Waste"—very much a "Little Eve Edgerton." To my mind she is the most domestic woman of the "whole boiling." Eleanor Abbot says, or would say: "It takes a real woman to make a home of the whole wide world.

"Jade"—good soldier. Still searching for the "Holy Grail." And how she can write!

"Blossom"—"Blossom" so truly represents the ideal of all men that in the name of all men I salute her with the salutation of the Ancient Serving Man to his mistress. It goes in this fashion: "Lady, who art in no wise bitter toward those who serve you with good intent, that which thy servant is, that he is for you."

And finally, Nancy Brown, we lie at your feet.

November 12, 1932   QUITE ELDERLY PERSON

* * *

I AM overwhelmed! I cannot picture myself in the light of a hero. That's what one is when folks lie at his feet, isn't it? I think it would be more comfortable for you to sit along with me in the firelit circle and chat pleasantly of our Column Folks and their problems, and of your own dear self. Your cheerful philosophy would be help-ful to the folks who are with us, within the fireside circle.

"Blossom" will love what you have said of her—and the others will, too. They are lovely tributes you pay. Thank you.

You will come again, won't you?

* * *

II

Nancy brown: I'm sorry, very sorry; but I guess you'll have to be a hero, even if you do say you are not of "hero-stuff." In the first place, about 99 per cent of the heroic acts are performed by every-day people in everyday circumstances. In your particular case, any woman who can, day after day, read our plaints and still remain kindly and sympathetic, is an extra special hero; so, with your per-mission, we will continue to "lie at your feet;" but you might heave me a cushion—my elbow gets sore.

I had to stop for a few moments. Wife brought in a cup of coffee and a plate of home-grown, sugared fried cakes. Sometimes that woman drives me wild. I have a notion to get a—all right, *all right*, quit fussing. I'll keep her.

Now I'll talk a while.

I gather from bits of conversation which I hear from time to time that there is a depression; that people are losing their money and their homes, and I might add—their sense of values.

Maybe there is a depression, but it seems to me that most of us have been pretty feverish for the last ten years and possibly we needed a depressant.

Nobody ever needed to lose his home. It may be that he is about to lose a house and lot, but that is something entirely different. A home consists of that indefinable something which surrounds a group of people who live together in mutual love, respect and consideration; and the particular kind of an edifice that covers it is unimportant.

Now, about losing that house and lot—oh! shucks, that isn't anything dreadful. I've lost two or three—maybe I'll lose more. Last summer I watched a pair of barn swallows that were setting up housekeeping on our porch. Just after they had completed their nest, a strong wind, or something, knocked it down. They didn't waste a minute, nor did they do any fussing. They just moved over to an old nest above the front door, patched it up a bit, hung the curtains, put up a couple of pictures, and went right ahead with their arrangements as though nothing had happened. I surely hope that I'm no dumber than a couple of barn swallows.

Now that you stop to think of it, isn't it true that the kitchen was awfully hard to work in, that there were nowhere near enough closets in the house? And you know perfectly well that you never did like that family next door. The next house I build is going to be in a good neighborhood and it's going to be right.

About money—well, it's a long while ago, and I can't remember very clearly—but the chap who lived in the next cave came over one day and said:

"Say, Neander, about that Diplodocus rib you was going to trade for my second best-stone hatchet—I ain't ready for the rib until the 'she' I'm living with fixes up our new cave. Well, here's the hatchet, and you just bite your teeth mark in that shell over there, and give it to me. When I'm ready for the rib I'll give it back to you."

That's the way this money thing started. I wrote two letters for a Swede who lives up the road, last week, and he brought me a bushel of turnips. Go and write a letter for a Swede, or even a Bulgarian. I'll bet you can do something.

And if anybody thinks that I'm so darned old that the thought of the "Flesh Pots of Egypt" don't make my nostrils quiver, they are completely hydrated.

That's all of the story for this evening. All right, children, kiss me good night and gwan to bed. Don't forget to say your prayers, and put clean handkerchiefs under your pillows. I don't want to get up in the night and get them for you. No, you can't say them in bed. It's not cold.

January 3, 1933   QUITE ELDERLY PERSON

* * *

I'LL heave the whole couch at you if you don't quit accusing me of being a hero, my friend! Not even the fact that you are a "quite elderly person" shall protect you.

I should like to know how that story of Neander and the rib came out. You know second chapters are a passion of mine.

I have no doubt in my own mind about the attractions of the flesh pots of Egypt for you, after reading about that plate of "home-grown, sugared doughnuts," and a cup of coffee. Also, I reorganized my idea of the elderliness that could digest them.

* * *

III

I MAY not live happily, nor die rich; labor may be hard, and I may have a home or just a place of residence—that, as it may be; but I'll bring up man-child to be as a man should; I'll have a friend or two; read a few books; and occasionally, perhaps, smoke a good cigar; so, here and there, I'll pick up a little joy. Finally, I believe that, when "30's in," a kindly Providence, knowing that life was hard, will make death easy.

November 24, 1932   QUITE ELDERLY PERSON

Why Did He Marry Me?

* * *

You know I just can't figure
　Why my husband married me.
Because I'm as small and homely
　As any girl can be.

My hair is straight and auburn,
　And though I do my best,
The more I try to curl it
　The funnier it gets.

My nose, it is a pug one,
　And I have freckles, too.
Of course I know I'm homely,
　But can't think what to do.

Perhaps because I'm Irish
　He thought that I would be
As sunny and good-natured
　As Irishmen can be.

But I was born in April,
　That month of sudden showers,
So I must change from smiles to tears
　At unexpected hours.

You know, I just can't figure
　Why my husband married me. . ..
I guess that I'll not bother,
　'Cause I'm happy as can be.

February 10, 1928

CONSTANT READER

Cornflower

* * *

D<small>EAR</small> <small>NANCY</small> <small>BROWN</small>: Tonight is one of those nights when I feel
that I must write or burst . . . and so here I am. Writing a letter to
you and the Column Family is my idea of making a speech, without
the audience and the jeers—at least they aren't audible.

I would like to have answered "Friend of the Poets'" questionnaire, but can't find it, and I had some perfectly grand answers, too.

Now would you like to know what one of my pet dreams is?
Just this: To while away about one year in a charming little villa
overlooking some blue bay in Italy, with nothing at all to worry
about, such as coal, gas bills and the dentist. I have a friend who did
just that, and every time he tells me about it, I go off into a swoon.
I think if I continue to subscribe to all these circulars describing the
lure of Italy, I shall become a violent Bolshevist.

When I get in my "Italian mood," I haunt the steamship booking
offices, with a mad look in my eyes, devouring all the literature in
sight, and grandly enquiring the sailing dates (of the best boats, of
course), and the rates. It seems that the agents themselves are in
league to torment me. The price of a trip to Italy seems to decrease
as my desire increases. Now is there any justice in the idea of a
measly old $295 standing between me and the desire of my heart?
So much for one of my dreams.

My ambition is to write poetry and actually receive American
currency for it. Is that a laudable . . . and hopeful ambition? I am
planning on repapering our living room with rejection slips, but
will have to write about 15 more poems so I can get enough of the
horrid old rejections for the ceiling.

Confidentially, I am of the opinion that editors may have some grounds for rejecting my brain children. But the knowledge that my beloved poetry will never put the world on its ear, is not going to prevent me from having a glorious time writing it.

I am one of the species of poets that I have dubbed "The Nocturnal" . . . can't you guess? I know several, besides myself, who always get their best inspiration late in the night when the lights are out, and the stillness is conducive to clear thinking. But it's such a nuisance, climbing out of bed, turning on the light, and writing it down quickly before it slips away. I think I might solve this problem by acquiring a dictaphone, and when inspired on a cold night, when a northern gale is sailing around one's ears, just reach for the tube and preserve the ideas, without moving.

Mother says I can think of the most ingenious devices for avoiding manual labor, and on certain auspicious occasions inferred that I was lazy.

One thing I have made up my mind about, though, Nancy, and it is this: If I ever fall heir to any money, I am going to hie myself to the printer's, and have all my poems published and bound in tree calf, with elegant gold lettering, and dedicate it to an undeserving public.

I have a friend who writes really exquisite poetry but who shudders at the thought of having it published and pored over by an unfeeling and unappreciative public. That may be a genius's reaction, but not mine. I yearn for recognition . . . and cash. I suppose that is a mercenary remark for me to make, and unsentimental, but I have quite a practical strain, which is a balance for me. I am very sensitive to criticism, but am not nursing a grudge that I am misunderstood.

Outside of writing fourth-rate poetry, and mooning about Italy, I am really quite a sane person. I know perfectly well that I will likely fall in love, marry some nice man who is dull but dear, have

11 children, and sew rompers, make pies, and try to save money for a decent burial. It can be interesting, and more satisfactory, eventually, than dreaming and yearning. But I assure you, Nancy, that at my advanced age of 23, I am not enthusiastic about a career of nose-wiping, dish-washing, economizing and sock-darning. I'll come around and with a bang, I expect, but in the meantime, I am having a grand time dreaming.

Do you suppose I will wake up some dreary day, when I'm 35, and wonder what I have been missing, and with all decent chances of marrying gone?

From what I have seen of marriages, it takes a woman with an angelic disposition, and a man with the patience of Job, to survive. Perhaps I will mellow with the years, and become wise, but at present the subject of marriage is a cry to battle, with me. The few happily married couples that I have known either were so unbearably smug, or had such lovely dispositions, that I despaired of ever achieving such a perfect state. Will this bring an avalanche of re-bukes upon me? Perhaps I can learn what formula a happily married couple use, to attain a state where they do not get on each other's nerves, but enjoy the same things, love their in-laws, and dwell in peace and harmony.

I could entertain you for several more pages, with the details ot why I have fallen out of love, or ceased enjoying the company of certain men. But I would immediately be called intolerant and picky, so I won't lay myself open to such abuse. But just to give you an idea of how utterly ridiculous I can be, I present this particular case as typical.

Once upon a time I was very much in love with a handsome young man, who had all the graces. A very commendable young man, who was kind to his family, loved children, went to church, read Dr. Eliot's Five Foot Shelf, and had few, if any, faults. I was urged to the right and left of me that here was the chance of a life-time, here was a jewel among men, here was a man who would make a perfect husband. I idealized him, and worshipped at the shrine of such perfection. (I was 20 and thought age creeping up on me, and that I had better attach such an exemplary young man before he returned to circulation.) ... But, dear Nancy, this is the reason I did not marry him; he had the most maddening way of clutching at my elbow, nearly throwing my arm out of joint, and propelling me across the street. He was an elbow-steerer. Any woman who has had her elbow clutched in this grim fashion, and been forced to walk at an impossible angle, will sympathize with me.

He also cherished the delightful (to some) illusion that women are of the delicate (mentally) sex, and should be treated as infants. Women were made to be looked at, but not listened to, and as to the remote possibility of a woman having a mind of her own, oh dear, that was too negligible to even discuss.

That, Nancy, was one of my blighted romances.

Should I have overlooked his elbow-steering (I begged him with tears to dispense with the formality and tried to convince him that I daily crossed streets in the thick of traffic, without being dis-membered ... but to no avail) and his belittling of the feminine mind in favor of his virtues? It does not matter what you say.

The wretch, after swearing eternal devotion, and calling upon heaven to witness that I would always be the *only* woman for him, has married a pretty little girl who is a wonderful wife to him, and from all reports he is very happy. I would have led him a dog's life and I think he must know it now. Fortunate man!

I have been requested by my maternal parent to please confine my typing to civilized hours, and go to bed at a sensible time. I had so much more to tell you, too. May I come again? I have enjoyed the visit, and hope you have not been too bored.

Am I one of the Family now? I send my warmest regards to the Column, and an especially affectionate greeting to you, Nancy.

November 17, 1932 CORNFLOWER

P.S.: My poet friend calls me that in his more lyrical moments. I like it, do you? I know he doesn't read the Column so I am practically safe from detection. He would faint if he were to read this unburdening of my mind.

* * *

I ENJOYED the visit very much, too, Miss "Cornflower"—very much, indeed. Too bad Mother interfered and broke up the discussion. Come back whenever you wish and finish it.

I am afraid I agree with you about the impossibility of overlooking the annoying elbow-steering habit and belittling of the feminine mind that belonged to the perfect young man you describe. He probably is happier as he is—and you, too. So that makes things all right, doesn't it?

The subject of marriage a "cry to battle" to you? It is with many people. However, let me tell you, Miss "Cornflower," that "battling" is not one of the qualifications for marriage. The contracting parties may be combatants or congenial companions—the choice is theirs. My happiest wish for you is that the plebeian career of dishwashing, sock-darning and other "garden variety" of occupations that you mention may be yours, either before or after you are 35. It is the happiest career for a woman.

There are not many women with "angelic" dispositions, or men with the patience of Job. They just don't exist. But there are countless happy marriages in spite of that. It seems to me that intelligence, courtesy and consideration, placed on a firm foundation of love, will uphold the house of happiness in married life. Doesn't sound so difficult, does it?

You are a member. You will come again, won't you?

Feuille de Livre

* * *

Dᴇᴀʀ ɴᴀɴᴄʏ: I have being a silence reader of your Column since I am in the U. S. that is about 11 years ago in fact I find your Column so interesting that, though I learned to read and write very little it is true Englisch but I never haved chance to go to the skool since I am U. S. Little I know then when I was reading Tʜᴇ Nᴇᴡs, that now I will come to you with my trouble. I need you so.

First of all Nancy what can you do if you cannot go to nobody you know with your trouble. I like every body and help every body if possible but went came my time to confide to someone I cannot and it is why I came to you with my trouble. You wont see my blusches of shame when I tell you my histoire.

I was born Nancy in a small citée of France the only child of a well to do famillie. But when I was only a little child yet my father die and there was only me, mother and grande mother. Mother never married again and spent her live giving me enough education to make me independent. Our live was a verry quiet one. Until one day.

The churches started to ring the tocsin. O Nancy I dont know if you ever hear such lugubre sound. To hear in every corner of the city that ring that chill your blood. Every body was excited. What was the matter? I was only 10 years old then but I tink that smaller of me will never forget that day.

The war was declared. Mothers cried for there son. Wifes there husbands and so.

Me I dont haved nobody verry close relations going but seeing every body else crie I cried to.

And started the hard time mother and grande mother looked

what they can stay without, to give to the soldier. Grande mother went to help in the farme where some niece was alone making her husband work, and taking care of 6 little ones.

Then our fund get small, living going hight, mother went as book keeper in the factorie.

And our hopes rise again. U. S. was coming, help us, never I have see such celebration—the first solder that came in France where carried we was so glad now was the end of the war in verry short time.

Between those brave solders there was my future husband. We engage when I was only 15 and he promised my mother to wait 1 year before we get married. In the mean times Armistice was signed and he came back to the U. S.

True to is promise after one year he came back but the same day he landed in France mother die. So we married quietly and we came and make our home in Detroit.

I dont tink you never hear the little I know to speak Englisch. I forget and he the same in French. But love can work miracle and I tried so hard to learn. When we came here we only haved 2 dollars in our name.

No home, no furniture, no job, that was in September 1920. We started housekeeping and he get a job small pay but enough for us and then I was so home sick I never went no place.

Before one years my baby boy born. I was contented with my husband and baby never going nowhere except to show some Sunday night.

Then one night in 1922 my husband got a accident he got both tumbs cut of in factory. 4 months after, my twins baby girls born, and 6 months after 1 of them die. And always alone except my husband. That was to much for a 19 years old since that time my nerves are shaky.

After is accident he get a compensation and we buy a home to put in our famillie—than our trouble get worst. Children keep on coming. I have now 4 boys and 1 girl.

And our only ambition was to pay for our home. If I wanted to go to show I remember the mortgage and I stay out. If I wanted to buy a dresse again that mortgage. In the grocerie the same, my children never ice cream all summer the only place they go was to Sunday skool. And use was only save, and save until I begain to hate that home who was taking all our enjoyment we was living like people 200 years ago. But I haved hope soon after that mortgage was pay the first ting I was going to buy a car to take my famillie out. 11 years in Detroit and never was to Montclement or Pontiac or Ecorse nowhere. And then I am going to buy clothes. O joy sure I earned to buy a new out-fit and furniture my chair are all broke.

And then Nancy that big day came. Do you know that feeling? When I came from the bank the deed in my hands I was blind with joy. I tink I was saying ullo to every body, me whow is so distant. Not because I want to be that way but I cannot be friend to fast why I dont know.

But that feeling was not to be mine for long. My husband get let off and there were are without debt but without penny—even my husband bonus went for the house. Now all is gone even hopes—noting is left.

We are now living on the 18 dollars per month compensation that my husband get from the government. With that pay gaz, light, water, feed and dress 7 peoples.

So much sacrifice for noting. 12 years of privation all for noting —if only I have enjoyed life when I haved. I be in the same boat like I am now but I'll be able to say that my children used to have.

Go to the welfare, go in the line like mendicant for meal tiket.

My children to see their father go like beggar. No better die. I cannot accept that I want them to learn they have to earn their bread or die. I have falled low enough without cloth or anything but my pride was safe. I dont own noting to nobody.

Last Christmas I promesse them a Christmas tree this year we never had one yet. Hèlas that to is going, no toys this Christmas, no candy. Are we going to have to ear I am afraid no. Big boy now 11 years old—keep a cross in is poket and said God is going to feel sorry for us. Blesse is heart I wishes I have is faith, that to is almost gone.

There are so many strong men without work can a cripple get work? O Nancy it is to much for me to carry, I have to show my husband I dont worrie so he wont suffer so much, O tanks God yet we still love each another. Winter coming children are with out cloth I dont complaint about myself—is all my fault I dont have no right to make those little ones to suffer so. They haved the right like very children to have what they need. I take that out of them with that foolish idea to pay a home that I am going to loose now for taxes.

Please give me a word Nancy if I was wrong tell me I can bear that yet. To you I come like I was going to my mother who is no more. I dont take the Sunday NEWS but if you take time to read this letter and have the kindnest to answer me I will appreciate so much.

Please answer poor

November 18, 1932   FEUILLE DE LIVRE

* * *

SUCH a lovely, lovely letter, dear woman.

I have two great reasons for wanting to send it on to the Column Folks. In the first place, in writing to us you have joined our big family and are one of us, and we can help each other both spiritually and materially. Each of us can bring an offering in one way or another, can't we?

You bring the spiritual with your courage and sweetness in the face of so many difficulties; your love for your husband and his for you that still abides after so many years of trial and sorrow; your cheerful acceptance of life and living in a strange country, away from your friends and home folks, with little or no recreation. All these lovely qualities that you have shown will help our Column Folks who are struggling with similar problems of their own.

This is one great reason why I wanted the Columnites to be sure to read your good letter. The other reason is that they may extend the hand of friendship to you—and they will, I know.

It does seem that you have had too much to carry, indeed, dear, but haven't you noticed that when we apparently have carried all we can, something nice always happens by way of relief? I think the "something nice" in this case is going to come from your letter to me and to the Column. I am sure it is, in fact.

I am just as sure that those dear little folks of yours are going to have a Christmas tree, and that Santa Claus is going to find them, as I am sure that Santa Claus comes on Christmas Eve. Maybe it is the cross that little son has carried so trustingly in his pocket that will bring about the Christmas miracle—but I am sure his confidence in Santa Claus is not going to be shaken.

You would like to help little boys and girls to have a happy Christmas, wouldn't you? I am sure you will not refuse us the same privilege. We all love little boys and girls. Not one of us would see a child deprived of Christmas if it were within our power to help. Even a mother's pride will break down before the "Santa Claus appeal" in babies' eyes, won't it?

There was a lump in my throat and a mist in my eyes when I read about your coming out of the bank with the deed to that little home in your hand, saying "hello" to everybody—diffident, reserved little foreign lady that you are. I want my Column Folks to know you. They will take you to their hearts and you will never be alone or lonesome again.

Now I am going to ask you for a favor. Will you write to me and give me your name and address, just for me? No one else will know it, I promise you. I want to write you a personal letter and tell you many, many things that it is not possible to write through the columns of a newspaper. You will send it right away, won't you? I shall watch for it.

[EDITOR'S NOTE: *She sent the address, and the children had their Christmas. The little lad's faith that the cross in his "pocket" would bring Santa Claus was not shaken.*]

*

Prodigal

I'm back! dear God, I'm back!
I'm here—in ashes and in sack.
Remember me, dear God?

It's me—I let you down,
Remember?—just to kid and clown—
But all in fun, you know.

Well, all that now is past.
And anyway, it couldn't last—
I knew it never would.

But gee! dear God, I pray
You'll never let me down, but say
To me, "Well, son, you're back—
I told you so!"

November 27, 1932   SQUALL

Henpecked

* * *

DEAR NANCY BROWN: How far is it from here to the nearest divorce court?

As sentimental ballad composers have so picturesquely portrayed it, my wife and I have come to the parting of the ways. It is indeed a pathetic story, but I am compelled to divorce either my wife or my typewriter and, after due deliberation, I have decided that the former must go, inasmuch as the latter cannot give me any back talk.

Every family has its ghosts in the garret or its skeletons in the closet, hence I am happy to be numbered among the fearless few who dare permit the invisible members of Columnland to lift the veil of secrecy or to brush aside the tangled skeins of cobwebs and penetrate into the deepest recesses wherein their shattered dreams are housed. In the ready unfolding of this dreary chapter of my earthly existence, I conscientiously believe that I merit a life membership in that great fraternizing brotherhood, the Order of Woebegone Husbands.

Possibly certain of the more matured members of Columnland will have guessed the truth, though reiteration here for the benefit of the In-Betweens will not do any particular harm. I am a married man, like a large number of my fellow straphangers. The depression has fathered a program whereby most husbands have become martyrs to a losing cause.

With no steady monetary job available, aside from the Big Shots, it is a case of stay at home and help wifie to peel potatoes, clean carrots, dust the furniture, hang out clothes, wash windows and do a multitudinous array of other penurious and perspicuous tasks—not to mention cleaning wallpaper where Junior's hands have cunningly deposited the goo from an all-day sucker while still learning to walk, vacuuming and brushing the rugs to remove dog hairs where the precious little pet has been permitted to do his daily dozen, gathering dandelion hearts and other wild fruit for the canary, in order that its feathers may glisten with the perpetuity of youth and that it may register the proper decimal point of blood pressure.

The entire week is replete with thrills. Comes Sunday morning. Wifie must have her beauty sleep, and thus permit the highly perfumed face creams and other alluring cosmetics applied the previous night to do their full work of removing that careworn look that marred her facial masterpiece.

I have learned my lesson by heart. I spring out of bed, take my morning ablution, slip into my garments and make a bee-line for the kitchen. With a song of thanksgiving on my lips for the privilege of living, I brew the coffee, fry the bacon and eggs (when we have them), make the toast, prepare the cereal, and then lightly tiptoe into my helpmeet's bed chamber, with an apology at my fingertips for thus so rudely disturbing her sweet slumber, and whisper in her delicate ear that the morning refreshments are about to be served.

Breakfast over, I tidy up the table and help with the dishes. Being short of change for the collection plate, we decide to remain at home and derive our spiritual uplift through the facilities of the National Broadcasting Company and its associated stations, WWJ or WJR.

After a diligent perusal of the Sunday News, I have an inspiration to transmit a brainy story, and straightway seek out my trusty friend, the contentious typewriter, when my dear little rib smilingly informs me that it is almost lunch time, and will I please set the table and bring the raw fruit out of the refrigerator?

At her behest I sidle over to the cupboard, and decorate the table once again with specified pieces of silverware and eating utensils. The repast is brief, but the session is not wholly in vain, since I am given the highlights of the discourse to which we have just listened, with wifie's personal opinion thrown in for good measure. The snow-blanketed treetops and silver-studded frost on hillside and in valley are simply darling, and would I mind taking a drive out into the country to commune with Nature? Well, Adam obeyed, so why shouldn't I? His Satanic Majesty sorely tempts me to take along my typewriter and do my stuff while wifie converses with her sparrow friends, but in a moment of weakness I succor sufficient courage to tell him to get behind me and not mess in our affairs.

Thus the afternoon is spent and, with the evening meal in view, Frank and Helen drop in for just a minute, though graciously (you know what I mean) are invited to have dinner with us. (Graciously goes like this: "Oh, but you must stay; we'll be so disappointed if you don't; it's no trouble at all; I'll have the table set in a jiffy. Dear, don't stand there so dumblike, take Frank's things.") Well, we make the best of it, realizing that we have unwittingly cheated the canine member of our family out of a few choice tidbits in our eagerness to keep up false appearances.

Somewhat strengthened in body and mind, Frank and I light up, and wallow through politics, the depression, and various and sundry forms of retrospective hieroglyphics and, when we shake hands in parting at midnight, we discover that despite our boasted cure-alls for humanity's grief, Old Man Depression is still hanging oodles of crêpe.

Monday morning—six bells—wash day has arrived. My fair one peeks at the sky, O.K.'s the weather. I jump into my running togs and rush to the basement to start the machinery rolling, and ere I have swallowed my last bite of burned toast the soapsuds are mounting high. With the lines full of glistening white paraphernalia, I don my dusting coiffure and settle down to a week of practical housework, extending from garret to basement.

[263]

The same momentous routine on Tuesday, Wednesday, Thursday and Friday—then comes the break. In the midst of my cleaning-up ceremonies the phone rings. The switchboard operator at the office is on the line. Will I come to work on Monday? Will I? Say, I am so delirious with joy that I pick up an old shoe and throw it through the garage window just to celebrate my good fortune.

How did I find time to write this narrative? It's a secret. I had to give my wife a sleeping potion and then steal out of bed while her reasoning faculties were still a bit hazy. But the typewriter works.

December 4, 1932   HENPECKED

* * *

You are a cheerful victim, Mr. "Henpecked"—just a bit too gay, I am afraid, to join the Order of Woebegones.

One of the outstanding blessings of the depression is that husbands are learning how to do housework. Some are even becoming experts—able to have the coffee and the bacon and eggs and the toast all come out together, in time for breakfast, without burning any of them.

It was a brave gesture on your part to refuse to yield to the temptation to take the typewriter along when you communed with Nature. Maybe that was a lesson taught by the depression, too. In fact, I am inclined to think there are some husbands who have benefited by the hard times. However, I am very glad for the phone call that summoned you back to work on Monday.

Come again. We shall put you among the cheer leaders, along with "Connecticut Yankee." Oh, I forgot. The nearest divorce court I can recommend to you is in Nevada.

Injustice to Man

* * *

Dear Nancy, all the girls we see
Are free at neck and free at knee,
    While all the men we chance to meet
    Are muffled up from neck to feet.
This, to my senses, seems to be
A most unjust disparity.

With sun-kist neck and air-bathed knee
I do most heartily agree;
    And so why mummify us men
    In sunless, airless wrappings, when
Our bodies starve for sun and air?
Oh, Nancy, this is hardly fair.

Can not you girls, your freedom won,
Think now of husband, brother, son;
    Your many-sided influence use
    To end the reign of this abuse,
And change the duds of man, till he
Has freedom at the neck and knee?

From torturing collars free his throat,
Yank off his sacred, padded coat;
    Your nifty scissors flourish free
    And bob his pants above the knee.
Indeed no effort spare, nor cease
Till he is tunicked like old Greece.

October 11, 1927

INSURGENT

Cup o' Tea

* * *

DEAR NANCY: Am enclosing $1 for your Goodfellows' Fund. It is only a little, but what can I do? So many of my friends are down and out, and I must help them as much as I can. I'm down myself, but if I'm not out, I'm nearly all in.

I've got a book. It is lovely. I'll tell you what I think of it when the Christmas rush is over, but just now I'm not in the mood for it. As a matter of fact, I'm in what you might call a "helluva" mood, and I got it over a nickel.

On Saturday I was over on Woodward Avenue. It was cold and snowing. I went into a restaurant for a cup of coffee. It was one of those places with a horseshoe counter. There were four of us in the place, scattered far apart around the horseshoe.

A little bit of a girl came in. She was, as I remember, wearing a brownish coat and a little red felt hat, and she had a muffler around her neck. She couldn't have been more than eight years old. She was selling candy.

She walked up to the first man and started her little stock speech. It began, "Please, Sir," and ended "only a nickel apiece." The man shook his head and went on with his steak and chips. She moved down to the second man. He looked flustered for a moment, then shook his head. Then the little red hat moved over to the side where I was sitting and approached the third man. "Please, Sir——only a nickel." He saw her coming and took a sudden interest in his paper. He ignored her. Then she came to me and I, I shook my head and let her go away. And so she went out into the cold, a gallant little figure in spite of the shabby coat. She was so small that she could hardly pull open the heavy doors.

When she was gone I could still hear, in imagination, the little childish voice, "Please, Sir——only a nickel apiece." I wanted to rush out after her and buy all her candy, but somehow I couldn't. I felt those other men would know—that they would wink at each other—another sucker!

So I let her go and stayed where I was and spent a damn bad quarter of an hour. And all for the sake of a lousy nickel.

She wasn't, by any means, hungry looking or ill or undernourished—by no means a pitiful little figure. And yet, I kept asking myself, "Must I wait until she is hungry and ill before I do anything?" Maybe it was the little profit from this candy that kept her well and properly nourished. Perhaps if she didn't sell the candy she would get a licking when she got home. Maybe she had a sick mother or a drunken father. Maybe she really needed the money badly—and maybe she was better off than I am myself—which wouldn't be so very hard. How do I know?

Everywhere the newspapers are exposing this sort of thing as a racket. Just before I went into the restaurant a man lurched out of the shadows. "Could yer spare the price of a sandwich an' a cup of coffee?" I looked at him. It was the same one that had approached me the Sunday before in exactly the same place, with the same old battle-cry. I had given him something then. A regular panhandler. That is why I turned the little girl down. I know it was. What's to do about it, Nancy?

Afterwards I went to church and felt like a damned hypocrite all the time I was sitting there. Fortunately there was no sermon. The minister gave a talk about some places he had visited in Europe, giving it a religious background. Thank God for that! What if he had taken for his subject: "Suffer Little Children"? It doesn't bear contemplating. "Please, Sir——only a nickel apiece." Oh, Nancy! It isn't fair. It isn't fair for people to use children for this sort of

[267]

thing. It isn't fair to the children. It isn't fair to us who would give everything we have, if we only knew for certain it was really needed.

The regular panhandler, we can sometimes spot—but a child's voice hurts. Why can't we use our heart strings for shoe strings, where they could be of practical use?

December 16, 1932   Cup o' Tea

P.S.: I've decided to enclose another dollar, making it two. Don't thank me, Nancy. Thank the little girl in the shabby coat and the little red hat with her box of fudgy candy. She didn't do any good for herself, but she sold me into scraping up another dollar—and so some little kiddie will have a little something that she—poor little soul—should perhaps have had, herself.

* * *

Your letter made me cry. That little girl with the shabby coat and the little red hat, with her candy and her "only a nickel apiece" made an appealingly pathetic picture. I agree with you that it is not fair to use children for such purposes, and yet, "Cup o' Tea," probably the homes of these pitiful little wage earners are desperately destitute. I am sure no mother in the world would send her little eight-year-old girl out on a winter night, selling candy from door to door, unless stark, staring necessity demanded it.

I spoke an "Amen" to your "Thank God that the minister did not choose as a text, 'Suffer little children'." It was hard enough, just to think of it, wasn't it?

I am adding the two dollars to our Christmas fund, as you request. But deep in my heart, "Cup o' Tea," I rather wish it was just the one.

He Sez, Sez He!

* * *

When I was a youngish fellow,
It seemed to me—I remember—
The old world was hardly big enough
For me to go hot-footin' in;
And I spent most of plenty years
A-goin' up and down it
On salt-crusted tramps at sea
And two good legs ashore,
To see what I could see.

All of a sudden I came, kind o' tired,
To them blue hills of old age
That all the time laid hazy away off
At the end of the road
Plumb on the edge of the world.
It was so quiet there and restful like,
I squatted down, lit my pipe,
And stayed put.

And now that I am here
My own door yard is plenty big enough—
I seem to be right sure—
For me to go a-wanderin' in,
Or just to sit in of a summer's day
And sort o' contemplate the shade
And listen to the sounds:
The rattle o' dishes just inside the door,
My old woman singin' to herself,

The junkman's horn up the alley,
The saw mill whinin' by the river,
Engine bells down in the yards,
And long whistles out in the harbor.

Yep, my door yard's plenty big enough—
I seem right sure—
Only, sometimes, for them bells a-whimperin'
And them rowdy whistles callin',
Especially at night time
When fog's driftin'.

July 3, 1932   EPH DEE

*

Ramblin' Cogitations

I've been in the woods where the violets bloom
    And smother their heads in their own perfume.
I've heard the soft laughter of fairies and elves
    Whose laughter is caused by a look at themselves.

I've been where the lily-bell swings in the breeze,
    And a lone bumble-bee with his sugary knees
Goes mumblin' an' grumblin' an' stumblin' along,
    A-payin' for sweets with a dolorous song.

I've been where the tree-tops reach up to the sky
    Like the stairways to heaven for those who pass by,
I've heard the still music of murmurin' streams
    That carried me backward to yesterday's dreams.

August 19, 1928   JIM

Querida

* * *

DEAR NANCY: If you had a husband with whom you were deeply in love and to whom you had been married for eight years and he suddenly told you that he had just simply "fallen out of love with you," if there is such a thing, what would you do?

Circumstances, regardless of arguments to the contrary, and conditions shape our whole life I think. We were so very much in love —frighteningly so—when as a couple of kids we turned our faces to the sun and defied the world to down us. Youth and love and understanding carried us to the very heights—hence the fall is quite far and, on my part, unexpected.

We have watched the sun rise from the top deck of an ocean liner and we have held hands and thrilled at the sight of the moon coming out of the Mediterranean—and now we figure hard to try and apportion a sufficient amount of the income to take care of necessities.

Money and folks are at the back of a great many tragedies, aren't they? We're young, very young, and I have a mother and father to take care of—not just to "help" but actually to take care of their every necessity. They're terribly selfish, but then, when I reach their age and life holds so very little, I shall probably be more so—if I have children to feel that way toward.

All through these last few years I've worked—had to. Of course, I like it a great deal (thank God) and it therefore hasn't been as much of a hardship as it might be if I didn't like it. The money has to come in. A wife that comes home tired, crabby, ready to fight at the drop of the hat over nothing (and then feels miserable over it for hours), and one whose life is more or less wrapped up in making a success of the job to take care of necessities, isn't very interesting, I know.

I'm entirely wrong and I'm not blaming him a bit.

We've never lived alone except for a very few months, when we were first married. That was heaven, but I got sick and we went home "for a few months." We're still there. We had all the fun and all the realization of our dreams anyone could ever have. Ever since then it's been a case of working and going places and doing things so that we could get a home and perhaps welcome a towhead.

We've been at home so long the folks just don't treat us like married people, but rather as sister and brother. It's impossible to do anything alone or have any little conversation unless others join in. You'll think I'm exaggerating, but I'm not.

He tells me there isn't any other person in the world but that he just can't feel toward me as he used to—that he's just "out of love," and he can't stand being around and seeing me hurt. It does hurt. He's discouraged over his business—says he wants to end things—and that we just aren't getting anywhere except to be commonplace in our attitudes every day and accept things as a matter of course, and that we're just not married. We aren't, in lots of ways.

He says he wants to go away, to find out if it's just that we've been together too much and yet not enough—which really doesn't make sense but is true. He says he can never tell whether he can love me again in the same old way unless he goes away, because he's felt this way for more than a year now and hasn't told me because he didn't want to hurt me.

I think the world just stopped going around when he told me that. He seemed so miserable. Funny, the same people are around, the same desk, the same work, the same signs on the street—but just empty, oh, so empty.

I begged him not to go. I felt that if he could just stick it out a while longer until something happened so we could get alone together, perhaps he would find that that was all that was wrong. He said he'd do anything I wanted, but he couldn't stick it out any longer. That he had loved me madly and then, after years together, circumstances just seemed to make it wear off, and now he just didn't feel toward me at all except terribly sorry that he had to hurt me. And he said that, since we had had so many wonderful times in our life together, he thought it would be better if he went now because he could always remember that, and if he stayed, he might just come to hate me and that would be the end of everything.

He hasn't any plans—doesn't know where to go or what to do, and doesn't seem to care about a thing.

I know that I should have let him go, but I just couldn't. I've never felt like this before. It's just as though everything were in one huge bowl and the bowl were slowly slipping off the table. He looks at me and his eyes are so sad and he doesn't eat a thing and he's far off when I speak to him and he tries to smile and he even kisses me —empty, cool and meaningless kisses which just tear right down inside me.

If we could only leave and get a little place and put up our own pictures and paint dragons on the table again and make big fluffy omelets for each other and get a funny little quivery feeling inside when we did something 'specially nice for the other one, I think perhaps things would adjust themselves. I only think this, because you see I'm so fatally in love with this boy I call "husband." He might not be able to do it. I don't know.

Anyhow, it's out of the question, for there's the mother and father. They've never let me down and I just couldn't do it to them, but if he were willing, I think I could live in one of those rooms that you walk up flights of stairs to get to, and sleep and eat and cook all in the one place.

If there was only something to fight—but there isn't. He says it's just all blank and he can't lie to me any longer.

So here am I and there is he—just a couple of kids with the wrong sense of direction. Perhaps it would work out all right if he went away. Somehow I feel I would never see him again. Perhaps it is only right that this should happen. I've evidently made a miserable failure of things. People always think life has been cruel to them when these things happen, don't they? Well, I think life has been worse than that. Besides making me the sole support of the whole family for two years, with all the incidental unhappiness that comes with it, such as not having the things you need in the way of clothes, Fate comes along with *this*.

He says he's going right after Christmas, so I'm presuming enough to think you may have some suggestion to make. You helped me wonderfully once before. I can't let him go, Nancy, or life will just stop. Say "So sorry" to me or something, will you, for I'm just a little "kid" wife whose husband has "fallen out of love" with

December 23, 1932   QUERIDA

* * *

I BELIEVE, dear, it would be better to let your husband go away for a while. Indeed, I think perhaps it is the only way. You want him back just as he was before all this trouble, don't you? I believe you cannot achieve that purpose without being absent from each other for a while.

Conditions have gotten on his nerves until everything seems all wrong, even you. I believe being "absent one from the other," will be the best start toward readjustment.

But I would stipulate certain conditions about that absence, to which I am sure he will agree. I would tell him that perhaps it would be better for him to go for a while, and you are willing, providing he will promise to keep in touch with you. That would be the least he could do to save you the suffering of uncertainty and worry about him.

You might set the length of time of his first absence, also. Make it three months or six months, whichever he wishes. Being away from you for a while will serve as a connecting link between the old times and the new that I think you may honestly hope for.

I would ask him to wait until the first of the year before he goes.

I truly believe that he still loves you and, if he is away from you, will realize it himself.

If he were in business partnership with another man, he would not feel that he could break loose any time he wanted to and run away and shift the burden of responsibility onto his partner. Business men do not do that. And yet, no other business in the world is half as important as this marriage business. I am sure you have been a fair and square partner, deserving of his consideration.

I do not believe fighting will do a bit of good, unless, like our dear "Connecticut Yankee," you "fight nice."

You are right about the responsibility for your mother and father. It is yours. On the other hand, it does not seem right that their care should wreck your life. I do believe that in a home of your own, your trouble would not have happened. Perhaps when times are better and your husband can find his place in the working world again, you will be able to be in a little home of your own and care for your mother and father separately in theirs.

Your husband, like other men, does not know the priceless treasure that he is losing in casting your love aside. Some day, something, perhaps in the guise of a calamity, perhaps in the absence that he wishes, will open his eyes. We are hoping so, and that hope will keep up your courage, dear.

[EDITOR'S NOTE: *A second letter from "Querida" revealed that her husband had held to his purpose, and left her.*]

Kindest Acts

* * *

ONE of the Columnites, who signed "Benedict," suggested that husbands and wives write the kindest acts each had done for the other.

A few resulting letters follow:

DEAR NANCY: In looking back over my married life and thinking of the years of happy companionship, the enduring peace and love-liness of home, I am convinced that the nicest thing my husband ever did for me was to marry me.

October 26, 1931   SANS SOUCI

* * *

DEAREST NANCY: The kindest act my husband ever did was not scolding me when I threw ten dollars in the stove, the only money we had to our name, years ago when the children were small.

I had to hurry to get my work done. Had the ten dollars in my hand, and was looking in the library table drawer for my insurance books. The drawer was all messed up with papers the children put in there. I started to clean out the drawer and forgot I had the money in my hand. It went in the stove with the papers. I was just sick over it.

When Hubby came home he saw I had been crying. He asked what the trouble was. I told him, "I did something terrible. I burned up the only money I had." He said, "Is that all? Now don't you go crying about that. You didn't do it intentionally and it's gone and that's all there is to it. I'm working and we'll have some more money soon." And I expected him to scold me for being so careless.

October 31, 1931   MARQUETTE

[276]

DEAR NANCY: The kindest act (or one of them) by Daddy was once when we only had a little bit of butter, just enough for his lunch. I put it on his bread and when I got up he had taken time to scrape it all off and leave it for my breakfast. He is like that in everything.

November 15, 1931   PLUMB DISCOURAGED

* * *

DEAR NANCY:

> Just thoughtful little things
> But thought of every day,
> Nothing spectacular;
> What less, then, could I say
> In all sincerity
> Of one so sweet and true?
> Her "kindest act" to me
> Was when she said, "I do."

November 8, 1931   ICHABOD

* * *

BELOVED NANCY: There are so many kind and dear acts that the Boy Friend bestows upon me that it is terribly hard to pick out any one for distinction. I shall select the one that involved the most sacrifice on his part.

We had a radio that was not very decorative and not too dependable. As we had just bought our home, we were economizing with a capital E. Nothing was purchased that was unnecessary. Still, the radio did not fit in with our other furniture and I casually hoped that some day we could have a nice new one. It was to be one of those distant millenniums when everyone could have all they ever wanted. It was in the summertime when I expressed my wish.

Christmas Day we went out of town to Mother's, and had just

[277]

the loveliest Christmas ever. When we came home, I felt so happy with everything I ran into the house with all my treasures and stopped dead still, for there in the corner was the dear little radio I wanted. I just gasped for breath, I was so surprised. Then I got my brain collected and wondered where that Boy Friend had annexed the money to pay for such a gift. He simply answered, "Oh, I just missed lunches for a few days, Honey." The truth of it was that he had been missing lunch for months to get my radio. The tears came to my eyes when I realized how inexpressibly dear he was. And *is*.

November 17, 1931   KITTEN

*

Dawn

(Upon meeting a celebrated poetess)

Yesterday,
dawn was like
a somber-garbed,
voiceless apparition!

Today,
dawn was like a prism
breaking into
a thousand rays
of refracted light—
each seemingly delirious
with the joy of flight!

I saw your name
etched upon every ray!

January 12, 1932   TOYO

Shortest Letters

* * *

ONE of our writers, who signed "Wee Dundonian," suggested that the contributors see who could write the best letter in the fewest words, the outstanding ones to be published in "Dear Nancy."

The chosen ones follow:

DEAR NANCY: How will this do for a short letter?

The depression didn't catch up with me until last week, but when it did I counted up my expenses and the money in my pay envelope, and there I was with four cents and no place to put it. "And so the Lord be thankit."

Your own   LANONE

*

IT will "do" very nicely. Thank you.

* * *

DEAR NANCY: I am an almost silent admirer, having received much help and a better understanding of human nature. This is my short letter:

> I do leftovers, makeovers, hand-me-downs—thin;
> "Pal" does heroics without any din,
> Walking his beat, with a happy grin.
> Boy Scouts three—are pals of me,
> And do their daily deeding,
> For any badly needing.

A fair division of labor. Yes?

A POLICEMAN'S WIFE

*

A FAIR division, indeed, and cleverly told. Thank you.

DEAR NANCY: *Beer again*—Drear again, fear again; tear again!

FINNEGAN

*

OH dear again!

* * *

DEAR NANCY: Here's my "wee letter." I love you.

LOU'S GRANDMA.

*

I THANK you, "Lou's Grandma."

* * *

DEAR NANCY: No foolin'—I can't be "short" with you.

RAG CARPET

*

THANK you, "Rag Carpet."

* * *

DEAR NANCY: (My "short"):

Out of the dirt and scum of things,
Something always, always sings.

TRINKET

P.S.: Don't know if you have a "Trinket" or not, but I'll change
—if you'll only let me belong.

*

WE have no "Trinket" and we are happy to have you belong.

* * *

DEAR COLUMN: My wee letter—Depression, repression, impression,
all give rise to expression.

Do we like it? And how!

STEAM

*

WE do. Very much. Thanks.

[280]

NANCY DEAR: After "listening in" to the Secretary of the Treasury last week (sounding brass and tinkling "symbol"). How's this for a "wee"?

The music of my cash-ed notes, now long past due, is what I'd like from Woodin! Now Woodin' you?

CANZONE

*

IT's fine for a "wee," "Canzone," and there will be plenty who will join in on the chorus.

* * *

DEAR NANCY AND FAMILY ALL: My short letter:

I have always been reprimanded for being foolish. I am foolish, I know I'm foolish, I want to be foolish and I wish I was foolish-er. I never could see any sensibility of sense. If I had been sensible I would have saved more money; had I saved more money it would have been with what I saved; if it had been with what I saved, it wouldn't be saved. Is there sense in sense or sense to sense? Is the sensible foolish or the foolish sensible?

QUESTIONING EYES

*

ALL right, Miss "Questioning Eyes."

You win. It was more sensible to be foolish than sensible.

* * *

DEAR NANCY BROWN: My short letter:

Boy. Roy. Joy.

LAZYBONES

*

IT couldn't be shorter—or better—"Lazybones." Congratulations.

[281]

On Attempting Authorship

* * *

Write! Write! What can a mortal say?
I met a young and pretty girl today.
Her hair was wavy, soft, and loam-earth brown;
The free-limbed rhythm of her stride a-down
The street was glorious . . .
              Can words convey
This beauty that I passed along the way?

I love and hate, I scorn, and sometimes fear;
Hold this thing lightly, find that thing most dear;
Thrill in my passions—thrill to beat them down—
Then try to write, and find my pen a *clown*.
Why, I can't even tell the tale that lies
In but a moment's glance from passing eyes!

And when the summer lightning scars the sky,
Or when the sun's retreating banners fly
Their boldness 'gainst the vanguard of the night,
My life is full . . .
              but if I try to write
I learn my folly in the trial to pen
This greatness. Not I can make death life again.

November 8, 1928   JAWN